# School-University Partnerships in Action

## CONCEPTS, CASES, AND CONCERNS

# School-University Partnerships in Action

## CONCEPTS, CASES, AND CONCERNS

*EDITED BY*

**Kenneth A. Sirotnik**
**John I. Goodlad**

Teachers College, Columbia University
New York and London

Published by Teachers College Press, 1234 Amsterdam Avenue,
New York, NY 10027

*Library of Congress Cataloging-in-Publication Data*

School-university partnerships in action.

   Includes index.
   1. University cooperation — United States.  2. Public
schools — United States.  3. Universities and colleges
— United States.  4. Interorganizational relations —
United States — Case studies.  5. Cooperation — United
States.  I. Sirotnik, Kenneth A.  II. Goodlad, John I.
LB2331.5.S36   1988       378'.103       87-33575


ISBN 0-8077-2893-4
ISBN 0-8077-2892-6 (pbk.)

Manufactured in the United States of America

93  92  91  90  89  88     1  2  3  4  5  6

# Contents

# Introduction

KENNETH A. SIROTNIK and JOHN I. GOODLAD

This book represents a working commitment to a rather deviant idea—an idea that by many accounts should probably not succeed. By our account and the accounts of several others, however, we hope to demonstrate that the idea of equitable, constructive, and productive partnerships between schools and universities is, indeed, viable—that is to say, viable *enough* to warrant substantial commitment and further investigation.

The idea of recognizing formal or informal connections between individuals, groups, and/or organizations as a means of furthering the interests of at least one or more of the members is not new. Yet, currently, on the heels of major educational reform reports directed first at public schools and then at schools of education and higher education generally, a flood of "partnerships" has covered the educational landscape as though the concept had been recently invented.

Several reasons probably account for this flurry of activity. First, the politics of educational reform have created the need for at least symbolic associations between educational stakeholders. For example, businesses wishing to show their concern for public schooling have created adopt-a-school "partnerships," and colleges of education wishing to demonstrate their connection to school practice have created school-university "partnerships." Second, the relatively sudden transformation of our society from one dependent upon industry to one dependent upon information and services has forced a raising of consciousness regarding institutional interdependency. Third, and most germane to this book, there may be some good theoretical and practical reasons for collaborative activities between institutions struggling with related aspects of common problems. Such is the case, we argue, for the institutions we call public schools (and their school districts) and schools, colleges, or departments of education (and their total university contexts).

Are the various past and current "coalitions," "collaboratives," "consortiums," "cooperatives," "networks," "partnerships," basically the same types of operations with different names? The answer is clearly no according to Richard Clark's review of attempts to link universities and schools. Any one of these terms — "partnership," for example — has been used to denote linking endeavors ranging from mostly symbolic, "on-paper" arrangements, to relationships based upon patronage and small monetary grants, to one-sided, noblesse oblige, service agreements, to information-sharing systems, to mutually collaborative arrangements between *equal* partners working together to meet self-interests while solving common problems. It is this last form of school-university *partnership* in which we are most interested — a form of institutional collaboration that rarely (if ever) has occurred in practice.

This is not to suggest that partnership efforts of this type are hopeless; indeed, we and our colleagues have been directly or indirectly involved in a number of comparable efforts that continue to hold a great deal of promise. While these school-university partnerships have not reached the ideal collaborative state, they represent a significant improvement over those "partnerships" of a more superficial nature. Moreover, the partnerships in the group that we discuss in this book have developed in different ways and have their own case histories of successes and failures. Thus, although we propose an ideal paradigm for collaboration between schools and universities, this paradigm will be only approximated in practice. Nonetheless, we conclude that reasonable approximations of the collaborative paradigm have the potential to effect significant educational improvement not ordinarily possible without such relationships.

In this book, therefore, we address the following aspects of school-university relationships: (1) detailing the kind of collaborative, partnership paradigm that we see emerging as the most viable form of school-university relationship; (2) clarifying terminology, past and present, and reviewing the literature on and efforts at linking schools and universities; (3) analyzing a selected set of case histories of school-university relationships that have attempted to approximate the kind of partnership proposed; (4) developing a research and evaluation perspective compatible with the tenets of the emerging paradigm; (5) critically appraising the viability of the school-university partnership concept; and (6) guiding future endeavors with whatever tentative lessons we have learned thus far.

The chapters of this book have been organized to coincide with the agenda of concepts, cases, and concerns. In Chapter 1, John Goodlad confronts explicitly this difficult but crucial question: What is a genuine, collaborative relationship between schools and universities? Persuasive arguments undoubtedly exist for at least several such conceptions.

The conception offered in Chapter 1 grows out of over forty years of thinking about and participating in various configurations of relationships between schools and universities. This conception relies heavily upon the positive features of symbiotic relationships and the power of support structures for educational renewal and change.

In Chapter 2, Richard Clark presents a summary of an in-depth foray into the tangle of literature on interinstitutional relationships, with particular emphasis on schools and universities. To facilitate this review both conceptually and organizationally, Clark distinguishes between two broad classes of connections: networks and partnerships (or consortiums, collaboratives, coalitions, etc.). He then reviews the history of each of these classes of relationship, focusing eventually on partnerships and analyzing the extent to which they appear to approximate the kind of collaborative endeavor outlined in the first chapter.

Across the nation, there exist several school-university collaborations that have attempted (and are attempting) to develop these partnership concepts in the arena of practice. The partnerships selected for analysis in Chapters 3 through 7 were not chosen at random; they were selected because we knew something about them, either through personal experience in their development and operation or through our collegial association with key individuals in the partnerships. Ann Lieberman and Robert Sinclair were colleagues in an earlier, prototypical partnership effort known as the League of Cooperating Schools developed by John Goodlad in the mid to late sixties. Each went to the East Coast and became involved in similar collaborative efforts. At Teachers College, Lieberman assumed the leadership role for the Metropolitan School Study Council, perhaps the oldest extant school-university partnership of its type. At the University of Massachusetts, Sinclair developed the Massachusetts Coalition for School Improvement, patterned very much after the League but with a specific focus on classroom instructional practices and student learning. The experiences of these partnerships are recounted in Chapters 3 and 4 (with Anne Harrison), respectively.

Following on the successes and problems of the League experience, John Goodlad developed The Partnership (later called the Southern California Partnership), a consortium of twelve school districts (and their schools), two community colleges, five county school offices, and the University of California at Los Angeles. Over the five to six years during which we were associated with this partnership, our colleague Paul Heckman spearheaded the liaison connection between the university and the schools. His account of this experience is presented in Chapter 5.

Finally, based in substantial part on the partnership in southern California, two newer school-university collaboratives were developed, the Brigham Young University–School District Partnership and the Puget Sound Educational Consortium. In Chapters 6 and 7 respectively, our colleagues David Williams and Pamela Keating and Richard Clark detail the shorter but revealing histories of these collaborative efforts.

Readers of these five chapters will find an interesting and varied array of partnership experiences that attest to the importance of *not* trying to package and disseminate detailed models of how partnerships function best. Nonetheless, readers will recognize common themes running through all five analyses that suggest there are similar rewards to be gained and lessons to be learned across these various struggles with school-university relationships. When we enlisted the writers of each of the cases presented in Part II, we suggested the following guidelines for their analyses:

- Avoid a "show-and-tell" presentation only; provide just enough descriptive material (e.g., premises, philosophy, operating principles, activities) to contextualize a critical analysis of the partnership experience.
- The phrase "critical analysis" is meant to suggest an interpretive history of each case that reflects critically but constructively on the problems, issues, dilemmas, and frustrations associated with the attempt to get schools and colleges/universities to collaborate with one another.
- Assuming we all have some stake in making such partnerships work, the critiques should be constructive. That is, based upon successes (as well as apparent failures), what are the lessons learned? What kinds of things would you do differently if you had it to do all over again, and why? Given the pitfalls, what are the possibilities?
- We suspect that there may be dilemmas that are generic throughout school-university partnership efforts. Many of these center on the institutional barriers/cultural clashes between places called districts and schools and places called schools, colleges, or departments of education (and their host universities). Please consider, if relevant, the possible conflicts among: (1) philosophies of organizational change; (2) reward systems; (3) research and practice; and (4) individual and organizational interests. Other generic issues/concerns might include such things as getting partnerships "off the ground," getting something going at the building level, involving teachers, involving faculty, selecting common issues on which to work, evaluat-

ing successes and failures, securing necessary resources (human and material), communicating within and between schools and the university, dealing with interpersonal attitudes/behaviors.

- One issue that may emerge and be of particular concern is the role of the "idea champion": do partnerships tend to "rise and fall" due to the presence/absence of a significant and charismatic individual? To what extent are partnerships dependent upon such individuals? How can "cultural regularities" be built into such collaborations so that they can survive/evolve effectively from one leadership cycle to the next?

Given the varied settings, local exigencies, and lengths of partnership experiences, we are generally pleased with the authors' analyses in response to these guidelines.

One of the most salient findings of Richard Clark's review was the dearth of attention that has been paid to documenting and evaluating network and partnership activities. Thus, we begin Part III with an attempt to construct a design for inquiry into school-university partnerships that befits the concepts developed previously in Chapter 1. Kenneth Sirotnik argues in Chapter 8 that partnership participants must be active agents in their own evaluative self-study through the process of collaborative inquiry. A central concept of collaborative inquiry is the legitimation of *critique* as knowledge-producing and effort-improving evaluative activity. A critical inquiry into partnership activities constructively challenges existing knowledge in terms of the values and human interests in the enterprise.

Many writers — some who have worked with partnerships, and some who have not — have been highly critical of the prospects of schools and universities being able to effect truly viable and collaborative working relationships. Phillip Schlechty is among those who speak from experience; moreover, he and colleague Betty Lou Whitford have been experimenting with alternative ways to bridge the school-university "gap," particularly with respect to pre-service teacher education. In Chapter 9, these authors provide an interesting and useful extension of partnerships as symbiotic relationships between schools and universities, using the professionalization of teaching as a case in point.

Finally, in Chapter 10, we attempt to sort out what the future holds for school-university partnerships based on an analysis of what our contributors have had to say. But it is also based on calculated, reasoned self-interests — appropriately so, we believe. For it should come as no surprise to readers who have glanced at the list of author affiliations that we and most of the contributors are university-based educators. Moreover, we all share a profound belief that the purpose, and perhaps existence, of schools and colleges of education depends upon the quality of their connections to educational practice. Our commitment, therefore, is to preserving schools, colleges, and departments of education as viable entities in institutions of higher education, but only to the extent that substantial attention is accorded to thought and action in collaboration with school-based educators.

Our conclusion, then, is positive; we see the cup of potential for productive school-university partnerships to be at least half full. To be sure, developing and realizing this potential will not be without attendant problems and conflicts. One can almost count on a common core of issues that will bear upon the quality of the interinstitutional relationships. The list will include at least these concerns, many of which were already anticipated above: top-heavy coordinating structures, securing adequate funding, conflicts between approaching symbiotic organizational relationships while balancing individual with institutional interests, using but not overly relying upon key individuals, getting something going while still attending to process, and, of course, developing a functioning collaboration marked by shared philosophies of organizational change and school improvement. It is our view that the experiences shared by the contributing authors of this volume suggest that struggling with these issues can be well worth the effort.

Many people with whom we have worked either directly or indirectly have helped considerably to shape our thinking and our practices. Let it simply be said that without the willingness of hundreds of educators in schools, districts, and universities to risk experimenting with partnership ideas, there would have been nothing to fill the pages of this book. We extend our sincerest thanks to these people and institutions.

# Part I
# CONCEPTS

# CHAPTER ONE

# School-University Partnerships for Educational Renewal: Rationale and Concepts

JOHN I. GOODLAD

Things left unattended deteriorate. Things attended to in desultory fashion stagnate. This is as true of institutions and those who run them as it is of gardens, shake roofs, and swimming pools. What was once lovely and/or functional becomes ugly and dysfunctional when not cared for. With respect to decaying institutions, yesterday's innovations become today's rigidities and tomorrow's anachronisms.

There is no way of assuring that deterioration and stagnation will not set in, but much can be done to delay or prevent them. Careful attention will keep a garden beautiful indefinitely, double the life of a shake roof, and enhance the inviting appearance of a pool. Humans wear out with aging, but changes in life-style can slow the process.

Institutions are concepts as well as entities. Those persons who conceptualize institutions and those who run them are continuously being replaced, usually with the young and vigorous picking up from those who have become comfortable with prevailing ideas and established ways. Yet, to borrow the words of Rodgers and Hammerstein's King of Siam, there is a puzzlement here. Rigor mortis often grips institutions even as new blood replaces the old. Some institutions appear to become comatose in performing their functions although workers and clients come and go.

There are other puzzlements. Some workers appear comatose even as they begin their careers. Some who began wide-eyed and eager soon become glassy-eyed and indolent. Some who began listlessly come alive with enthusiasm and effort, sometimes late in their careers. It is difficult to sort out the impact of humans individually and collectively on institutional culture, and it is equally difficult to unravel the reverse. Clearly, there is much more to institutional vitality in a given institution than the traits, knowledge, and skills of individuals.

This book addresses the vitality of educational institutions and those who work in them. This and several other chapters are devoted

3

primarily to the idea that the prospects for both individual and institutional renewal are vastly enhanced when the workplace is continuously infused with both the craftmanship of those similarly engaged and relevant knowledge from both inside and outside the setting. Other chapters recount, from the perspective of the several authors, early experiences with an educational change strategy designed to promote such infusion. The strategy involves large-scale collaborations among universities and school districts and their constituent schools. This chapter describes the rationale and concepts underlying a particular kind of school-university partnership and a nationwide network embracing a dozen such partnerships.

## Alternative Views of the Educational Improvement Process

The United States is currently undergoing still another cycle of attention to educational reform — first of elementary and secondary schools, then of teacher education and general education in universities. I say "still another" because cycles such as this one have occurred several times during the century.

What is frustrating and even dismaying about these cycles is that they regularly address virtually the same issues and pose such similar recommendations for reform. The recommendations for improving the schools that surfaced most frequently between 1983 and 1986 paralleled closely those attracting attention between 1957 and 1960. An analysis of reform reports in teacher education reveals repetition of many of the same recommendations since the late 1800s (Su, 1986). The same inadequacies and reminders have been the focal point for reform agendas in undergraduate education as well.

Perhaps the most puzzling aspect of these reform cycles is the disjuncture between the target of the rhetoric and the targets singled out for improvement. Almost invariably, it is the institution or program — schooling, schools, teacher education, schools of education, general education — that requires attention. But it is the teacher or, ironically, the student who is to be reformed. We are led to believe that all will be well if we select brighter teachers, put them through tougher programs, and test them during their careers. Similarly, we are to give students tougher tests, more often, or raise the expectations for passing grades, or both.

Such proposals are seductive; they possess a modicum of rationality. Further, they satisfy our need to do something. We buttress them with a few passes at getting better salaries for teachers, the slogan for getting taxpayer support being "better schools mean better jobs" (National Governors' Association, 1986).

There is something pathological about all of this. It is akin to believing that we can eliminate juvenile delinquency by incarcerating and rehabilitating delinquents. Certainly we must seek to rehabilitate juvenile delinquents, but sociological theory has been directing our attention for decades to the malfunctioning community ecology that fosters delinquency. Failing to respond to the implications of such theory and focusing only on the unfortunate individuals parallels attacking the mosquito problem without going to the ponds and ditches where mosquitoes breed. Failing to look deeply into the institutions where our young are taught and their teachers teach and are prepared to teach is a similar folly, but one of much greater significance.

We do not take readily or comfortably to the idea that our institutions, because of faulty initial conception or subsequent human neglect, are malfunctioning. If they are, as Eiseley suggests, "the bones of the societal body" (1969, p. 169), then to fault them is to cast doubt on the wisdom of our forebears, heroes included. To point to the weaknesses and inadequacies of contemporary workers is more comforting. Pick better people and subject them to tougher rules of accountability and our institutions will hum as they once did. Reluctant to prepare or engage in comprehensive overhaul, we make a few modest changes and add a few new people. No wonder that periodic proposals for reform tend to be repetitive regarding the identification of both problems and solutions.

The editors of this volume hold to the proposition that recurring, strident attacks on schooling, teacher education, and undergraduate curricula and teaching, in the form of commission and task-force reports, are symptomatic of inadequate renewing behavior in large numbers of schools and universities. We believe, further, that reform proposals directed only to the rehabilitation or replacement of individuals in these settings, however accurate the diagnosis of incompetence or inadequate effort, are doomed to failure and will serve only to assure, later, still another round of similar reform proposals.

We propose an alternative paradigm embracing simultaneous individual and institutional renewal. We believe such renewal to be feasible with or without an infusion of new personnel—which means, of course, belief in the capability and potential for renewal among persons now perceived not to be salvageable. It may be necessary to develop mechanisms for helping people move so as to achieve a better fit between individuals and institutional settings. And the process of renewal probably would progress more quickly and smoothly if those now perceived to be beyond redemption were summarily removed from the scene. But agreeing on who these people are would become extraordinarily difficult, even if we were seriously to seek such agreement. And then removing those about whom we agree is a task most of us would prefer to delegate.

Let us assume, then, that we must proceed with the faculty — teachers and administrators — we have. Let us quit wringing our hands over an aging cohort and rejoice in the realization that so much seasoned experience is available to us. Let us extend best wishes and encouragement to the Holmes Group (1986) and the Carnegie Forum on Education and the Economy (1986) and hope that their work ultimately will produce the most promising and best educated recruits for teaching in our schools (without closing off the possibility that some of their recommendations, if implemented, might be counterproductive). And let us refrain from the easy, melancholy disclaimer, "We've tried it before and it doesn't work"—because frequently we have not, and, because we have not, we do not know.

## Bureaucratic Growth and Educational Decline

There is little point in embellishing here the obvious fact that both our society and our institutions have become extraordinarily complex. What is less obvious, particularly to the young, is the extraordinary speed at which this complexity increased. When I went to school, there was no superintendent presiding over the five elementary schools and one high school in the district. When I began teaching, the secretary-treasurer of the school board and a clerk constituted the central staff in a district three times the size of the one where I had been a pupil. The shape of the things to come could be seen only in the still larger urban districts where superintendents were beginning the process of building administrative and supervisory staffs. Today, the bureaucratic model prevails in school districts, large and small. This is characteristic of our society generally, not just a perverse accompaniment of aggrandizement in the field of school administration.

Growth in both the size and complexity of our institutions led to bureaucratization and, in turn — virtually by definition — the transfer of decision-making authority from thousands of individuals in cottage-type enterprises to far fewer individuals in corporate centers removed from the arenas of daily human interaction. More and more, workers functioned by rules fashioned by others in remote and usually inaccessible places. Often, the rules did not fit the circumstances for which they were intended (usually because these circumstances were only dimly understood by those who fashioned the rules). Worse, the workers usually were powerless to change the rules to fit them to the circumstances. Today, it is astonishing for corporate executives to encounter the single sentence "policy manual" of Nordstrom, a large specialty clothing retailer: "Use your own best judgment at all times."[1]

The shift in decision-making authority, with its questionable claims of increased efficiency and cost-effectiveness, appears to be particularly inappropriate and dysfunctional in education, resulting in what Wise (1979) terms "legislated learning." Teaching involves not only thousands of decisions of cumulative impact made daily by just one teacher but also thousands of largely unpredictable human interactions occurring daily in and around a single school. Efforts to regulate, systematize, or standardize these decisions and interactions are doomed at the outset and, when implemented, are hazardous to the well-being of individuals and institutions. The role of management is to do everything possible to assure that individual judgments will be not only the worker's (student's, teacher's, administrator's) best but also the best possible under the circumstances. This means that management's attention is addressed to both increasing the worker's decision-making capability and making the circumstances more hospitable to the exercise of the worker's best judgment. When management does this well, we call it leadership.

Ironically, during several recent decades of growing bureaucratic size and complexity, management in education, as in other enterprises, was preoccupied with coping with growth itself.[2] For several years during the 1950s, to cite one example, it was necessary for Los Angeles to provide additional student seating space every Monday morning equivalent to building a 500-pupil elementary school. Not surprisingly, the implications for schooling as an institution were ignored. It was more expedient to make decisions centrally and quickly than to have second, let alone first, thoughts about the erosion of decision-making authority at school and classroom levels. Principals increasingly took their cues from the district office and not from carefully assessing the health of the cultural entities in their care. Central issues of curriculum and instruction were less and less on the minds of those in management roles in the central office and at school sites. Worse, by the 1970s when growth was stalled, the fundamental questions of what education is for and what is worth knowing, left unattended, were fading from the educational scene.

---

1. J. Nordstrom (personal communication), January 5, 1987.
2. For an informative account of this growth in both state departments of education and urban school districts, see Frazier, 1987, pp. 99–117.

Throughout the 1970s, criticisms of the schools intensified. Attacking the schools in newspaper headlines was in fashion. Some thoughtful students of education began inquiries which proved later to be useful. It was not too difficult to predict a breaking point and the form it would take. The widely publicized release in 1983 of the National Commission on Excellence in Education's report, *A Nation at Risk*, had an effect on American education comparable to that following the Russians' launching of Sputnik in 1957. *A Nation at Risk* was a goad to action, not a very accurate diagnosis of the circumstances into which schooling had fallen and, therefore, not a very useful prescription for fostering good educational health in schools. But a spur to action it certainly was.

Almost simultaneous publication of several more thoughtful, data-based analyses of and recommendations for schools provided powerful evidence to support the demand for "excellence." But the data and recommendations from these studies gaining the attention of policymakers and top administrators were those most easily used to support a "toughen up" approach to improvement, quite like the one following the launching of Sputnik. The message embedded in the research-oriented books of Boyer (1983), Goodlad (1984), and Sizer (1984) and increasingly in the major educational journals, to the effect that more fundamental questions had to be asked and answered, was largely ignored.

Currently, however, still another shift is apparent. There is little criticism of the schools to be said that has not already been said. Politicians, whose fate is attached to the short-term, already have reaped such personal gains as can be obtained. Top officials from the president of the United States on down have pointed with pride to how quickly the "rising tide of mediocrity in our schools" has been replaced by a rising tide of reform. But the truth is that the steam already has gone out of the top-down school reform effort, the money to support "more" — more time in school, more pay for teachers, etc. — has not been forthcoming, and the so-called improvements have been largely at the edges. Recent newspaper headlines are derived from another cyclical attack on teacher education.

Interest in and concern about the schools has not disappeared, however. Professional educators, initially skeptical and somewhat reluctant to get seriously involved, have been drawn in on many fronts and, to a degree, at all levels. Schools and colleges of education in the universities have played more of a waiting game, their interest being stimulated by talk of needed reforms in preparing teachers. Caution and cynicism are perhaps more evident than are bold initiatives directed toward change.

In communities across the land, there is not yet anything resembling a surge of support for a common public school, serving all comprehensively and equally. Indeed, school officials, particularly in urban districts, hesitate to tamper with the "shopping mall" (Powell, Farrar, & Cohen, 1985) array of curricular and organizational caterings to special interest groups and adaptations to students' assumed needs, which, in effect, makes a mockery of the common school concept. More than in suburban districts, many urban students are in private schools; the parents of others threaten to remove their children from the public schools if what they see to be in their special interest is removed or not added. Nationwide, the prospect of client-driven schools supported by public funds and similar in many ways to private schools, looms as a topic to be debated as well as a not-unlikely alternative to the model usually connected with our form of democracy.

There are those among us who believe, however, that the Great American Experiment with public, comprehensive, universal schooling is not over; indeed, it may be just beginning (Goodlad, 1985). What we need is a reaffirmation and, probably, a redefinition of the role of education in a democracy, with particular attention to what is required for successful enculturation of the young; a much clearer delineation of the desired function of schools in this process; a clear articulation of the goals, substance, length and breadth of the schooling deemed necessary; and a fresh commitment to both excellence and equity and how these can be forwarded simultaneously.

These essentials are not the central subject-matter of this book. But they lie just beneath the surface throughout and, from time to time, provide either a backdrop for the narrative or are addressed specifically. This chapter places them within the framework of an educational improvement strategy deliberately designed to bring to the forefront issues appearing on the surface to be somewhat less profound. The approach reflects the personal belief that we are a highly pragmatic culture. We have a passion for what works. While not entirely eschewing the whys and wherefores, philosophical dialogue tends to be rationed out along the linear stages of how. Too often, this dialogue is prolonged and is only deep enough to assure us that it is important to have reasons for doing what works.

A change strategy focused on issues that are significant and at the same time practical in their apparent implications has considerable potential for gaining serious attention. If, at the same time, these issues are the above-the-surface manifestation of something more fundamental, then they should lead us to the questions raised above regarding the role of education and schools in a democratic society — if the strategy maximizes opportunity for sustained, informed dialogue at all levels of the system and in the surrounding context.

These are extraordinary expectations; one has no assurance of achieving them. But if the strategy is based upon sound educational concepts and principles and uses human energy and resources that would normally be directed to improvement efforts anyway, the gains are likely to outweigh the losses regardless of whether or not the strategy fully lives up to its promises. We are addressing, then, a social experiment in educational improvement involving the use and refinement of a strategy that has strong heuristic underpinnings.

## School-University Collaboration: A Non-Event?

The foregoing discussion implies that institutions do not stand still for long; they renew or decline. Individuals collectively sustain the renewing process or are carried along by the decline. Individual and institutional well-being go hand in hand.

Two essentials of renewal were identified on preceding pages. First, the workers — at all levels — must have optimal opportunity to infuse their efforts with the expertise of others engaged in similar work. This notion has long inspired quiltmakers, boatbuilders, glassblowers and other craftspersons to come together for purposes of sharing designs and techniques. Second, there must be continuous infusion of both relevant knowledge and alternative (indeed, countervailing) ideas for practice stemming from inquiry into the enterprise. Universities increasingly have played a significant role in producing knowledge relevant to professions and occupations and in designing mechanisms for linking theory, research, and practice. The closer these linkages, presumably, the greater the probability that the agenda of research and the agenda of practice will be parallel and significant — the right agenda, so to speak, for their time and place in history.

For a host of reasons — some of which are addressed in this volume — the schooling enterprise is at best only weakly characterized by these essentials of renewal. The egg carton structure of schools effectively isolates teachers from one another (Lortie, 1975). Administrators and supervisors, not teachers, show up most regularly at conferences. Local opportunities for in-service education tend to be district-inspired and conducted and, ironically, take teachers away from the institutional settings so in need of renewal (Tye, 1981). Serious proposals — "serious" in that funding is included — for teachers to have time for planning within their own buildings have surfaced only in recent years. The rhetoric regarding the school as the most significant unit for change is not new (Goodlad, 1955), but the gap between rhetoric and reality remains formidable.

The record of relating research and practice in medicine, public health, dentistry and other professions is not without its warts and blemishes. Yet at only six-month intervals in our visits, most of us find in our dentists' offices evidences of advances that add to our comfort and well-being. Close alliances between schools of agriculture in universities and the practice of agriculture have produced hardier wheat, eliminated plant diseases, and enormously increased productivity. Leading businesses and industries devote a share of their income to research and development; employees attend university-sponsored institutes and workshops, with costs borne routinely by their companies.

Circumstances in the schooling workplace are quite different. The budget for research and development, if it exists at all, is rarely more than a fraction of one percent of the total. A few days of in-service education for teachers are scattered over the year and usually are taught by district staff, with an occasional speaker or consultant from a university. Attendance at a university is on one's own time and money. Rarely is there a long-term contract between a university and a school district for the renewal of employees and institutions.

Conversation among teachers and administrators rarely lauds their university preparation programs or the role of universities in enhancing practice. Yet, ironically, the knowledge base about both teaching and leadership is to a large degree the same whether used to prepare personnel for schools or for a wide range of business enterprises (Peters & Waterman, 1982). In the major universities, education professors eschew both the preparation of teachers (Judge, 1982) and sustained involvement with schools, their prime source of reward being publication in refereed journals. But schoolteachers and administrators rarely read these journals and, indeed, inhabit a culture that values action over reading, reflection, and dialogue about alternatives.

The gulf between the essentials for individual and institutional renewal and the conditions and circumstances of schooling, as well as the gulf between schools and universities, is formidable. Presumably, it is the persistence of this gulf that motivates periodic orgies of school reform. And since it appears that the malaise lies deeply embedded in the structure of institutions and, therefore, is structural and bureaucratic in character, one begins to see why reform directed at individuals alone is relatively unproductive. But one also begins to understand why productive change, even if directed at institutions, is and will be exceedingly difficult. Sarason (1972) has taught us a great deal about the resistance of school cultures to change and the difficulties inherent in seeking to replace old settings with new ones. Further, even modest attacks on the basic structure of bureaucracies alert the defensive and self-serving mechanisms of all those persons who perceive themselves to be well-served by the way things are and have been.

The above paragraph addresses the structural rigidity of schools. Substitute "colleges and universities" for "schools" and closing the gulf described becomes even more formidable. Institutions of higher learning gain much of their credibility from a unique combination of institutional stability and individual autonomy. One tampers with these characteristics at the possible peril of institutional integrity and accompanying restraints on individual productivity.

Yet, as previously noted, some university-based professional schools have been creative in maintaining their integrity as knowledge-producers while establishing relationships with practice oriented to change rather than to maintaining the status quo. Sometimes, the latter has been accomplished in part through establishing "bridging" units — notably the experiment station in agriculture and the field station in architecture and urban planning. And, of course, the health services have their hospitals and clinics. In each instance, the university has been organizationally integrated, acting as more than just an agency of goodwill or noblesse oblige.

Although professors of education have served frequently as consultants and conducted research in schools, Clark's (1986) review of the literature (see Chapter 2) reveals few arrangements within which schools and schools of education, *qua* institutions, have been organizationally linked to achieve shared purposes. An exception in intent has been the Metropolitan School Study Council described by Lieberman in Chapter 3. University-based laboratory schools were intended to link theory and practice but lacked an organizational arrangement with surrounding schools. Further, they increasingly succumbed to the university's self-interests in preparing teachers at the expense of designing alternative school practices (Goodlad, 1980). In the history of laboratory schools, we see once again preoccupation with individuals far overshadowing concern for institutional renewal. The arguments and actions directed at abolishing them rarely were countered by arguments and actions directed toward replacing them with viable alternatives.

The history of school-university collaboration is not so much, then, replete with failure as it is short on examples of carefully crafted agreements and programs accompanied by the ingredient considered by Clark (1986) to be essential for success — namely, individual and institutional commitment on both sides. In short, the joining of schools (and school districts) and universities in commonly purposive and mutually beneficial linkages is a virtually untried and, therefore, unstudied phenomenon. But, if tried, the history of educational reform in schools and in schools of education need not necessarily be a prediction of its future.

## Evolution of an Educational Improvement Strategy

In Chapter 2, Clark endeavors to sort out of confusing usage some agreement on the meaning of "network" and "partnership." He arrives at a useful conclusion regarding what a network is not: "[I]t is not a deliberately designed, collaborative arrangement between different institutions working together to advance self-interests and solve common problems." What a network is *not*, a partnership *is*.

In my lexicon, a network is a very useful arrangement of exchanging information and ideas — as among boatbuilders, engineers, sociologists, teachers, deans, and so forth. These networks are characterized by likeness of interest or job and camaraderie rather than by confrontation. They are not ordinarily designed with change — especially radical change — in mind; if change occurs (as it most assuredly does), it is more by serendipity than design.

The joining of individuals, schools, and even school districts in networks is becoming increasingly common. Accompanying usage of the term "partnership" for naming such networks is, in my judgment, unfortunate. Further, and more important, the goals frequently set for such arrangements, implying significant change and even institutional renewal, are unrealistic, portending failure and erroneously discrediting the use of partnerships as a change strategy. Schools or school districts, whatever their differences in degree (e.g., size, demographics of the student population, resources), are nonetheless similar in kind (e.g., purpose, function, structure). McNeill (1986, p. 16) has pointed out that, throughout civilization, fundamental change tends to be the result of different cultures impinging on one another. It is rare for members of a given culture not to become introspective about their customs after exposure — even abrasive exposure — to the customs of another culture. The differences between two schools or two school districts may be productive of refinements in practice through communication but usually are insufficient for challenging the validity of practices already characteristic of both. Consequently, "network," not "partnership," appears to be the better term for linkages among like institutions.

A major reason for promoting partnerships that include at least one university is that schools (or school districts) and universities differ not in degree but in kind. They differ in purpose, function, structure, clientele, reward systems, rules and regulations, ambience, ethos; schools and universities are markedly different cultural entities. Herein lie both the promise of a productive school-university partnership and the sandtraps, swamps, and quicksands standing in the way of a successful marriage.

Symbiosis is a provocative concept. Viewed positively, it refers to unlike organisms (or institutions) joined intimately in mutually beneficial relationships. For there to be a symbiotic partnership, presumably three minimum conditions must prevail: dissimilarity between or among the partners; mutual satisfaction of self-interests; and sufficient selflessness on the part of each member to assure the satisfaction of self-interests on the part of all members. Regarding partnerships between schools and universities, the first condition is clearly present. The others must be created and require resolve, commitment, planning, creativity, leadership, sacrifice, and endurance. A steady flame requires continuous replenishment of the lamp oil.

What follows is a recounting of those cumulative learnings from experiences spanning four decades that laid the groundwork for the partnerships and National Network for Educational Renewal (NNER).[3] Since 1947, I have been involved in school-university collaborative efforts of one kind or another, efforts to improve teacher education or schools or both simultaneously, and in research or some aspect of one or more of these. Elsewhere, I have described evolution during these years of the educational improvement strategy built into the NNER (Goodlad, 1987). Several of the lessons learned are highly relevant to understanding this strategy.

## The Atlanta Area Teacher Education Service

The Atlanta Area Teacher Education Service (AATES), created at the close of World War II, joined six rapidly growing school districts and six colleges and universities in a collaborative effort to upgrade the qualifications of practicing teachers, many of whom did not possess baccalaureate degrees and formal preparation to teach (Goodlad & Jor-

---

3. The NNER combines two time-honored strategies designed with educational purposes in mind — namely, partnerships and networks. Each partnership consists of at least one university (at present, primarily their schools and colleges of education) and up to a dozen school districts (with their member schools). Currently 14 in number in as many states, these school-university partnerships embrace 17 institutions of higher education and 115 school districts. The Network comprises all 14 partnerships, each viewed as a separate, unique entity.

dan, 1950). It served this purpose well. Teachers registered for degrees at the institution of their choice and poured into courses conveniently located and taught by the professor best qualified, regardless of his or her institutional affiliation. But the AATES was, indeed, a "service." It was not built structurally into the existing bones of the institutions. Individuals, not institutions, were the focus and locus. Perhaps because of the magnitude of the enterprise, some institutional changes occurred by serendipity.

Two subprograms of the AATES provoked my thinking about the change process, however. One was a renaissance in the arts in schools which had its genesis in the fact that the esteemed artist and chairman of the art department at the University of Georgia, Lamar Dodd, became motivated about the possibilities while teaching one of the AATES courses. He introduced into the art department a vision of cultivating the abilities of large numbers of teachers to develop the artistic talents of their students. This vision was translated into a built-in departmental function and an encouraged faculty activity. *Unless working with children, teachers, and schools is legitimated within relevant units of the university — that is, those units with present, potential, or latent self-interests pertaining to schools — relations with the schools are likely to be marginal and maintained only in a spirit of sporadic goodwill.*

The other subgroup was a rather accurate version of the sequence in child study meticulously designed by Daniel Prescott, first at the University of Chicago and later at the University of Maryland. Its structure differed markedly from that of the courses offered routinely and, usually, on an *ad hoc* basis through the AATES. First, there was a three-year sequence, beginning with the detailed study of a single child and proceeding through the study of a child and children in a larger social context. Second, each cohort was brought together initially and subsequently in a two-week summer workshop, serving to anchor the yearlong study and class sessions at both ends. Third, and perhaps most important, a principal and a group of teachers from a single school formed a sub-cohort as a condition of participation.

I joined Lynn Shufelt, director of the AATES child study program, in an experimental fourth year for school-based clusters that had completed the standard three-year sequence. Our purpose was to address the question of what child development, as we had come to understand it, meant for school and classroom practice. Again and again during that year and the next, when we again worked with a fourth-year cohort, dialogue turned to frustration over school-based regularities some perceived to be at cross-purposes with the principals' and teachers' insights into the developmental processes of children.

During a nine-year association with the AATES (on nearly a full-time basis from 1947 to 1949 and a substantial part-time basis from 1949 to 1956), I experienced recurring, persistent questioning of the regularities of schooling only among these cohort groups and only after they had worked together for a considerable amount of time in developing some common values and agreements regarding learners and learning — a philosophy, if you will. And, by 1954 or thereabouts — some eight years after the founding of the AATES — the schools beginning to stand out for their exemplary (and often innovative) practices were staffed by a principal and core of teachers who had come through the complete child study sequence.

There are several learnings here:

1. For a school to become renewing, there must be at least a core of teachers and the principal engaged continuously in inquiry about the nature, quality, and relevance of the educational enterprise in which they are engaged.
2. There must be "detached" time — time away from daily demands, as in summer workshops (with no children to teach) — for periods of sustained dialogue and reflection.
3. It is highly desirable and perhaps even necessary for there to be some interpenetration with other cohort groups, "alternative drummers," and countervailing ideas on provocative questions.

### The Englewood Project

For the last two or three years of the period just described and for the next six years, I directed the Englewood Project. With funds provided by the William Vanderbilt family and full approval of the superintendent and board of the Sarasota, Florida, county school district, I worked with the principal (more than one over the years) in designing a new elementary school program and a new building unit to accommodate it. Growth in enrollment demanded a change in the one-grade-per-class-per-teacher structure which the old six-room building and graded structure of the Englewood elementary school had accommodated so comfortably. Instead of having one teacher teach the overload of 30 or so students in a multi-graded class, all teachers transited to a multi-grade, then a multi-age and ultimately a nongraded class (Goodlad, 1958). Experiencing and anticipating more growth, we turned our attention to designing new space that would accommodate cooperative teaching. There has emerged no evidence to challenge the claim that this was the first nongraded, team-taught elementary school in the United States (Goodlad and Anderson, 1959). It was an early experiment, too, with a peer review system of teacher evaluation (Bahner, 1960).

The necessary but not sufficient conditions for school renewal summarized above were built in from the beginning: a cohort group (in this instance, the principal and all the teachers) engaged continuously in serious inquiry about the school's central business; detached time (but not much, given district constraints); and an alternative drummer who worked with the staff several times a year, observed and critiqued classes, provided written evaluations and suggestions, and so forth. Further, the enterprise enjoyed the enthusiastic support of the superintendent and chairman of the board, as well as modest funds to be used at the discretion of the project's director.

Aware that the school's structure and program were increasingly deviating from conventional practice (a fact broadcast in part by the moderately innovative new building), the principal in particular worked very hard on communications — with parents, self-appointed guardians of personal and community values, and especially other principals. For the most part, these efforts were successful. The school became sufficiently built into the community and its program sufficiently satisfying to parents and students for scattered criticisms to be blunted. The principal was elected president of the district's administrators' association; new buildings in the district borrowed upon and extended concepts built into the Englewood addition; modifications of the nongraded, team-taught pattern of organization were developed in other schools.

But it was entirely upstream paddling from the beginning. Positive reinforcement from the district office was short of district promulgation of values compatible with the Englewood effort. Sporadic dissemination to other schools was quite different from being part of a network of schools, each committed to inquiry into its business and all joined in the discussion and exchange of practices and ideas. Neither of these nor any other deliberately designed support mechanisms existed in the district. Indeed, the in-service education pattern of drawing teachers away from the schools for district-wide institutes and the like — common in the United States at that time and still today — worked against the kind of institutional renewal characterizing the Englewood school from the beginning of the project.

Two significant learnings emerged for me from the experience:

1. Just as the culture of the individual school can powerfully resist changes imposed upon it, that same culture can be a potent force for change, given proper conditions (Goodlad, 1977).
2. One of these conditions is a supportive infrastructure that not only encourages the principal and teachers to design the best possible settings for learning and teaching but also provides the necessary resources and supporting mechanisms.

Left alone, a school faculty that runs against tradition and convention consumes so much time and energy defending its accomplishments that it soon has little of either left for continuing the process of renewal.

### The League of Cooperating Schools

The League of Cooperating Schools in southern California was deliberately designed (in 1966) to provide this infrastructure. I have described elsewhere several of the key elements: the individual school as the center of change, a network (18 schools in 18 districts), a long-term commitment signed and approved by each district's superintendent and board, a rather substantial supporting "hub" independent of the districts and loosely connected to a major university, and a data-gathering process capable of providing useful information for formative evaluation at both the school and network level (Goodlad, 1975). This hub provided the League with staff members who maintained direct linkages to the schools, conducted monthly meetings of principals focused directly on their problems of leadership, published a newsletter, provided research summaries in areas of interest and demand, organized all-League conferences, served as a switching-station for exchanging information and bringing together small groups of teachers with like interests, occasionally brought in speakers and consultants, provided information to superintendents and arranged periodic meetings for them, and gathered various kinds of data.

The prime locus of attention throughout the six years of the League's formal existence was the school as the center of change and the cultivation within it of individual and institutional renewal. To the degree possible, each school was to be a renewing entity through development and refinement of an inquiry process commonly referred to as DDAE—for dialogue, decision, actions, and evaluation (Bentzen, 1974). The monthly meetings of principals frequently addressed their role in fostering such a process. Hub staff members assisted a school faculty with problem-solving, sometimes infusing into the dialogue data on DDAE in that particular school.

The hub served as a major part of the Research Division of the Institute for Development of Educational Activities (/I/D/E/A/), then an arm of the Kettering Foundation. This organization built into its Individually Guided Education (IGE) program key elements of the strategy developed in the League of Cooperating Schools. IGE, in turn, became a nationwide school improvement strategy.

Those of us who were most intimately involved with the Study of Educational Change and School Improvement, the research activity accompanying the League, became convinced that DDAE, the inquiry process encouraged in each school, is the most important and, at the same time, the most underrated and least understood part of the strategy which the /I/D/E/A/ staff sought to adapt and incorporate into IGE. Essential to inquiry (inquiry is meaningless without it) is generating and acting upon knowledge. This, we believe, was the most neglected ingredient in the IGE schools, cut off as most of them were from research-oriented institutions such as universities. Although the hub of the League was only loosely tied to the University of California, Los Angeles, it performed in many ways the role one might expect of a university in what Sirotnik refers to as "collaborative inquiry" (Chapter 8). It was especially useful in promoting the importance of generating and using knowledge.

A second shortcoming in the IGE adaptation was the looseness and disparateness of the network. /I/D/E/A/ should have served as the central hub for the hubs of a dozen or a hundred Leagues of Schools, each with its own identity and infrastructure. Instead, /I/D/E/A/ sought to monitor a widely dispersed collection of schools, depending greatly on films and written materials to convey concepts and processes. There was little or no opportunity to build the level of trust and candor that characterized the meetings of the principals of League schools. Indeed, more than a dozen daylong, monthly meetings took place before the League group even addressed an agenda of problems owned by principals as genuine and real.

Likewise, the geographic disparateness of IGE schools strained /I/D/E/A/ resources in seeking to maintain communications with all of the schools, to say nothing of cultivating support for each at the district level. This proved to be a serious shortcoming in the League as well. We had placed most of our chips on the individual schools and on cultivating the network of 18. We did not omit concern for the superintendent and the district, but we also did not cultivate them. Some superintendents remained highly supportive throughout, but some were skeptical and even hostile. Several saw their principals enjoying intellectual benefits they did not have; several saw elevation of the principal's leadership role as a threat to their authority. Only a handful of superintendents deliberately cultivated support for their League school with other principals and schools. Not surprisingly, several principals of League schools experienced the hard knocks of being regarded as "rate-busters" in charge of "funny farms."

Mostly, experience with the League of Cooperating Schools and the Study of Educational Change confirmed the learnings gleaned from the AATES and the Englewood Project built into the strategy from the beginning. But it strengthened several learnings immeasurably and added several more. Chief among these are the following:

1. Although certain of the concepts are more seminal and important than others — for example, developing the renewing capacity of those closest to students, the individual school as the center of change, the process of inquiry — potency for change lies in combining all of these and more within a supportive infrastructure which includes ample access to alternatives and relevant knowledge.
2. The most significant elements, such as collaborative inquiry (Chapter 8), are also the most difficult to achieve and, simultaneously, the most deceptively subtle in their mature functioning. Consequently, they usually are the ones least likely to be diligently cultivated and most likely to be sacrificed to "packages" or quick-fix panaceas.
3. In efforts to achieve the positive potential of symbiotic partnerships between schools (or school districts) and universities, the latter are least likely to perceive the relationship as relevant to their self-interests and, therefore, least likely to enter seriously into the marriage and to make it work.

## A Study of Schooling

The fourth and last contributor to the partnership strategy that evolved was A Study of Schooling, an intensive study of 38 schools (1,016 classrooms) conducted nationally during the late 1970s. The study strengthened a number of postulates about the conditions and circumstances of schooling summarized on preceding pages: relatively impotent, haphazard, short-term staff development activities focused on individuals and removed from school sites; little time or stimulus for site-based renewal; little evidence of attention to and encouragement of long-term planning at either the school or district level. The study revealed, also, the prevalence and persistence of instructional, curricular and organizational regularities running counter to a rather large body of literature that has for some time pointed to the need for alternatives. The fact that these regularities have fared so well in the face of contrary authorized opinions[4] and cyclical attacks attests to both their virility and their usefulness to some educators and school patrons alike. Practices that serve well the special interests or beliefs of those most closely attached to them are not easily changed.

---

4. For a discussion of the concept of authorized opinions, see Buchman, 1987.

Ironically, although professors of education have produced a good deal of the knowledge about learning, teaching, questionable school practices, and the like, neither professors nor schools of education were in the forefront of reform initiatives immediately before or after Sputnik (1957) or "Sputnik 1983" — *A Nation at Risk*. Their critiques of the reform literature of both eras have been voluminous, however. Clearly, the university culture possesses those characteristics of reflective inquiry that are at once lacking and needed in schools. Further, units such as schools of agriculture, as noted earlier, have organized themselves so as to participate in the collaborative inquiry endorsed by Sirotnik in Chapter 8. It would be highly desirable (and probably in the interests of their survival) for schools of education to do likewise.

The thesis emerging in my mind, then, as the findings from A Study of Schooling began to fall into place (Goodlad, 1984), was comprised of several interrelated themes:

1. Juxtaposition of the action-oriented culture of the school and the inquiry-oriented culture of the university offers promise of shaking loose the calcified programs of both (e.g., how teachers teach and how teachers are prepared to teach.
2. A school-university partnership offers promise of stimulating collaborative inquiry into both the problems of the schools and relevance of various research paradigms.
3. The agenda of instructional, curricular, and organizational improvements needed in the schools and of the relevance of teacher education and research programs in schools of education appear to overlap and thus to satisfy the criterion of mutual self-interests characteristic of a potentially powerful partnership.

## School-University Partnerships and the NNER

This thesis and the learnings about individual and school renewal, networking, supportive infrastructures, and the like contributed significantly to the creation, between 1980 and 1985, of the Southern California Partnership, Brigham Young University–School District Partnership, and the Puget Sound Educational Consortium, all described in subsequent chapters. And experiences with these school-university partnerships led to communications and, ultimately, transactions with persons in other settings interested in or already engaged in various school-university collaborations. These, in turn, led to creation of the National Network (of School-University Partnerships) for Educational Renewal.

The balance of this chapter presents, in somewhat abbreviated fashion, the document now referred to as "the mission statement" of the NNER — essentially a set of concepts and arrangements agreed to by the constituent partnerships. Chapter 8 places these within an evaluation framework. Chapter 10 includes, among other things, some caveats and some reflections on the issues and problems likely, in the future, to somewhat temper one's enthusiasms for what appears to be an idea whose time has come.

The learnings summarized on preceding pages emerge all too neatly from the complex contexts from which they were derived. Putting them all together in a comprehensive educational improvement strategy is an undertaking of great difficulty and uncertainty — a social experiment.

### The NNER Mission Statement

There is little in the history of school-university relations to suggest that collaboration has served to solve tough, persistent problems. Often, the relationship has been self-serving, bypassing areas of *mutual* self-interest calling for give-and-take and joint inquiry. Schools, for example, have sought university-based consultants to help them do better what they are already doing. Universities have sought out teachers in schools to supervise their student teachers, and these "cooperating teachers" have passed along the conventional wisdom to their future colleagues. Neither the schools nor the teacher education programs have been fundamentally changed in the process. Yet, the criticism of both seldom has been more intense. It is hard not to conclude that more than tinkering is necessary.

Consequently, universities and school districts in 14 settings have entered into long-term agreements to work closely with one another *as equal partners* for purposes of addressing long-standing, tough problem areas in which both sets of institutions have a stake. Recognizing the difficulties and complexities of working together on overlapping self-interests, which in themselves are complex, the institutions have made substantial commitments to the partnerships of which they are a part. Recognizing that networking has proven to be a useful strategy for strengthening local, collaborating entities, each school-university partnership has joined in the National Network for Educational Renewal. Again, a serious commitment is involved, the minimum essentials of which are detailed subsequently.

Before proceeding with further elaboration on both these partnerships and the network joining them, it is essential to emphasize a fact that has been largely overlooked in the current rhetoric of educational reform. It is true that many of the most serious problems of schooling and many of the most persistent problems inherent in preparing educators for the schools have been around for a long time. Reform movements have come and gone, leaving very little mark on either educators or schools. But what has changed and is changing rapidly is the context within which institutionalized forms of education function.

Not only have the coalitions that created and sustained the educational system withered, but the institutions represented in these coalitions have weakened significantly. The family rivals the school in its loss of stability. Home, school, and religious institution no longer join as they once did in rearing the young. Further, a secondary school that once enrolled only a fraction of the age group — and those young people most supported by other institutions in the coalition — has become part of the common school. The problems of dealing with student diversity grow even greater. Perhaps most serious of all, the parental and solid-citizen role models of an intimate community and the heroes of virtue of earlier times have been largely replaced by the glamorized lives of "beautiful people" and athletes whose exploits are made exotic and larger than life by attentive media. The role of education in enculturation is threatened by serious imperfections in the culture itself.

One major implication of all this (and more) is that we must look beneath the often-cited problems of low test scores, for example, in seeking an agenda worth the time and energy of the teachers, principals, professors, superintendents, and deans embraced by a school-university partnership. Another is that the changing context briefly sketched above will not become more amenable to educational processes — especially the moral imperatives embedded in such processes — unless the educative role of other institutions is maximized. Although this document focuses on the minimum essentials of a healthy school-university relationship, it is assumed that each partnership will join with other agencies committed to the idea of educative communities. The drug problem, for instance, will not be solved by school-based classes, counseling, and student searches, however useful these may be. If it is to be resolved at all, the solutions will come from recognizing and addressing this problem and others attributed to schools as clear signs of pathology in the community and, indeed, the larger society.

It is assumed that the partnerships being entered into are symbiotic in nature — that is, two different kinds of organisms (institutions) are joining for the satisfaction of mutual self-interests. The obvious differences between schools and universities, which undeniably complicate and frustrate collaboration, are strengths, not weaknesses to be overcome. Without them, collaboration would represent redundancy. Nonetheless, there are overlapping self-interests (schools need better teachers; universities need better sites in which to prepare future teachers). The agenda of collaboration grows out of the points of overlap. For a partnership to be successful, each partner must see satisfaction of the self-interests of the other(s) as essential to the satisfaction of its own. Consequently, to see to it that the self-interests of the other(s) are met is to be both selfless and self-serving. It is realistic, not cynical, to suggest that partnerships lacking this balance of selflessness and selfishness are short-lived.

It is assumed that each partnership is to be characterized by efficient and effective sharing of information and knowledge, either produced by its members or coming from other sources. Schools and universities in collaboration for the improvement of schooling and education must maintain a commitment to quality information and knowledge *in context* — that is, in terms of relevant historical, current, and projected social, political, and economic circumstances and conditions at local, state, national, and international levels. Consequently, the results of both previous research and new research (including formative evaluation) will infuse ongoing processes of renewal.

It is assumed that each partnership will seek to clarify and promulgate a small set of beliefs about what education is and what this conception means for priorities, programs, and practices. This set must be small enough to maximize near-consensus of endorsement, and yet permit maximum flexibility for local initiative and creative response. Leaders, therefore, must be willing and able to empower others with the time and autonomy necessary for individual creativity. For example, it is assumed that each partnership is committed to assuring equal access to knowledge for all students. But what blocks access and, therefore, what must be done to remove the blocks may differ from institution to institution.

It is assumed that individual schools and individual preparation programs are the units of improvement. Research shows that change does not come about and is not sustained through intervention and installation techniques. Rather, persons in schools and persons responsible for programs must learn how to effect improvement as a built-in characteristic. They take care of their business in increasingly better ways. Therefore, resources are essential to a renewal process that involves dialogue, decisions, actions, and evaluation. Unless the conditions for renewal marked by inquiry are created, improvement once more will be at the edges, not fundamental.

The paths to truly effective partnerships between schools and school districts and universities are not at all clear. Indeed, the literature suggests that symbiotic partnerships, as defined above, have scarcely been attempted. It is assumed, then, that there is much to be learned by everyone involved. Consequently, "staff development," as in-service education has come to be called, is for everyone — superintendents, deans, and professors, as well as teachers and principals — not just those at the base of the organizational pyramid.

Efforts to attribute accountability signal pathology in the system (Cronbach & Associates, 1980). Consequently, it is assumed that the partnerships entered into will eschew in their operations any search for persons or places for the affixing of blame. Instead, every effort will be made to develop values and practices that promote a system of shared responsibilities. Clearly, the largest source of power and energy for educational improvement is at the base of the organizational pyramid referred to above. We see once again the enlightened role of leadership in empowering teachers and principals in schools and those who have responsibility for teacher education and other preparation programs so that the process of change becomes one of continuous renewal.

The cards are stacked against improvement that is anything other than glacial or cosmetic. Policy makers frequently berate educators for their apparent inertia and then often enact mandates that encourage inertia. It is assumed that the current opportunity to restructure schooling and the education of educators will pass us by unless the policies enacted (and not enacted) succeed in unleashing the energy of educators and then providing the infrastructure by means of which this energy will be constructively guided and supported. In some cases, this means rolling back state legislation already on the books. In some instances, it means providing the financial resources for local planning and action. Consequently, the partnerships cannot afford to remain mute with respect to the larger educational context of which they are a part. Some of them represent up to 30 percent of the student enrollment in the state. It becomes obvious that partnerships can and must play a significant role in the advocacy of policy to support sound educational practices. Likewise, the National Network for Educational Renewal assumes such advocacy as one of its major functions.

### Minimum Essentials for Each Partnership

CONCEPT.  A school-university partnership represents a planned effort to establish a formal, mutually beneficial, interinstitutional relationship characterized by sufficient commitment to the effective fulfillment of overlapping functions to warrant the inevitable loss of some present control and authority on the part of the institution currently claiming dominant interest.

PURPOSES. The intent is to create a process and an accompanying structure through which each *equal* party to a collaborative agreement will seek to draw on the complementary strengths of the other *equal* parties in advancing its self-interests. Each partnership is a means to this end and not an end in itself.

The central purposes boil down to just three:

1. The exemplary performance by universities of their educational responsibility to those seeking to become educators or to enhance their present performance as educators. (Increasing the usefulness of the university research function is a major part of this responsibility.)
2. The exemplary performance by schools of their educational function and the accompanying exemplary performance of school districts in providing the necessary support.
3. The exemplary performance of both universities and schools (and their school districts) in collaborative arrangements and processes that promote both of the above purposes.

AGENDA. The agenda grows out of fulfillment of the above purposes. It must not be allowed to grow out of a preoccupation with sustaining a partnership for its own sake. Nor is the partnership to be the vehicle for solving all of the problems of schools or all of the problems of preparing educators for the schools. Rather, the partnership is to be used as a device for bringing together institutions that need each other for the solution of tough problems.

The tough problems emerge naturally as an agenda of the times. One need not be Sherlock Holmes to identify clues and underlying mysteries contributing to educational unrest, especially in times of increased educational reform activity. As we approached the 1970s, many of the problems and issues of both research and practice were tied to court-ordered desegregation of schools. Now, as we approach the 1990s, the educational focus shifts to problems inherent in the curriculum, organization, and teaching practices inside schools brought sharply to the surface because of the need to accommodate diverse student populations. One begins with such problems because they are there; they are real to large numbers of people; they won't go away. But one does not pursue for long either the problems of the 1960s or those of the 1980s without coming to the realization that they are manifestations of educational and, indeed, sociopolitical issues of long standing. What appears to be quite contemporary is found to have a long lineage.

The following agenda of our time grows out of rather simple detective work carried out in our own Study of Schooling, by Boyer (1983) and Sizer (1984) in their studies of high schools, and in some other of the more thoughtful analyses appearing in the last decade. It also grows out of mutual institutional sensitivity to those problems that have largely resisted previous attempts to resolve them, whether mounted by single institutions or institutions in unison. The specifics will change but the following emerge as worthy of concerted attention and action:

1. The creation of exemplary sites in which future teachers are educated that demonstrate the best we know about how schools should function.
2. The creation of internships and residencies for educational specialists (including administrators) through which these professionals may observe and gain experience with the best possible educational practices.
3. The development of curricula that truly reflect the best analyses and projections of what young people need.
4. The assurance of equal access by all students to these curricula.
5. The cultivation of site-based staff development activities designed to foster continual school renewal, particularly of the curriculum and accompanying pedagogical practices.
6. The restructuring of schools to assure increased continuity of students' programs, decreased accumulation of partial and inadequate or misdirected learnings, decreased alienation and dropping-out of students, and more effective utilization of varied teaching resources, including technology.
7. The continuous infusion of knowledge relative to provision of good education in schools and in programs preparing educators.
8. The creation and utilization of opportunities to promote in the community a continuing, informed dialogue about what education is and why it has more to do with the welfare of both individuals and society than just preparation for jobs.

STRUCTURE. Although there probably is no one best way to organize school-university partnerships, experience and careful thought suggest at least these minimum essentials (or their equivalents) for structuring each partnership:

1. A governing board, preferably but not necessarily composed of the superintendent of each collaborating school district and the dean(s) of the participating school(s) or college(s) of education.
2. A modest secretariat composed of an executive director reporting to the governing board, and charged with performing both leadership and management functions; and necessary support services provided by a secretary and, preferably, a research assistant — all paid from the partnership budget.
3. An operating budget providing both money and specifically assigned personnel from participating institutions (N.B.: Should any institution volunteer to provide for the executive director, for example, it must be clearly understood that this person reports directly to the governing board in performing partnership functions, not to the institution contributing this resource.)
4. Top-level endorsement and support from each institution's chief executive officer and, ultimately, university involvement beyond the school or college of education.
5. Task forces or working parties, each charged with developing plans and strategies for addressing the most critical and most calcified problems of improving schools and the education of educators, and each staffed with appropriate representation of schools, district offices, and universities (and with consultants from outside any given partnership, as appropriate).
6. An orderly process within each partnership of endorsing and encouraging all projects and activities undertaken in the partnership so as to assure widespread understanding and a minimum of bureaucratic procedures and control.
7. An ongoing effort to document, analyze, and communicate successes and failures and possible reasons for successes and failures (preferably through designating and supporting an individual to take the lead in assuring that the gathering of relevant data is built into the functioning of the partnership).
8. The establishment and maintenance of connecting linkages with the NNER for purposes of giving help to and receiving help from other partnerships in the network.
9. A deliberate effort to secure additional funds from external funding sources (particularly those in the state or region).
10. The redirection of existing funds within and across institutions for purposes of securing the time necessary for educational renewal.
11. A formal time commitment of at least five years.
12. Arrangements for sharing information, ideas, and even resources

within and across partnerships, including the sharing of responsibility for advocating the best in educational policy and practice.

## Minimum Essentials for the NNER

In the same vein, a set of minimum essentials is proposed for a network of school-university partnerships focusing on educational renewal:

1. Exchange of ideas, practices, information, and personnel among partnerships.
2. Provision of data and analysis of experiences for purposes of contributing to our knowledge about change and improvement.
3. Task forces addressing common self-interests.
4. A communications network among partnerships.
5. Support from the Center for Educational Renewal[5] in the form of consultants, exchange of information (for example, through a newsletter), organization of task forces, periodic meetings and conferences, networking of expertise, and assistance in securing supplementary funds.
6. Use of the totality of the NNER in advocating the importance of education and securing sound educational practices and policies that support renewal, as opposed to sporadic efforts to upgrade the delivery system.

## Conclusion

In this chapter, I have endeavored to construct the argument for school-university collaboration by reviewing the growth of schooling as we know it today and the largely unsuccessful efforts to intervene signifi-

---

5. With regard to funding, each partnership is to be a "tub on its own bottom." The Center for Educational Renewal, with headquarters at the University of Washington, will assist in every way possible to secure additional resources. The budget of the Center for Educational Renewal, with support from private foundations, pledges five years of support for a newsletter, consultants, meetings of executive directors of the partnerships, and the work of network task forces. The director of the National Network and his associates will endeavor to maintain close communication with all partnerships and to improve their well-being. Staff members of the Center and several continuing consultants will assist in coordination and in their areas of expertise. The ultimate source of human resources lies, however, within the network itself. Consequently, a major activity of the Center for Educational Renewal is the networking of resources.

cantly into the regularities of schools or those of universities ostensibly connected to them; by sharing a personal account of my own intellectual growth and development of school-university partnership principles through intensive experiences with several such projects over the last four decades; and by outlining the commitments and working assumptions we have developed for school-university partnerships as members of a national network.

It is my sincere hope that readers do not mistake what I have presented here as a public relations piece for the NNER. The concept and vitality of *partnerships* between schools and universities are much larger and far more important than any one organizational effort. I have used my own experiences and the NNER because they are close at hand and because they may be representative of the kind of structural, behavioral, and attitudinal changes we must risk if we are to make more than marginal impacts on schools and universities.

My colleagues and I are engaged, then, in an ongoing learning experience. I encourage others to do the same in their own ways. Together, we will have much to share regarding the problems and possibilities of collaboration between schools and universities.

## References

Bentzen, M. M. (1974). *Changing schools: The magic feather principle.* New York: McGraw-Hill.

Bahner, J. M. (1960). *An elementary school faculty at work.* Unpublished doctoral dissertation, University of Chicago.

Boyer, E. L. (1983). *High school.* New York: Harper & Row.

Buchman, M. (1987). Reporting and using educational research: Conviction or persuasion? In John I. Goodlad (Ed.), *The ecology of school renewal,* 86th yearbook of the National Society for the Study of Education, Part I, pp. 170–191. Chicago: University of Chicago Press.

Carnegie Forum on Education and the Economy. (1986). *A nation prepared: Teachers for the 21st century.* New York: Carnegie Forum.

Clark, R. W. (1986). *School-university relationships: Partnerships and networks.* Occasional Paper No. 2, Center for Educational Renewal, College of Education, University of Washington, Seattle.

Cronbach, L. J., & Associates. (1980). *Toward reform of program evaluation.* San Francisco: Jossey-Bass.

Eiseley, L. C. (1969). Alternatives to technology. In A. W. Warner, D. Morse, & T. E. Cooney (Eds.), *The environment of change* (pp. 165–180). New York: Columbia University Press.

Frazier, C. M. (1987). The 1980s: States assume educational leadership. In John I. Goodlad (Ed.), *The ecology of school renewal,* 86th yearbook of the National Society for the Study of Education, Part I, pp. 99–117. Chicago: University of Chicago Press.

Goodlad, J. I. (1955). The individual school and its principal: Key setting and key person in educational leadership. *Educational Leadership, 13*, 2–6.

Goodlad, J. I. (1958). In pursuit of visions. *Elementary School Journal, 59*, 1–17.

Goodlad, J. I. (1975). *The dynamics of educational change.* New York: McGraw-Hill.

Goodlad, J. I. (1977). An ecological approach to change in elementary-school settings. *Elementary School Journal, 78*(2), 95–105.

Goodlad, J. I. (1980). How laboratory schools go awry. *UCLA Educator, 21*(2), 47–53.

Goodlad, J. I. (1984). *A place called school.* New York: McGraw-Hill.

Goodlad, J. I. (1985). The great American schooling experiment. *Phi Delta Kappan, 67*(4), 266–271.

Goodlad, J. I. (1987). School-university partnerships: An idea whose time is come? Unpublished manuscript.

Goodlad, J. I., & Anderson, R. H. (1959, revised 1963; reprinted 1987). *The nongraded elementary school.* New York: Harcourt Brace Jovanovich; reprinted, Teachers College Press.

Goodlad, J. I., & Jordan, F. (1950). When school and college collaborate. *Educational Leadership, 7*, 461–465.

Holmes Group. (1986). *Tomorrow's teachers: A report of the Holmes Group.* East Lansing, MI: Holmes Group, Inc.

Judge, H. (1982). *American graduate schools of education: A view from abroad.* New York: Ford Foundation.

Lortie, D. C. (1975). *Schoolteacher: A sociological study.* Chicago: University of Chicago Press.

McNeill, W. H. (1986). *Mythistory and other essays.* Chicago: University of Chicago Press.

National Commission on Excellence in Education. (1983). *A nation at risk.* Washington, DC: The Commission.

National Governors' Association. (1986). *Time for results: The governor's 1981 report on education.* Washington, DC: National Governors' Association.

Peters, T. J., & Waterman, R. H. (1982). *In search of excellence: Lessons from America's best-run companies.* New York: Warner Books.

Powell, A. G., Farrar, E., & Cohen, D. K. (1985). *The shopping mall high school.* Boston: Houghton Mifflin.

Sarason, S. B. (1972). *The creation of settings and the future societies.* San Francisco: Jossey-Bass.

Sizer, T. R. (1984). *Horace's compromise: The dilemma of the American high school.* Boston: Houghton Mifflin.

Su, Zhixin. (1986). *Teacher education reform in the United States (1890–1986).* Occasional Paper No. 3, Center for Educational Renewal, College of Education, University of Washington, Seattle.

Tye, K. A. (1981). Changing our schools: The realities. In *A study of schooling,* Technical Report No. 30, Graduate School of Education, University of California, Los Angeles.

Wise, A. E. (1979). *Legislated learning.* Berkeley: University of California Press.

# CHAPTER TWO

# School-University Relationships: An Interpretive Review

RICHARD W. CLARK

The average person who is not part of the public schools or the various institutions of higher education in this country probably has the commonsense point of view that these organizations are in the same business — education — and assumes that they work together to achieve complementary if not identical goals. The average person would undoubtedly be surprised if told that, in reality, these are very different kinds of organizations with cultures so different that professionals working within them have difficulty understanding one another's needs and values. Since all professionals in schools and universities have at one time or another been active participants in precollegiate education — as students if not as faculty or administrators — it is even more surprising that these people have a lack of knowledge of each other's culture and a lack of awareness of how they can work together to achieve more than can be accomplished by working separately. In spite of commonsense points of view and lack of knowledge about each other's institutions, collaboration among school and university personnel is now one of the most frequently talked about approaches to the reform of education.

Recently, Goodlad (1984) completed his extensive A Study of Schooling, reporting on results of in-depth investigations in 38 schools covering more than 1,000 classrooms, 1,300 teachers, 8,600 parents, and 17,000 students. In that work he described actions needed to reform schools, and called for the creation of a national network of local school-university partnerships. After describing The Partnership he had initiated with surrounding school districts while he was dean at the University of California at Los Angeles (UCLA), Goodlad went on to say:

> Needed is a critical mass large enough to make a visible difference — a really sizable network of partnerships, if you will. Each partnership must be small enough to be conceptually and logically manageable and large enough to include the essential components of the community arena — but

no more. The network to which the partnerships belong must be a binding, communicating one sharing a reasonably common agenda. (1984, p. 356)

While the ideas of partnership between and networking of these institutions are relatively old, instances of schools and universities actually working together to renew schools are still relatively rare. However, there is a substantial and growing body of literature concerning networks and other types of school-university relationships. This chapter seeks to provide an overview of that literature as background for further consideration of specific examples of relationships and as a resource for people actively engaged in creating and operating partnerships and networks for school improvement. Since there are many articles, books, and other documents on the subject of school-university relationships, it would be presumptuous to suggest that this chapter summarizes the findings of *all* studies. It does, however, represent the results of an extensive review of the literature on the subject and provides bibliographic information for those who wish to explore the subject in more depth.

After a thorough investigation of this literature, it seemed useful to organize this review into three main parts:

1. A clarification of terminology and definitions.
2. A historical review of school-university relationships dating as far back as the late 1800s and continuing up to the present.
3. A more specific discussion of the purposes, problems, and possibilities in these relationships as they emerged from the historical review.

## Terminology and Definitions

One of the complications of investigating this subject is that different terms are used to describe similar activities, and, on the other hand, different meanings are attached to the same term. Authors speak of partnerships, collaborations, consortiums, networks, clusters, interorganizational agreements (IOAs), collectives, and cooperatives, frequently without definition and often without distinguishing their chosen descriptor from other possible terms. In fact, these are different kinds of relationships, and, at least to some extent, it is important to define them before attempting to discuss school-university relationships. This collection of terms and meanings can be most easily sorted out by distinguishing networks from the array of remaining configurations.

*Networks*

Of the various terms used, *network* represents the most complex concept and has the greatest record of scholarly investigation. Sarason, Carroll, Maton, Cohen, and Lorentz (1977) observe:

> The word *network* has been used in more than a dozen fields, including sociology, anthropology, psychiatry, psychology, administrative sciences, geography, city planning, and communications engineering. Although there is little cross-indexing among fields, network has surprisingly similar but not identical meanings across these disciplines, each discipline emphasizing different points, and certainly various disciplines studying dissimilar phenomena. Most usages are not mutually exclusive and reflect the same underlying idea, that is, that each person or organization has a wide array of interrelationships, the bases of which can vary in the extreme. (p. 126)

While relying primarily on material from administrative sciences and sociology, this review will examine some materials from all of the above mentioned fields.

Historically, Jacob Moreno (1934) provided basic methodological tools for analyzing networks as he developed sociograms to provide graphic representations of social relationships among individuals. Sociology has continued to focus on the study of such relationships, expanding the size of the networks and the sophistication of tools used for the study. Role theory, exchange theory, and structural-functional theory have all contributed to this development of sophisticated methodology (Smith, 1983). Networks became the focus of such studies with the publication of Katz and Lazarfield's *Personal Influence* in 1955, with the work by Coleman, Katz, and Menzels (Sarason et al., 1977, pp. 158–159), and with the investigations by Homans which focused on dyads for communication. Such studies have expanded so that now relationships are mapped not only between individuals and pairs of individuals, but between groups and organizations.

In 1977, Miles offered this definition of a network:

> At the most abstract, a network is simply a set of nodes or points connected by lines or links. There is often the implication that various things (such as messages, objects, energy, etc.) travel along the lines, which thus serve as channels. . . . In social networks the nodes are persons, groups or organizations. The things which travel between the nodes are *socially* relevant . . . objects, labor, affect, evaluation, knowledge, prescription/opinion, influence and power. So a network is a connected set of social actors exchanging socially relevant material. (p. 2)

Lortie (1977) provided a somewhat less abstract definition, suggesting that when

> sociologists and other social scientists study networks, they are examining the composite activities of individual scientists, job seekers, underworld figures, migrants, etc., as they go about their daily concerns; the patterns of interactions developed by such persons can be conceptualized as social circles or networks, and analysis is revealing that they have particular properties which set them apart. (p. 8)

Parker (1977), based on a study of 29 networks, observed that there are many types of social networks — kinship, diffusion, natural helping, person-to-person — and informal establishment cliques (otherwise known as "old-boy" networks). His particular focus (and of particular interest here) was on problem-solving and innovation networks. These he defined as networks that

> facilitate the sharing of information and psychological support among independent innovators and problem solvers who link together voluntarily as equals seeking assistance not provided by established systems. (p. 25)

Similarly, Schon (1977) defined informal social networks as

> patterns of relationship and interaction among persons or collectivities. These patterns are regular and persistent and, in that sense, law-like, but they are not governed by formal rules. They lie outside the boundaries of formal contact, formal regulation, formal organization. (p. 3)

Smith's (1977) definition of network introduces the notion of spatial separation and again raises the question of the difference between networks and formal organizations:

> A network is an interrelated set of members separated in space so that direct face-to-face interactions tend to be sporadic or episodic rather than regular or frequent. As such, a network can be roughly distinguished from a group . . . a network tends to be more diffuse, less hierarchical, and less goal centered than a formal organization. (p. 4)

However, writing from the perspective of a political scientist, Peterson (1977) takes exception to Smith's differentiation of networks from groups:

To understand the significance and implications of social networks, one must appreciate how closely this concept in contemporary writing approximates the social group, as understood by Dewey, Bentley, Mead and the progressive/pluralist tradition more generally. (p. 4)

The spatial dispersion of members of a network is also present in Huberman's (in Devaney, 1982) overview of the concept:

Network theorists . . . usually talk about interrelated sets of members who are separated organizationally or geographically so that direct, face-to-face interactions tend to be sporadic or episodic. And networks are typically made up of "homophiles," people who share a common background, common experiences and common understandings or convictions. (p. 91)

Huberman (1982), Lortie (1977), Parker (1977), Sarason et al. (1977), and Schon (1977), are among those who emphasize the difference between networks and formal organizations. Generally, these authors emphasize that networks are alternatives to established systems. Lortie goes so far as to express doubt that networks can be artificially created because, as he notes:

Informal networks grow out of the decisions and behaviors of hundreds and thousands of persons — they have a spontaneous, unconstructed quality, or, at least, a limited degree of intentionality. . . . I personally find it hard to see how anyone, acting from the outside, can create such systems, but it may be possible. (p. 9)

Huberman (1982) and others discuss the way networks are used by their members to bypass formal institutional channels in order to cope better with day-to-day problems. Parker (1977) distinguishes networks from formal organizations in noting that if a network stops meeting participants' needs, it disintegrates or becomes latent.

One further way that various people have attempted to characterize networks is to describe commonalities. For instance, Parker (1977) has suggested that all problem-solving and innovation networks include certain common ingredients:

1. a sense of being an alternative to established systems
2. a feeling of shared purpose
3. a mixture of information sharing and psychological support
4. a person functioning as an effective facilitator
5. an emphasis on voluntary participation and equal treatment. (p. 10)

Sarason et al. (1977), on the other hand, suggest that there are three "distinctive attributes" of networks:

1. every unit in a network does not interact with every other unit in a network;
2. the units in a single network do not have a clear boundary from the rest of the world; and
3. the only common characteristic of units in a network is their relationship (direct or indirect) to the ego [the center of the network]. (p. 128)

In identifying these attributes, Sarason is suggesting, as do others, that a characteristic of networks is the separation of major units; however, his notion that the only commonality is the link to the ego — while quite possibly accurate — is not consistent with the lists compiled by others (e.g., Schon, 1977) of commonalities by which networks can be defined. This set of attributes also limits the concept to one kind of network; other types of networks, as Sarason acknowledges, may not have a central node serving as ego for the network.

Thus, while there are similarities and linkages in the ways in which the term *network* is used, it should be obvious by now that even when authors stop to define the term, they fail to agree on it. This lack of agreement is compounded by the heavy contemporary use of *networking* as a verb describing ways that individuals gain power and advancement. Within the field of education, informal networking has had a long history of significant impact. In fact, as will be discussed later in reviewing the history of school-university relationships, it may have had more influence on the development of the current system of schooling than any of the constituted networks spawned by federal agencies or colleges in recent years.

Whatever the nature of agreement or disagreement on the features constituting a network, it should be clear what a network is *not* — namely, it is not a deliberately designed, collaborative arrangement between different institutions working together to advance self-interests and solve common problems. This latter kind of *partnership* arrangement between schools and universities is the focus of this book. However, even in these relationships the terminology of *collaboration*, *cooperation*, and the like has quite different meanings for various conceptual, political, and operational reasons.

## Collaboratives, Consortiums, Cooperatives, and Partnerships

There has been much written, particularly in recent years, about school-university relationships, described variously as collaborations or partnerships. Much of this material consists of brief descriptions of individual arrangements, generally by one of the key participants in the relationship. While there is often an effort to offer generalizations about such relationships, there is much less serious scholarship and therefore less theoretical framework for considering them. That is not to say that there are not a number of theoretical constructs in sociology, organization theory, and other fields that may be relevant; but most of the people writing on the subject have not given much attention to these constructs.

One exception to this is work done by Hord, who for several years has focused not only on school-university relations, but on trying to categorize different kinds of relationships. In 1978, she defined *collaboration* as "a term that implies the parties involved share responsibility and authority for basic policy decision making." She suggested that *cooperation*, on the other hand, is "a term that assumes two or more parties, each with separate and autonomous programs, agree to work together in making all such programs more successful" (Hord, 1986, p. 22).

Hord (1986) compares these definitions with the following, which were developed by the New England Program in Teacher Education in 1973:

> Collaboration — development of the model of joint planning, joint implementation, and joint evaluation between individuals or organizations. Cooperation — two individuals or organizations reach some mutual agreement but their work together does not progress beyond this level. (p. 22)

An essential point of difference often appears to be the extent to which the relating agencies function as equals, and in so doing are willing to give up some of their autonomy. That issue has been, and continues to be, central to the entire question of school-university relationships.

Gehrke and Parker (1983) speak to the looseness with which such terms have been used, then identify two types of collaboration:

> The literature implies that collaboration should involve pure collective initiation, planning, and implementation, and that all parties should have similar roles and responsibilities in all facets of the change. This model of collaboration could be called egalitarian. Its distinguishing characteristic is parity. . . . Collaborative planning can appear in yet another form that we call *dialectical collaboration*. It is distinguished by an integration of the top-down, grass roots, and joint planning modes. (pp. 50–51)

For these authors, each model has its own utility depending on the situation. Thus, rather than all partners in a collaboration needing to be equal in all ways, these authors propose alternatives that can be deployed according to the subjective needs of the partners.

The literature in organizational theory may also help clarify the reciprocal nature of collaborative relationships. In particular, Thompson (1967) describes three different ways in which interdependent parts of an organization can be related: (1) pooled interdependence, (2) sequential interdependence, and (3) reciprocal interdependence (p. 54). This typology may be helpful in categorizing different kinds of school-university relationships as well. In a pooled relationship, each organization — school or university — would make its unique contribution to the whole of educating our citizenry, but would do so in a relatively independent manner, being concerned with sufficient standardization of activities to allow each to complete its task. Historically, as will be noted in more detail later, much of the effort toward school-university relations has been devoted to facilitating their sequential interdependence — that is, to assuring that the entrance requirements of the colleges are clearly enough specified so that elementary and high schools can keep the sequence moving productively forward. Reciprocal interdependencies are those situations in which the outputs of each become the inputs for others.

Much of the relating between schools and universities appears to have been based on the premise that their interdependence (if indeed there was any) was pooled or sequential. However, it is the premise of much of this book that schools and universities can shift into reciprocal relationships and that there are viable strategies for sustaining such relationships. As Thompson (1967) notes, standardization can provide for coordination of pooled interdependence and planning can suffice to coordinate sequential relations, but mutual adjustment is essential for situations of reciprocal interdependence. Thompson goes on to point out:

> Coordination by mutual adjustment is more costly, involving greater decision and communication burdens, than coordination by plan, which in turn is more costly than coordination by standardization. (p. 57)

Since organizations seek to minimize coordination costs, Thompson suggests they will seek to group their internal organizations in such a way as to reduce the need for mutual adjustment. Again, examination of the historical relationships between schools and universities supports the notion that they have tried to avoid (or at least have ignored) the fact that they are reciprocally interdependent — which has reduced coordinating costs, but which has not necessarily helped them achieve their common goals.

Today, as different authors describe partnerships and consortiums involving schools and universities, they are speaking more and more of the need for the relationship to be one of equality. Hord (1986), for example, reports that the North Carolina Quality Assurance Program is an effort involving colleges and public schools that defines collaboration as

> shared decision-making in governance, planning, delivery, and evaluation of programs. It is a pluralistic form of education where people of dissimilar backgrounds work together with equal status. It may be seen as working with rather than working on a person. (p. 24)

Trubowitz, Duncan, Fibkins, Longo, and Sarason (1984) also emphasize working with schools rather than on them as they describe the collaboration between Queens College of the City University of New York and the Louis Armstrong Middle School in their book *When a College Works with a Public School*. Goodlad (1985b) has proposed perhaps the most stringent partnership concept by specifying that the relationship must be symbiotic. In general usage, as defined by the dictionary and by many biologists, such a relationship would be one in which the mutual interests of the two parties were equally well served. This symbiotic mutualism is more than "working with"; it is working with in order to satisfy the mutual self-interests of the two (or more) agencies involved. It is not enough that the agencies are equal in the relationship; they need to be mutually benefiting each other.

In sum, whether or not there is mutual adjustment in the coordination of school-university relations, or there is mutualism in the extent to which the relationship is beneficial to both schools and universities, there clearly have been close and frequently repeated interactions between these institutions. Moreover, there is ample evidence that most institutions of higher education have tried something that they have called collaboration or partnership with schools within the past twenty years — particularly since the rash of national criticism of common schools has appeared and the problems of tax support have manifested themselves for both schools and higher education. Perhaps partially because of the large number of such arrangements, it is virtually impossible to tell from the name given a particular relationship what its characteristics are. Although many have offered suggestions as to what should characterize these relationships, one finds the same characteristics urged for those known as collaborations, consortiums, cooperatives, and partnerships.

## Conclusions About Terminology

What generalizations can be made about the meaning of various terms used to describe interinstitutional relationships? First, and perhaps most obvious, individuals who seek to understand this topic, when studying the writings of others about these relationships, must not be lulled into the belief that they are studying the same things because they have the same name. While it may be possible to say a rose is a rose is a rose, one cannot conclude that a partnership is a partnership is a partnership. As different relations are examined, it will be necessary to consider each in terms of its operating concepts and practices, not its title.

Second, the term *network* is more apt to be used to describe relations between similar individuals, groups, or organizations. *Partnership* or *consortium* may describe relations between dissimilar entities—but not always. Networks are essentially antiestablishment. When networks become formalized, the line between a network and an organization becomes very blurred; therefore, those members forming networks need to beware of overly specifying governance, unless they seek the benefits of a formal organization instead of those attributable to a social network.

Third, examination of the varied ways these relationships are described should lead one to recognize that value positions cannot be immediately inferred from the terminology alone. Turk (1970) has emphasized this point, and it seems worth emphasizing here. Networks can be used for "good" and "bad" purposes. People may collaborate to produce change or to resist it.

Fourth, since there is particularly little agreement on the meaning of "partnership," it is necessary to select one definition as a basis for discussion. Throughout the remainder of this chapter, Goodlad's definition will be used. In doing so, particular reliance has been placed on a recent manuscript by Goodlad (1985b). Note that his concept is *not* "value-free." Specifically, he identifies three basic characteristics for partnerships:

1. The partners need to have a degree of dissimilarity,
2. The goal should be mutual satisfaction of self-interests,
3. Each party must be selfless enough to assure the satisfaction of these self-interests. (p. 1)

Goodlad suggests that school-university partnerships can meet these three tests if they begin with a recognition that the responsibilities of these two institutions for the quality of schooling are "virtually inseparable" (p. 5). Specifically he says:

> The argument for school-university partnerships proceeds somewhat as follows. For schools to get better, they must have better teachers, among other things. To prepare better teachers (and counselors, special educators and administrators), universities must have access to schools using the best practices. To have the best practices, schools need access to new ideas and knowledge. This means that universities have a stake in school improvement just as schools have a stake in the education of teachers. (p. 6)

Partnerships such as those Goodlad suggests are not easy to locate. In the following review of the history of school-university collaboration, the reader should keep this concept of partnership in mind. There are many instances of collaboration, but there are few, if any, examples of symbiotic relationships as proposed by Goodlad.

## Historical Perspective on School-University Relationships

### Early Collaboration

One of the earliest and best known efforts at school-university collaboration was initiated in the late nineteenth century by a committee under the chairmanship of Charles Eliot, president of Harvard. This committee, known as the committee of ten, issued its recommendations in 1892 and included among them a call for:

> a conference of school and college teachers of each principal subject which enters into the programmes of secondary schools . . . to consider the limits of its subject, the best methods of instruction, the most desirable allocation of time for the subject, and the best methods of testing the pupils' attainment therein. (in Cohen, 1974, p. 1931)

The conferences were convened and included 47 individuals from colleges and universities and 42 school people. Their recommendations spoke to the need for an earlier introduction of basic elements of all the disciplines, interdisciplinary instruction, emphasis on study skills and critical thinking, upgrading of grammar school studies, and uniformity of teaching for all students — college-bound or not. In addition, they called for improvement of teacher preparation for both elementary and secondary levels. These improvements were to be obtained through a cooperative program involving local school officials and the universities.

> ·As to the colleges, it is quite as much an enlargement of sympathies as an improvement of apparatus or of teaching that they need. They ought to take more interest than they have heretofore done, not only in the secondary, but in the elementary schools. . . . They should take an active interest, through their presidents, professors, and other teachers, in improving the schools in their respective localities, and in contributing to the thorough discussion of all questions affecting the welfare of both the elementary and secondary schools. (in Cohen, 1974, p. 1944)

Fuess (1950) describes one of the outgrowths of these efforts to provide for articulation between high schools and colleges: the development of the College Entrance Examination Board. In November 1894, Charles Eliot suggested that the colleges organize a board of examiners to conduct admission examinations throughout the country. By 1899, many of the eastern colleges had accepted this idea. Nicholas Murray Butler claimed that the debate generated by this testing would "usher in an era of educational cooperation which will increase the effectiveness of our existing machinery manifold" (in Fuess, 1950, p. 24).

However, by the time the first Scholastic Aptitude Tests were administered in 1926, the colleges' domination in their relationship with the schools had extended beyond determining course and instructional materials to the establishment of their right to prescribe what was good for the schools because of superior expertise on the part of college personnel. This led to direct conflict with the schools. In 1934 the board acknowledged that it "should be ready to cooperate with the secondary schools and colleges in this period of important change in secondary school work" (Fuess, p. 114).

Division among the ranks and mistrust continued, and what had begun as a collaborative venture between the colleges and secondary schools became a battle between the new experts in psychological testing and those devoted to more traditional methods of achievement testing.

In April of 1930, the Progressive Education Association initiated a commission on the relation of schools and colleges to explore possibilities of better coordination of school and college work and to seek an agreement that would provide freedom for secondary schools to attempt fundamental reconstruction. This commission's work led directly to the Eight-Year Study which was designed to allow high schools to be freed from some of higher education's restrictions. While it quickly became evident that the schools were not quite sure what to do with their newly found independence, Aiken (1952) suggests that "everyone involved in the study was convinced that some means should be found by which teachers in the schools and professors in the colleges should work together in mutual respect, confidence and understanding" (p. 16).

The study, under Ralph Tyler's leadership, demonstrated that schools could make significant gains in educating students if freed from college restrictions. It also demonstrated that traditional course titles provided colleges with little information about what students had learned. The study provided other information that might have led to better communications between schools and colleges if the onset of World War II had not distracted the nation from concern about its schools.

While these examples of school-university interaction focus primarily on the articulation of programs, the nation's schools were also greatly influenced during the first half of the twentieth century by a number of networks—many of which included representatives from schools and universities. Tyack and Hansot (1982) discuss these networks in some detail. They also observe that terminology is difficult:

> Networks resist definition. The word itself is a metaphor for a connecting web with much open space. As we use the term here, we mean an informal association of individuals who occupied influential positions (usually in university education departments or schools, as policy analysts or researchers in foundations, and as key superintendents), who shared common purposes . . . who had common interests in furthering their own careers, and who had come to know one another mostly through face-to-face interactions and through their similar writing and research. (p. 130)

Many of these networks consisted of individuals who attended the same schools and worked under a particular professor who served as their sponsor. To get an idea of how pervasive these networks became, consider the fact that at one time "sixteen of the eighteen superintendents in the largest American cities were former students of Strayer" (Tyack & Hansot, 1982, p. 135). George Strayer of Teachers College—and, later, Paul Mort of the same school—Ellwood Cubberley of Stanford, and Charles Judd of the University of Chicago, were among those whose early influence was spread through these managerial networks. One of the activities promoted by these networks was the conducting of surveys. This activity provided consulting fees for professors and training and connections for students, with the overall effect of making school districts look alike in the way in which staff were allocated and student programs were described. Considering the supposed extent of local control, these networks clearly contributed much to the development of a national school system.

But what of school-university relationships that can be described as being symbiotic? In this regard, Tyack and Hansot (1982) speak to the relation between university professors and their students:

> In return for assistance in moving ahead on the chessboard of superintendencies, the alumnus helped the professor recruit students, invited the sponsor to consult for or survey his district, notified him of vacancies, helped place graduates, and kept him in touch with the field. . . . His advancement often depended on pleasing his sponsor as well as the local school board. . . .
>
> The system employed by professors at Teachers College illustrated this symbiosis in its fullest development under George Strayer, Paul Mort and Nicolaus Englehardt. (p. 142)

The definition we are using as a point of reference calls for a symbiotic relationship between schools and universities that is at once both selfless and concerned with mutually meeting self-interests. While the sponsorship relationships noted by Tyack and Hansot were (and are) concerned with mutual self-interests, they would appear to fail the test of being selfless. They also serve to remind us that any kind of relationship can be used for a variety of purposes. As Tyack and Hansot (1982) note:

> The sponsorship system placed a premium on similarity of opinions and background characteristics and probably did much unconsciously to insure that the top positions in public education rarely went to women, to minorities, or to others deviating from the male, white, Anglo-Saxon Protestant norm. (p. 143)

Early networks were not limited to professor-student sponsorships. The Cleveland Conference, initiated in 1915, is cited as an example of a powerful private network of superintendents, university professors, and others in education who have had a powerful influence on the shaping of education in this country. As Tyack and Hansot (1982) point out, this was "indeed an old-boy network" (p. 133), with blacks first admitted in 1946 and women first becoming active in the 1960s. The group was in a position to determine who received key appointments, to influence the distribution of foundation grants and, through its deliberations on the need for a more progressive educational system, to contribute significantly to the shape of the educational program itself.

Members of a network such as the Cleveland Conference might

also be a part of sponsor networks, of networks within professional organizations such as the National Education Association, and political networks. Thus, the strength of individuals in one set of relationships could be extended beyond the immediate boundaries of that network.

Thus we see that school-university collaboration between the late nineteenth century and the outbreak of World War II can generally be characterized as follows:

1. College efforts to provide for articulation with the lower schools by prescribing entrance requirements, specifying courses, and establishing entrance examinations. School officials' involvement was largely in the role of determining how they could satisfy the colleges, with several noteworthy exceptions such as the Eight-Year Study.
2. Informal networks of university and school leaders that served to produce similarity among schools, to promote the personal power of individuals in the networks, and to establish conceptual, "scientific" approaches to school management. Often these relationships were symbiotic for the individuals involved—demonstrating that symbiotic relationships can be used for the benefit of the institutions involved or the enhancement of the individual's personal prestige.

## More Recent Collaboration

Following World War II, school-university collaboration was fueled by several forces. The end of the war produced a large group of GI-bill–supported graduate students who were utilized by the colleges to complete even more surveys and field studies than had been possible during the preceding decades. At the same time, the "baby boom" produced a rapid expansion of the public schools, which increased the need for the kinds of services the university survey teams could provide.

The boom also expanded the need for cooperation in the preparation of teachers as, by this time, most states had adopted a four-year degree as a minimum requirement for teachers, and colleges throughout the country were scrambling to produce enough credentialed graduates. Previous efforts to train teachers in campus laboratory schools were criticized as being unrealistic, and, besides, the schools could not support the number of students that the colleges needed to produce. Therefore, the colleges turned to public school settings for locations for cadet or student teachers. Curtis and Andrews (1954) cite Association for Student Teaching yearbooks written in the late forties and early fifties to support their contention that "more students are being placed in cooperating public schools for their student teaching experiences

[and] student teaching is rapidly becoming a cooperative enterprise between public schools and colleges" (p. 2).

Maeroff (1983), reviewing the history of school-university collaboration, noted:

> After Sputnik [1957] togetherness flourished . . . new curricula in biology, physics, English, and mathematics were prepared. Schools and colleges, together, pushed for excellence in education.
>
> The relationship was at times unhealthy. Colleges would often take the schools for granted. In paternalistic fashion, curricula would be packaged and teacher training programs planned with little or no consultation with the schools. (p. 2)

Maeroff observes that collaboration "came to a screeching halt" during the 1960s. But the many cooperative efforts reported in the literature for the 1960s tend to contradict his observation.

In 1966, for example, the Association for Student Teaching and the American Association of Colleges for Teacher Education sponsored a workshop which titled its report, *Partnership in Teacher Education*. In that extensive report, the participants explored issues associated with partnerships, such as the politics of school-college collaboration and new approaches to preparing teachers. They also included reports of several innovative, cooperative efforts, including the League of Cooperating Schools initiated by John Goodlad between the Graduate School of Education at UCLA and a number of southern California schools. As described in Smith and Goodlad (1966), this league was intended to develop intermediaries — persons who could facilitate interaction between the knowledge-producing function of the university and the service performed by the schools. It would also provide, through collaboration, an improved setting for clinical experiences in teacher education. Speaking specifically to the intention of creating intermediaries, they noted:

> We have very few "intermediate engineers" who can move back and forth in such a way that they truly serve to bridge the gap between theoretical conceptualization and practice. Worse, we have very few creative individuals who are committed to action and who have access to laboratories where they can effect their plans. (Smith & Goodlad, 1966, p. 17)

Goodlad (1975) discusses this league extensively and points out that while the League was able to accomplish some of its expectations, the effort needed to draw in central office support if significant progress was going to be achieved.

While the baby boom promoted the need for collaboration between universities and schools in order to find sufficient settings for training student teachers, the decline in school enrollment of the 1970s also promoted cooperation. As Davies and Aquino (1975) noted, major emphases during this time shifted to in-service education and continuing professional development. They summarized major projects of such agencies as the Chief State School Officers, the American Association of Colleges for Teacher Education, and the federal government, all of which were engaged in supporting collaborative efforts for such training. Among the most rapidly growing of the approaches to collaboration were teacher centers of which there were estimated to be 4,500 by the fall of 1975 with more on the way. While many of these centers did not include universities, most involved collaboration of several agencies and professional organizations. To some people, they were seen as a threat to established school district and college roles in developing professional personnel. Among those with such a view were many of the leaders of the centers (Devaney, 1982).

In 1985, the American Association of State Colleges and Universities reported results of an extensive survey of members' involvement in school-university collaboration (Roberts, 1985). Nearly one-third of the institutions said that the president or the chancellor was in regular contact with the schools, and that "virtually all education departments have regular contact with the schools" (p. 2). Seventy-three percent of the institutions responding reported they were involved "in a formal consortium or council which meets regularly with school officials to discuss school concerns" (p. 2). Teacher training and in-service education of teachers and administrators were the most frequent types of involvement among the 228 institutions responding to the survey. Seventy-two of these colleges mentioned that they were involved in specific programs targeted at local needs that were developed through cooperative efforts with the schools. Only 37 of these institutions were the sole providers of in-service training in their particular "market." In other words, 84 percent of these colleges had competition (in most cases with two other institutions) for their services to the schools. With the hustling for students to maintain faculty teaching loads, the competitive market became a new stimulator of growth for the idea of school-university collaboration. In short, if the college could get schools to join in a partnership, it could protect a market for its services. While this may be one way in which self-interests are served, it probably does not lead to the kind of symbiotic relationship discussed above.

In spite of all of these reports of collaboration, Maeroff (1983) concluded that "historically, the preparation of teachers has been dominated by higher education. The schools have had little to say about it and are rarely consulted" (p. 27).

Based on this general review of the long history of school-university collaboration, those who would seek to form such arrangements, or to study those already formed, or to derive the most benefits possible from those which exist, would also be wise to seek to understand the origins of the "partnership" in question. Those who believe they have discovered some bright new idea are doomed to spend considerable energy relearning the experiences of the past — and are quite likely to be dismayed by some of the obstacles they face that have been both generated and encountered over the years of interaction between these institutions. The review in the next section should be helpful in this regard.

## The Whys, Wherefores, and Whatnots of Collaboration

We will examine here the reasons individuals and organizations offer for seeking collaborative arrangements, and consider the benefits claimed for such efforts. Then we will turn to a review of the obstacles reported as creating difficulties for those who seek success through collaboration. Finally, we will discuss the suggestions that have been offered as to what conditions must be met for collaborations between schools and universities to be more successful.

### What Is to Be Gained from Collaboration?

In discussing definitions, we noted that schools and universities are reciprocally interdependent. Consistent with Thompson's (1967) explication of that concept, the outputs of each organization become the inputs of the other. This is a commonly cited reason for collaboration. For example, Hathaway (1985) notes:

> The university and the school district are each other's own best resources. Between them, school districts and universities cover virtually the whole range of human learning. That we are interconnected is undeniable. The challenge before us is to realize and build upon the extent, the possibilities, and the necessity of our connection and dependence. (p. 4)

In several instances, the rationale for collaboration has been expressed simply as survival. Andrews and Soder (1985–1986), Trubowitz et al. (1984), and Wu (1985) are among the authorities whose comments lend credence to the survival argument. Wu cites anthropologist S. T. Kimball to make his point that there are three conditions for collaboration:

1. there is a threat from the outside
2. there is an identification of a common problem
3. there is a combination of the threat and the need to investigate the problem. (p. 7)

As Andrews and Soder recite their case study, one quickly reaches the conclusion that the survival of their higher education unit was closely tied to collaboration with local schools, and that the schools were also faced with significant threats. De Bevoise (1986) quotes Goodlad as stating that "teacher education institutions are seriously threatened by the disaffection and sometimes outright hostility that educators in the nation's schools express toward them" (p. 9). De Bevoise then describes the conditions that the Louisville University president, Donald Swain, and the Jefferson County, Kentucky, school superintendent, Donald Ingwerson, saw that caused them to initiate a collaboration:

> Both institutions needed to change. The problems of desegregation and reorganization in the school district, the need to build public respect and support for all levels of education, and scarce resources encouraged an openness to risk-taking and to experimentation in seeking improvement. (p. 10)

Since collaboration is one strategy by which organizations seek to continue their existence or to strengthen it, it is worth noting Peterson's (1977) observation that participation in networks is most important to those with less income, status, and power. While Peterson is referring to individuals and various social and political groups, the same conclusion would seem reasonable in looking at school-university partnerships. However, in this case, all members may be in a weak position relative to their environment and need each other in order to develop a stronger position. In that regard, Ambach (1982) warned:

> Both secondary and postsecondary education . . . must address their connections with mutual support. Competition for government or private resources for the maintenance of education is so severe that it threatens to submerge the common interests and interdependence of the different levels of education beneath the drive for institutional survival. (p. 22)

Parker (1977) and others have pointed out that being part of a network has psychological advantages for participants. He said that participants feel a sense of shared purpose, and of being part of a special group (pp. 10–11). This kind of support was also reported by Goodlad (1975) in talking about the principals' response to the League of Schools project.

Another of the gains that one or all of the participants in a collaboration may obtain is that of money. Usually this is spoken of as increased resources or covered up in some other kind of jargon, but occasionally an individual reporting on the results of such an effort will acknowledge it outright. Botel, Glatthorn, and Larkin (1984) describe the benefits of a cooperative program to the Graduate School of Education at the University of Pennsylvania: "First, there was significant monetary profit: the participants paid more than $175,000 in tuition" (p. 565).

Early collaborative efforts and those that continue today report that these relationships allow the universities to support graduate students and faculty positions they would not otherwise be able to fund. Schools, too, benefit financially, obtaining training, curriculum development, and evaluation services, among other things, at lower than normal market rates. Shive (1984) puts it this way: "In a period of tight fiscal constraints and increased demands for educational excellence, the school-college partnership concept has much untapped potential" (p. 122).

Sarason (1977) looks at the question of resource benefits differently. He doubts that there will ever be the resources some organizations seem to think they need to deal with their problems. However, he thinks that networks can help:

> *Agencies learn to exchange resources in mutually beneficial ways and without finances being a prerequisite for discussion or the basis for exchange.* . . . What do I have that somebody else can use in exchange for something of his that I need? (pp. 21–22)

As will be seen in subsequent chapters of this book, one of the primary intentions of school-university relationships is to promote change. Lieberman (1986b) concludes that "in many cases we find that change efforts have been successful due to some type of collaborative relations between the participating parties" (p. 5). In two separate reports, Havelock (1973, 1981) notes the utility of collaboration in facilitating the exchange and diffusion of knowledge and in effecting change-oriented activities. Parker (1977) and others at the 1977 National Institute of Education conference on networking had different perspectives on the exact nature of networks, but all agreed that such arrangements had the potential for facilitating change.

Another specific benefit of school-university collaboration is the potential for research. Several authors, including Lieberman (1986b), speak to gains they believe can be achieved through this approach to research. Lieberman (1986a), for example, focuses on teams of school and university people created to engage in research and development and notes six benefits that can come from such teams:

- Collaborative research and development creates a structure for teachers that facilitates reflection and action on the messiness of teaching and schooling problems.
- The team unites teachers and encourages collegial interaction. . . .
- Both the process of group interaction and the content of what is learned narrow the gap between "doing research" and "implementing research findings." . . .
- Naturally occurring problems that teachers have in their schools may lend themselves better to this type of research and development than large-scale funded research, as it can respect the time lines of the school people rather than the research grant.
- A collaborative team provides possibilities for teachers to assume new roles and exhibit leadership. . . .
- Collaborative research legitimates teachers' practical understanding and their definition of problems for both research and professional development. (p. 31)

Several other authors have discussed various purposes and advantages for school-university relationships (e.g., Norris, Starrfield, & Hartwell, 1984). But the above discussion covers most of the commonly cited reasons for collaboration.

### What Are Some of the Problems?

In spite of the abundance of benefits demonstrated for cooperative efforts, there are obstacles to achieving success. One of the most commonly mentioned impediments is the notion that the two institutions are just plain incompatible. Martin Haberman (1971), for example, has identified twenty-three reasons why universities cannot educate teachers, the first being the impossibility of "college–lower school cooperation" (p. 33). He used the following analogy to help make his point:

Slow-witted, lumbering elephants circle each other for a century only to discover that they are both males and incapable even of friendship. (p. 134)

Haberman continues, less metaphorically, and asserts:

> Reports, books, and demonstration projects on how we cooperate have not affected any reality. . . . There are not budgetary, personnel, or other resources built into either institution that depend on cooperation; quite the contrary, the more either institution "cooperates," the more it costs and detracts from its own major purposes. (p. 134)

While our review might allow us at least to ask some questions about the notion that there is no financial benefit, Haberman's second reason why universities cannot educate teachers suggests another impediment to school-university cooperation. He maintains, flatly, that people in schools and colleges cannot work together:

> Public school people regard college people as too theoretical and more concerned with analysis than solutions, not capable of working within legal structures, incapable of hard work during regularly scheduled business hours. College people perceive public school people as too conservative in accepting research or responding to great social problems; fearful of superiors; of lower intelligence, status, and education. . . . In truth, *both groups are experts in maintaining their own organizations and espousing radical reforms in the other* [italics added]. (p. 134)

While he may be overstating the case, there is no question that some of the people in these institutions do have these attitudes and that these attitudes do get in the way of successful collaboration. Particularly troublesome is the notion that *both* school and college people know what is "best" for those in the *other* institutions. When collaboration is approached with this in mind — as it often is — defensive mechanisms begin operating almost immediately.

Haberman's list does not stop with these two broadsides. He adds charges that college faculty members are not capable of relating theory to practice, professional knowledge cannot be acted on in the lower schools, college leadership is not interested in the lower schools, and the public does not expect cooperative efforts. He adds that colleges cannot "change and improve themselves and schools through research, demonstration, creative proposals, and dissemination programs" (p. 136). As he puts it:

> Government agencies and private foundations have placed universities in the role of "mover and shaker" only to end up in the same place at greater cost. After much time and money, there isn't a single example of school

change which university faculty have researched and advocated that is now accepted as practice. . . . Any status survey will reveal that the proverbial third grade in Peoria grinds on pretty much as it did in 1910. . . . Our record for self-change is even more dismal. (p. 136)

Findings from A Study of Schooling (Goodlad, 1984) also support the notion that schools have changed little in the basic way teaching takes place in spite of the work done by universities. However, rather than demonstrate that school-university cooperation is useless, as Haberman suggests, these findings may help demonstrate why school-university cooperation *as it has typically been practiced* is not sufficient to bring about changes of the magnitude that is required. If, however, we discount the notion that schools and universities are incompatible and assume that they are willing to keep searching for a means of effective collaboration, what obstacles are apt to be in the way?

University people in particular assert that one of the major obstacles to successful collaboration is the lack of reward for people in higher education who become involved in such efforts. Haberman (1971), Hathaway (1985), Havelock (1981), Lieberman (1986b), Sarason et al. (1977), and Wilbur (1985) are just some of the many who comment on this problem. What is seldom mentioned, but is true, is that there is little reward for people in the schools either.

The issue takes on particular importance for the college teacher because his or her promotion, academic respectability, and feelings of self-worth are entangled in a peer review system that offers financial rewards, tenure, and titles for selected kinds of professional behaviors. Generally, greater emphasis is placed in universities on research and publication than on service or teaching. Some have suggested that this problem is more than just an issue of rewards and is due also to "an elitist view that values the problems and descriptions of researchers over those of practitioners" (Lieberman, 1986a, p. 28).

There is no denying that the reward system poses problems for collaboration — at least in the minds of some faculty members in universities. Nevertheless, one is struck by the relatively less problematic nature of bridging research and practice in other professional schools in the university. One hears few medical school faculty members complaining about lack of recognition for their work with surgery; few business school professors moan about lack of recognition for their time analyzing the practices of large corporations. Agricultural scholars developed the highly successful cooperative service programs that contributed greatly to the success (and downfall?) of the American farmer, but they are seldom heard to complain that working with extension services produces little recognition. It may be that part of the problem that individuals in the colleges of education have is that they see the work with the schools as "service" rather than viewing it as a really significant opportunity for research and publication. At times it almost seems as if they believe they can learn more about schools and schooling by reading what one of their peers has written about schools than by studying schools themselves.

But what about the lack of rewards for those educators in the school system? While they are not subject to "publish or perish" promotion routines, they undergo review by superiors and by lay boards regarding their success in accomplishing established priorities. This means, especially during times when finances are tight, that school people are not apt to want to continue something unless it is showing clear results. Havelock (1981), in commenting on the Metropolitan School Study Council, noted:

> Most of the resources it provided were also offered by other network-like arrangements and service agencies which abounded in the region. Thus it was generally regarded by superintendents as pleasant, worthwhile, but rather inconsequential among the rich and varied assortment of in-service and linking opportunities available to them. There was no district for which it could be said to have provided a service which was either essential or one which could not be provided from some other source. (p. 156)

Elsewhere Havelock noted:

> For the school people and the superintendents in particular, the activities of the IOA [Interorganizational Agreement] were harder and harder to justify within very stringent budgets because they appeared to be mostly intellectual exercises with few clear and concrete school benefits either in terms of on-site technical advice or materials, or credits for professional upgrading. (p. 139)

The typical school salary structure does reward advanced training (as, for that matter, does the college system which places non-doctorate-holding teachers in low-esteem, low-pay roles), and this makes participation in collaborative efforts as a graduate student something that is rewarding for school employees. However, nothing is built into the school's reward system that makes participation in a cooperative venture any more valuable to an individual than any other activity. In fact, such participation may be seen by some as failing to pay attention to primary responsibilities—particularly if the collaboration threatens the status quo in the schools. School people are less likely to use this lack of recognition as an excuse for not committing to a collaborative effort; instead, they tend to stress the lack of "concrete accomplishment," as Havelock noted above, as their way of dealing with the same issue.

Closely tied to the question of individual reward is the response of the institutions to collaboration. Havelock (1981), Huberman, Levinson, Havelock, and Cox (1981), Sarason et al. (1977), Wilbur (1984), and others emphasize that institutions often place low priority on such interactions or feel them completely unnecessary. Sarason points out:

> Agencies do not seek each other out for purposes of resource exchange; each agency sees itself as independent of all others, dependent only on its own subsidized resources to meet its goals, and energetically seeking new monies to purchase more resources. Each agency is an island, seeking ways to expand its land areas, fearing erosion from uncontrollable and unpredictable sources, and nurturing the fantasy that there must or there should exist the quantity and quality of resources that could ensure a safe and goal-fulfilling life. (p. 22)

It was this tendency that Seattle and the University of Washington's College of Education had to overcome in instituting the collaboration described by Andrews and Soder (1985–1986). In fact, this institutional view has to be overcome by any who would seek to form a true partnership.

Earlier we mentioned that college personnel members needed to overcome the notion that their work in the schools is only a "service." Seeley (1981) is emphatic in his insistence that this view must be changed, not because of the university reward system but because he believes the service-delivery model is inappropriate for education. He argues:

> The chief characteristic of partnership is common effort toward common goals. Partners may help one another in general or specific ways, but none is ever a client, because the relationship is mutual. Providers and clients can deal with one another at arm's length; partners share an enterprise, though their mutuality does not imply or require equality or similarity. Participants in effective partnerships may be strikingly different, each contributing to the common enterprise particular talents, experiences, and perspectives and sometimes having different status within the relationship and control over aspects of the work to be done.
>
> The concept of service delivery, unlike that of partnership, leads to conflict-producing ambiguities about whether provider or client wields more power in the relationship. "Client" is a word having two possible

contradictory meanings: in one, it means "slave," "dependent." . . . In the other, it is a synonym for "patron," "employer." . . . Education has instances of both kinds of client relationships — neither one healthy. (p. 65)

Unfortunately, our review of the history of school-university relationships showed the service-delivery model to be one of the most prevalent bases for the relationships.

An equally poor model of collaboration appears to be one based upon the competition for power and control. Davies and Aquino (1975) do an excellent job of describing the obstacles to improving teacher education caused when teacher organizations, administrative groups, colleges of education, and state departments of education insist that each must be in control of the enterprise. Hathaway (1985) concludes from his review of the history of collaboration that "institutions of higher education have tended to exercise control over most joint LEA/IHE [Local Educational Agencies/Institutions of Higher Education] ventures in this country" (p. 7). Maeroff (1983) expresses concern about what he considers to be the traditional academic "pecking order," warning that "colleges and universities have had — for many years — a 'plantation mentality' about the schools" (p. 3). Seeley (1981) quotes former U.S. Representative Barbara Jordan, describing relationships in which one gives the appearance of collaboration but attempts to maintain control as "networks of illusions" (p. 73). By definition, the situation in which one party is in control of the other is not a partnership of the type we are seeking.

Many network theorists, including Huberman (1982), Lortie (1977), Miles (1977), and Sarason et al. (1977), express concern about relationships becoming too formalized. They warn that the advantages claimed for network interaction are derived from knowledge of natural relationships, maintaining that efforts to formalize and codify such relationships quickly will create all of the problems experienced by large bureaucracies. Sarason et al. (1977) in particular express concern about possible negative consequences of legislating networks (p. 181). This warning is especially appropriate in light of recent attempts by a number of states to legislate cooperation as part of their school reform plans. Maeroff (1983) warns against focusing on the machinery of school-university relationships, saying that "time and time again, when people think about collaboration they focus on budgets and bureaucracy . . . this, of course is self-defeating" (p. 5).

One obstacle that has received less attention than others in the existing literature is the indirect influence of the societal milieu. Pressure from the external environment may have more influence than many of the participants in collaboration realize. While some authorities have pointed out that the environment may drive the schools and universities to collaborate in order to survive, relatively little attention has been given to the potentially significant effects of the context of the ongoing operation of a school-university partnership (see, however, Smith, 1977). Obviously, significant shifts in funding will have an effect, but what of major changes in the national political scene, or in social movements? For example, can anyone doubt that the focus of school-university interaction was drastically changed by the civil rights disorders of the late 1960s?

In discussing obstacles, others speak to the basic differences between schools and universities — not as proof of incompatibility, but by way of noting that these differences must be adequately recognized by participants in order to avoid serious conflict. Lortie (1977) calls attention to the differences in the ways policy is made in the two institutions. Wu (1985) provides a three-page listing, noting differences in how the two institutions deal with such diverse matters as research, control, policy making, personnel matters, public criticism, and expenditures of funds. Sarason has frequently written and spoken about the differences in the cultures of the two institutions and how unaware participants in one are of the life in the other. Hathaway's (1985) list of 18 obstacles includes similar concerns. But all of these writers appear to hold some hope that these obstacles can be overcome sufficiently for productive school-university relationships.

### Possibilities for More Successful School-University Relationships

There are many obstacles in the path of securing the numerous benefits promised from collaboration. Some of the suggestions for making collaboration successful simply direct schools and universities to overcome the obstacles. In addition there are other suggestions for what it takes to produce success coming from those who have studied networks and other forms of collaboration.

Many of the authors have provided summary lists of what they believe is necessary for collaboration to succeed. Interestingly, our review suggests that a major consideration in achieving satisfactory results is an ingredient not commonly found in the summary lists. This ingredient is best described by Sarason (1977) when he talks about Mrs. Dewar, whom he credits with initiating the Essex-type network described in his analysis:

> To start an Essex-type network requires a person who is perceived as
> important in some way, who is known to many people, and who has

persistence. . . . We would contend that it was her ideas, far more than affluence and status, that made the difference between the network's viability and an early demise. (p. 105)

In addition to noting the importance of Dewar's ideas, Sarason cites her persistence as a key ingredient. Later, he discusses another network and finds a person acting in a role similar to that of Mrs. Dewar.

The partnership between Queens College and the Louis Armstrong Middle School had several people in key leadership roles, but clearly owes much of its success to Sidney Trubowitz. The former Southern California Partnership involving UCLA and the Puget Sound Educational Consortium can identify numerous individuals who played roles in their creation, but most would probably admit to the central role of John Goodlad and his ideas and persistence in functioning as their Mrs. Dewar. In a Little Rock, Arkansas, collaboration, Sara Murphy functions as if she were Dewar's reincarnation. The long history of the Metropolitan School Study Council reveals that it flourished under the inspiration of Paul Mort, Paul Vincent, and Ann Lieberman, but struggled when it did not have the benefit of the ideas and persistence of its own versions of Mrs. Dewar. Peterson (1977) observes that successful collaborations often are initiated by a particular innovator who becomes their first leader. In short, it appears that a partnership is much more likely to be successful if it has leadership from a Mrs. Dewar whose ideas and persistence will provoke the kinds of interactions that are necessary to overcome the many obstacles present and secure for the collaboration the benefits that can derive from such arrangements.

The purpose of a relationship also helps determine its success. However, the experts have mixed recommendations concerning whether the purpose should be narrow and specifically defined or broad and multifaceted. Hathaway (1985), Maeroff (1983), Peterson (1977), and Shive (1984), are among those who argue for sharply focused efforts. On the other hand, Dalin (1977), Parker (1977), and Schon (1977) suggest in varying ways that a multipurpose network may have a better chance of survival. In any event, all agree that clarity of purpose is necessary. At the same time, several authorities warn against an overemphasis on defining very specific goals and objectives.

Lieberman (1986b) stresses the importance of paying attention to activities, not goals, in initiating a collaboration. Maeroff (1983) and Wilbur (1985) add their emphasis to this by stressing the importance of focusing on action and not machinery in the early stages of collaboration. While it is important to get on with the action, there is still a need to provide for adequate coordination among all stakeholders. Wu (1985) specifies the need to provide for the management of conflict, while

Lieberman (1986b), Mahlios and Carpenter (1982), and Shive (1984) discuss the importance of clarifying and coordinating the roles of different participants. The three case studies completed by Havelock, Miles, and Huberman also clearly demonstrate the need for such clarification and coordination (see Havelock, Huberman, Levinson, & Cox 1982).

Making sure that there are adequate resources is another necessary action. Hathaway (1985) and Shive (1984) speak to the need for adequate funding and the necessity of pooling funds. Each of the case studies reviewed spoke in one way or the other to this aspect of collaboration. Some reviewers have pointed out that it is not just a question of whether there are adequate funds. If these funds are controlled by one of the parties in the collaboration instead of shared, adverse relationships may develop. Time is another important resource. Schon (1977) points out that if there is not sufficient slack in the schedules of would-be collaborators, they will not get together sufficiently to build the necessary bridges. Lieberman (1986b) and Shive (1984) also speak to the importance of providing sufficient time to accomplish the interactions that are needed.

In the above discussion on obstacles to school-university relationships, the problems of lack of reward and recognition of individuals in schools and colleges for collaborative activities were emphasized. Goodlad (1975), Hathaway (1985), Havelock (1981), Havelock et al. (1982), Lieberman (1986b), Maeroff (1983), Parkay (1986), Shive (1984), and Wilbur (1985) are among those addressing these same issues. Parkay speaks more directly to the need for recognition of people in the school than most of the others who tend to focus on the problem in the universities. Interestingly, with the exception of Haberman (1971), most of these writers express the belief that such rewards can, indeed, be found in the system. At the same time, however, they acknowledge that the systems functioning as they now do will not provide recognition to collaborators. Several authorities, including Hathaway (1985) and Wilbur (1985), speak to a variation on this theme when they emphasize the importance of support from the top administration in the institutions. In his work with the League of Cooperating Schools, this same theme led Goodlad (1984) to conclude that school districts, not just schools, needed to be involved in the school-university relationships. Recognition of individual effort in a collaboration is much more apt to be obtained if the institutions' leaders are committed to the collaboration.

In the very definition of partnerships of the type we are discussing, an explicit condition for success is the recognition by the parties of each others' mutual needs. Hathaway (1985), Maeroff (1983), and Wilbur (1985) are among those who identify this as an essential condition for success in collaboration. Sarason (1982) has written and spoken eloquently of the need for the participants to understand the culture of the parties involved in a collaborative effort. Hathaway (1985) and Lieberman (1986b) are among others who have suggested this as a condition for success in collaboration. As this is considered, it becomes evident that, in addition to a Mrs. Dewar, school-university partnerships need intermediate engineers of the type described by Goodlad (Smith & Goodlad, 1966). Havelock's recital of the history of the Metropolitan School Study Council and Huberman's Midwestern State Case, as well as his review of the Teachers' Center Exchange, reveal individuals successfully filling this responsibility. These are people who are knowledgeable about, and comfortable with, the cultures of all the participants in a collaboration so that they can move freely between them, interpret the language, understand the reward systems, and translate the ideas of those in one culture to those in another. Of course, to some extent, these are the liaison positions described in classical network theory—the boundary spanners who permit otherwise independent entities to establish effective links.

Several other suggestions have also been repeatedly emphasized. For example, shared ownership of problems is urged, participants are reminded to provide training if new skills are needed for the collaboration, individuals are warned to expect problems, and collaborators are encouraged to recognize that they can achieve more together than they can by working alone. A point made by Parkay (1986) and by many others studying school change processes (e.g., Goodlad, 1975) is that success is more apt to be achieved if the university concentrates on working *with* the schools rather than imposing a particular solution *onto* the school.

Finally, if we consider the case studies of Havelock et al. (1982) and Huberman et al. (1981), the analysis of networks by Turk (1970), and other writings, we will recognize how important it is to learn from the past in dealing with these collaborations. Many of the mistakes and problems experienced by schools and universities as they seek to work together could be substantially alleviated if participants were aware of prior relationships and of attitudes that those relationships may have created.

### Conclusion

We began by noting the imprecise usage of terms to describe school-university relationships. This imprecision has been due, in part, to the varied aims that schools and universities have had as they sought out each other for collaboration. The inconsistencies in terminology have been further promoted by rhetoric that sought to describe a mutuality in interinstitutional relationships that was impossible because of the intention of one agency to control (or at least dominate) the other. Nevertheless, there have been many interactions between schools and universities, and the history of these relationships can provide insight into future cooperative efforts.

Ultimately, as we continue to study these relationships, we may find that we are watching two dinosaurs (not elephants) circling each other. We may watch as schools and universities parry and thrust, while other entities emerge as the providers of education and the trainers of those who educate. If such is the case, it is likely to be only because we fail to understand the potential of school-university collaboration or because we do not capitalize on what is already known about how obstacles can be overcome to achieve success within these relationships.

Successful partnerships will not be created by university people preoccupied with the need for personal promotion. Neither will they be developed by school people worried about professional survival in the bureaucracy of the school system. They will develop and flourish only if created and sustained by educators who are willing and able to find personal rewards in the satisfaction of the self-interests of others with whom they are working. Partnerships will be of value only to the extent that all parties seek to use them for the simultaneous reform and renewal of both schools and universities.

## References

Aiken, W. M. (1952). *The story of the eight-year study*. Vol. 1 of *Adventure in American education*. Progressive Education Association, Commission on the Relation of School and College. New York: Harper and Brothers.

Ambach, G. (1982, Jan/Feb). The high school/college connection: A state perspective. *Change, 14,* 22–25.

Andrews, R. L., & Soder, R. (1985–1986). University/district collaboration on effective schools. *National Forum of Education Administration and Supervision* 2(3), 33–48.

Botel, M., Glatthorn, A., & Larkin, J. (1984). Focused graduate studies: A new pattern of school/university cooperation. *Phi Delta Kappan, 65,* 563–564.

Cohen, S. (Ed.) (1974). *Education in the United States: A documentary history*. New York: Random House.

Curtis, D. K., & Andrews, L. O. (1954). *Guiding your student teacher*. Englewood Cliffs, NJ: Prentice-Hall.

Dalin, P. (1977). *Network for educational change*. Washington, DC: National Institute of Education.

Davies, H. D., & Aquino, J. T. (1975). Collaboration in continuing professional development. *Journal of Teacher Education, 26*(3), 274–277.

De Bevoise, W. (1986). Collaboration: Some principles of bridgework. *Educational Leadership, 43,* 9–12.

Devaney, K. (1982). *Networking on purpose: A reflection study of the teachers' center exchange.* San Francisco: Far West Laboratory for Educational Research and Development.

Fuess, C. M. (1950). *The college board: Its first fifty years.* New York: University Press.

Gehrke, N. J., & Parker, W. C. (1983). Collaboration in staff development: Variations on the concept. *NASSP Bulletin, 67*(461), 50–54.

Goodlad, J. I. (1975). *The dynamics of educational change.* New York: McGraw-Hill.

Goodlad, J. I. (1984). *A place called school.* New York: McGraw-Hill.

Goodlad, J. I. (1985a). *Summary: Work conference on school/university partnerships, Chicago, August 2, 1985.* Unpublished manuscript, University of Washington.

Goodlad, J. I. (1985b). *Reconstructing schooling and the education of educators: The partnership concept.* Unpublished manuscript, University of Washington.

Haberman, M. (1971). Twenty-three reasons why universities can't educate teachers. *Journal of Teacher Education, 22,* 133–140.

Hathaway, W. E. (1985, March). *Models of school-university collaboration: National and local perspective on collaborations that work.* Paper presented for Symposium at the Annual Meeting of American Educational Research Association, Chicago. (ED 253 973).

Havelock, R. G. (1973). *The change agent's guide to innovation in education.* Englewood Cliffs, NJ: Education Technology Publications.

Havelock, R. G. (1981). School-university collaboration supporting school improvement. *The eastern private university network case,* Vol. 3. Washington, DC: National Institute of Education, Research and Practice Program.

Havelock, R., Huberman, M., Levinson, R., & Cox, P. (1982). School-university collaboration supporting school improvement. *Cross-site analysis,* Vol. 3. Washington, DC: American University, Knowledge Transfer Institute. (NIE Contract No. 400-79-0063)

Hord, S. M. (1986, February). A synthesis of research on organizational collaboration. *Educational Leadership,* pp. 22–26.

Huberman, M. (1982). Making changes from exchanges: Some frameworks for studying the teachers' centers exchange. In K. Devaney (Ed.), *Networking on purpose.* San Francisco: Far West Laboratory.

Huberman, M., Levinson, N., Havelock, R., & Cox, P. (1981). Interorganizational arrangements: An approach to educational practice improvement. *Knowledge, 3*(1), 5–22.

Huberman, M., & Miles, M. (1982). How school improvement works: A multiple-site field study. In D. Crandall et al. (Eds.), *A study of dissemination efforts in supporting school improvement,* Vol. 3. Andover, MA: The Network.

Katz, E., & Lazarsfeld, P. F. (1955). *Personal influence: The part played by people in the flow of mass communications.* Glencoe, IL: The Free Press.

Lieberman, A. (1986a). Collaborative research: Working with, not working on. *Educational Leadership, 43*, 28–32.

Lieberman, A. (1986b). Collaborative work. *Educational Leadership, 43*, 4–8.

Lortie, D. C. (1977). *Networks and organizational rationality in American public schools.* Washington, DC: National Institute of Education.

Maeroff, G. I. (1983). *School and college partnerships in education.* Princeton: The Carnegie Foundation for the Advancement of Teaching.

Mahlios, M. C., & Carpenter, R. L. (1982, Fall). Political economy as a conceptual framework for the analysis of school-university cooperation. *Education, 103*(1), 15–21.

Miles, M. (1977). *On networking.* Washington, DC: National Institute of Education, Group on School Capacity for Problem-Solving.

Moreno, J. L. (1934). *Who shall survive: Foundation of sociometry, group psychotherapy and sociodrama.* Washington, DC: Nervous and Mental Disease Monograph 58, 1934; New York: Beacon House. Republished in 1953.

Norris, C. A., Starrfield, S. L., & Hartwell, L. K. (1984, April). Old adversaries united: Benefits of collaborative research. *NASSP Bulletin, 68*, 143–147.

Parkay, F. W. (1986). A school/university partnership that fosters inquiry-oriented staff development. *Phi Delta Kappan, 67*, 386–389.

Parker, L. (1977). *Networks for innovation and problem-solving and their use for improving education: A comparative overview.* Washington, DC: National Institute of Education, Group on School Capacity for Problem-Solving.

Peterson, P. E. (1977). *Schools, groups and networks: A political perspective*, rev. ed. Washington, DC: National Education Association.

Roberts, H. (1985, January). *American Association of State Colleges and Universities surveys school/college cooperative programs.* AASCU Special Report. Washington, DC: AASCU, January. (ED 257 797)

Sarason, S. B. (1982). *The culture of the school and the problem of change*, 2nd ed. Boston: Allyn and Bacon.

Sarason, S. B., Carroll, C., Maton, K., Cohen, S., and Lorentz, E. (1977). *Human services and resource networks.* San Francisco: Jossey-Bass.

Schon, D. A. (1977). *Network-related intervention.* Washington, DC: National Institute of Education.

Seeley, D. S. (1981). *Education through partnership: Mediating structures and education.* Cambridge, MA: Ballinger Publishing Company.

Shive, R. J. (1984). School and university partnerships: Meeting common needs. *Improving college and university teaching, 32*(3), 119–122.

Smith, E. B., & Goodlad, J. I. (1966). Promises and pitfalls in the trend toward collaboration. In *Partnership in teacher education* (pp. 13–34). Washington, DC: American Association of Colleges for Teacher Education and The Association for Student Teaching.

Smith, L. M. (1977). *Interorganizational structures as educational networks.* Washington, DC: National Institute of Education.

Smith, W. (1983). *A study of administrators' communication networks in a public school district.* Unpublished doctoral dissertation, University of Washington.

Thompson, J. D. (1967). *Organizations in action*. New York: McGraw-Hill.

Trubowitz, S., Duncan, W., Fibkins, W., Longo, P., & Sarason, S. (1984). *When a college works with a public school: A case study of school-college collaboration*. Boston: Institute for Responsive Education.

Turk, H. (1970). Interorganizational networks in urban society: Initial perspectives and comparative research. *American Sociological Review, 35*(1), 1–19.

Tyack, D., & Hansot, E. (1982). *Managers of virtue*. New York: Basic Books.

Wilbur, F. P. (1984, October). School-college partnerships: Building effective models for collaboration. *NASSP Bulletin, 68*, 34–49.

Wilbur, F. P. (1985, Summer). School-college partnerships. *Journal of College Admissions*, no. 108, pp. 20–28.

Wu, P. C. (1985, December). *School districts and universities and staff development: Is it a mixture that will work?* Paper presented at the National Staff Development Council Conference, Denver.

# Part II
# CASES

# CHAPTER THREE

# The Metropolitan School Study Council: A Living History

## ANN LIEBERMAN

It may be serendipitous that school-university partnerships are appearing during what some educators are referring to as the second wave of educational reform. I say serendipitous because these partnerships come at a time when research universities are being called to task for having grown distant from the real problems that schools are facing while school people are being criticized for having been so immersed in their daily problems that they have spent little time or energy reflecting on how schools could be improved. School-university collaboration, then, is being suggested as a way of meeting these mutual concerns and as a way of creating dialogue and interaction between these two very different cultures. At the very least this may be a time when there is enough activity connected with the organization of these collaborations to enable us to gain some understanding about how to mobilize these efforts and how to make them work for the mutual benefit of the participants while providing opportunities for those who work in them to understand better the cultures of both the school and the university.

It is within this context that I shall look at the history of the Metropolitan School Study Council (MSSC), which I, a professor at Teachers College, Columbia University, was associated with as Executive Secretary from 1977 to 1986. There is much to be learned from this school-university collaboration, from understanding the conditions that brought it into existence and that caused it to endure — through good times and bad — for more than 40 years. What follows is an analysis of some of the important events, key players, and the nature of the organization of MSSC, particularly from 1977 to 1986, with some of the lessons learned, persistent problems, new questions, and prospects for the future.

### Some Personal Learning

As a graduate student at the University of California at Los Angeles (UCLA) from 1966 to 1969, I had been one of 11 students who worked

69

with the League of Cooperating Schools, a collaboration between UCLA and 18 schools in southern California. The details of this collaboration have been written about elsewhere (Goodlad, 1975; Bentzen, 1974), but one important insight I gained from that experience was the enormous power of a collaboration between school and university people. Somehow, the sustained involvement of those who had the time for research, reflection, and significant discussion with those who worked actively, but had little or no time to think about their work, was incredibly powerful. Over time, people came to trust one another. Early periods of anger, frustration, and inability to communicate gave way to the growth of new norms of risk-taking together and shared high expectations for effecting constructive change. Many of the people involved in that collaboration took new risks in their personal as well as their work lives and, many years afterward, still spoke about the experience as one of the most enriching of their professional careers. (This was true for both the school people and those involved in the university setting.) As a student, I received a unique education. I was studying theories and concepts of organizations while I was experiencing them in the League of Cooperating Schools. I was to become a person who cared about reflection and the conceptualization of practice while being sensitive and empathic to the labor-intensive work of principals and teachers. Living professionally between two worlds, not totally comfortable in either but able to operate in both, I was, in a word, "bi-cultural."

## The Historical Context

Although I became executive secretary in 1977, the Metropolitan School Study Council had existed since 1941. Paul Mort, a professor of Educational Administration, had formed the MSSC as part of a larger plan for Teachers College. He had been very influential in the creation of the Ed.D., "a doctoral program whose foci lay in the advanced knowledge, the specialized understandings, and the practical skills required for broad professional competence in the field" (Cremin, Shannon, & Townsend, 1954, p. 140). Mort's particular interest was in the creation of a program at Teachers College that would be responsible for educating a new group of leaders in schools throughout the country. It was the era of the growth of the superintendency as the focus of leadership in school districts. The MSSC, under Mort, provided research assistantships where the students would do their studies "in the field." Sixty school districts in metropolitan New York represented the field. They were known as the "lighthouse districts." They were to be the districts that would be on the cutting edge of the new ideas that were being created at Teachers College. (Mort's own research persuaded him that significant improvement could only come about from wealthy districts with the tax base to support their schools at a relatively high level.) Many administrators got their degrees by doing research in the MSSC districts.

The central idea developed by Mort was an "index of innovativeness." The characteristics in the index were subsequently used by school districts as a tool for self-improvement (Havelock, 1981, p. 148). This provided the schools with a focus for seminars, training for the graduate students, and content for workshops and conferences. The development of the instrument provided the practical focus for research while its substance provided the ideas to be practiced and implemented by the MSSC schools.

The Ed.D. degree, then, which was to become a standard for the field, was more attuned to practicing administrators than to those who would become researchers. At the same time, through MSSC, Teachers College was legitimating the importance both of scholarship for school leaders and of research that had a practical focus. Mort's operation at Teachers College developed around three components: he had a *structure* within the college as well as one outside the college that mobilized support for his work (MSSC and other institutes); he had a strong *research focus* on finance which involved scores of students; and he eventually created a *network* of school superintendents in districts throughout the nation. Hundreds of administrators went through MSSC or one of the college's institutes.

For years Teachers College was seen as *the* place to go for the finest professional education. The ferment of new ideas, the large number of professors focusing on building professional knowledge, the growth of institutes, and the new degree for practicing administrators set norms at the college that continue, in some form, to this day.

Upon Mort's retirement, William Vincent, another professor in Educational Administration, assumed the leadership of MSSC. Vincent had gotten his experience in practical scholarship as one of the officers of the Citizenship Education Project, a large Carnegie Corporation project which was an effort to help schools aid teachers in getting their students to participate in civic activities (Cremin et al., 1954). The focus of Vincent's interest was on the development of what came to be known as the *Indicators of Quality*, in some ways an updated and expanded version of Mort's "index." Although "Indicators" was eventually to become a measurement instrument, the intent was also to involve the MSSC schools in building and designing quality schools. The focus of

MSSC activity was to describe in as detailed a way as possible what quality schools should be (an interest that was important to the schools) while figuring out how to observe these qualities (an interest and focus for the doctoral students who would use this as the basis for their dissertations but who would also activate this knowledge when they went to assume leadership positions). Vincent, like his predecessor, had structures both in and outside the college, a practical research focus, and a continuing number of students getting their education as administrators in the content of "quality schools." This program lasted for more than a decade.

Structurally, MSSC had been under the Institute for Administrative Research, another institute within the college, whose responsibility was to coordinate many independent projects that were carried on locally in the MSSC schools and nationally in the Associated Public School Systems (APSS). MSSC was a part of the college community that was heavily invested in working with schools in the creation of practical knowledge. Students became the missionaries of the new ideas being created at the college and used that knowledge as they became the leaders in districts throughout the country.

## A Changed World

MSSC had several other directors in the interim, but by 1977 the situation had changed at the college, in the profession, and in New York. Many professors had moved from research that involved practical and professional knowledge to more traditional university-oriented research. Although some professors had been involved in significant projects in the 1960s and 1970s (Passow, 1967), by the 1970s money was tight and the school programs of the Johnson Administration's "Great Society" were running down. Much had been learned, but unquestionably the world had changed. The idea of "lighthouse schools" was suspect since it connoted in real and symbolic terms, the enormous differences between city schools that were essentially serving the urban minority poor and suburban schools that were serving the middle- and upper-class white students who had left the city. Administering schools had become very complex. Many universities were involved in giving doctoral degrees to administrators. Administration departments were in disarray in terms of their focus, direction, and contribution to the field. The research community was beginning to talk about the "school improvement literature" that had been virtually nonexistent in Mort's era. Where Mort had created his own view of educational change (and it was the most salient view), many people were now involved in the study and understanding of change processes in schools (Berman & McLaughlin, 1975; Hall, Wallace, & Dossett, 1973; Lieberman & Miller, 1978). The dominance of male administrators, which was a hallmark of the early days of MSSC, was being seriously questioned by the growth of the women's movement and women's expanded opportunities in many typically male-dominated professions. New York City was suffering from serious financial problems, and teachers were being laid off or "RIFed" (due to a reduction in force).

Professional associations had formed for all members of the educational establishment, and clearly a major part of their agenda was to protect their own members. Superintendents, principals, and teachers all had their own organizations representing their interests. The relations between members of the educational establishment could best be described as adversarial. The American Educational Research Association (AERA) had become the principal organization for educational researchers and had distanced itself from the complex practical problems of the schools. Where Teachers College had been at the heart of the creation of practical knowledge, it too had, for the most part, taken the distanced stance of other research universities. As in several other periods of its history, it was having financial problems as well.

## Learning from the History

There are some important ideas embedded in the reconstruction of MSSC's history before its renewal in the late 1970s. There is no question that the notion of an "idea champion" was critical to the birth and formation of MSSC. Paul Mort was one of the leading figures at Teachers College during the 1930s and 1940s. His ideas took hold both structurally and intellectually in the Teachers College community. Before the establishment of MSSC, in writing about "the Advanced School" (which was to be made up of a group of researchers within the college involved with field projects in the schools), Mort made his values clear: "If the Advanced School is to fulfill its potential significance in American education, every step should be taken to prevent it from becoming academically minded" (Cremin et al., 1954, pp. 160–161).* Indeed, Mort held a strong philosophical orientation to research. It was to have *practical significance* for the field, but it was also to be recognized by the college as legitimate *cutting edge research*.

---

*For a fascinating account of the structures, personalities, and intellectual ferment of the growth of professional education at Teachers College, see *A History of Teachers College, Columbia University* by Cremin, Shannon, and Townsend (1954).

Mort's contribution to the Educational Administration Department was not only his concern with producing leaders in the field, but also with producing a new view of the type of credential these leaders should hold and a *structure* within the college to promote these ideas. In addition to MSSC projects, work conferences, seminars, and informal get-togethers were very much a part of college life for both students and faculty. All of these forms lent respectability to collaborative work that involved students, faculty, and lay people outside the college. Because much of the research was done by doctoral students, there was a changing staff of people actually running MSSC. As students completed their graduate work, others took over to begin theirs. This provided students with a way to finance their studies, while being schooled in a new way. It also insured the organization of a supply of new people and new ideas.

## The Renewal of MSSC, 1977–1986

Although I had not read about Mort and the history of MSSC, the folklore was still being discussed in the halls of Teachers College when I arrived in 1973. Superintendents that I met throughout the country talked about being "fellows" at Teachers College working for MSSC. But MSSC had, like the rest of New York, fallen on bad times. Only nine superintendents were still paying their dues to MSSC, and they were clearly dissatisfied with their membership and the college itself. There was much anger and frustration at what seemed to the school people to be a total disregard for their problems. They were tired of being used as "subjects" for someone's dissertation thesis. They were troubled with many complex problems which did not seem to be a part of the college's research agenda. Clearly much had changed since the days of Paul Mort.

Within the college, many of the structures that had been the hallmark of the Mort era were also in a state of decline. Within a few years, the Institute for Administrative Research was to come to an end. The Horace Mann–Lincoln Institute, which was supposed to be the umbrella for MSSC, was the last remaining institute that related to the field. Its purpose had been to "direct attention to the solution of critical educational problems" (Cremin et al., 1954, p. 238). The institute was still there, but it had only a few projects under its aegis. It no longer had a staff of professors doing work with schools. Most faculty members did not see the focus of their work as being primarily directed toward working with schools. The reward system in graduate schools of education had changed nationwide—and that included Teachers College. Research was something that emanated from the professorate, not from the field. Large-scale surveys of programs were legitimate, but these, for the most part, were being conducted by heavily funded corporations such as Rand or by the federally funded laboratories and centers. Research universities found it hard to compete with such places whose entire operation was geared to writing proposals and doing research. The definition of research, rather than being geared to the solution of critical educational problems, became the description of these problems. This was clearly very far from the early years at Teachers College.

But despite these changed conditions, many of the traditions still lived on within the walls of the college. Teachers College still held a broad view of professional education. The professors still represented a diverse, creative, and highly experienced group of people in a major metropolitan center, some of whom had been leaders in earlier reform efforts. A broader view of scholarship was still being debated in the college through some of its committees. Lawrence Cremin, president of Teachers College, spoke of how critically important it was for faculty to be "on the cutting edge" of what was happening in education, health, and psychology. His orientation was clearly supportive of establishing ties with the field (Havelock, 1981, p. 43).

## Using and Adapting the College's Traditions

Such was the climate when I became the executive secretary of MSSC. For the first time, then, MSSC was being run by someone in the Curriculum and Teaching (C & T) Department rather than by someone in the Educational Administration Department. Although I suspect that this happened not as a matter of policy but because I had had experience with school-university collaboration, it was important to the central thrust and underlying values of the early years of renewal. For a long time, the professors of the Educational Administration Department and the Curriculum and Teaching Department had disagreed on the appropriate role of the educational leader. In fact, there was disagreement within the departments as well (Cremin et al., 1954). (This had been the case in the 1940s and it continues to the present day.) The Educational Administration Department essentially created superintendents of schools and school principals—the leaders of school districts. The Curriculum and Teaching Department attracted students who had historically become the teacher education faculties, but in the 1970s these students were increasingly becoming assistant superintendents of curriculum, directors of staff development, or project directors of particular curriculum projects (many having to do with improving schools).

The C & T department had more of a teacher orientation, whereas educational administration was oriented toward top-level administration, often with a managerial approach. Although superintendents, principals, and teachers work in schools together, because of the separation of all members of the professional community, ideologies have become separated as well (Lieberman & Miller, 1984). This was as true in the college as in the field at large. In fact, several of us were fond of saying that if the curriculum and teaching faculty could work with the educational administration faculty, we might be able to model what was needed in the field.

## The Fellows

During the first year, the college gave money to support doctoral students. Ten students were asked to participate in the renewal of MSSC. With the exception of one student, they were all from the C & T Department. Most of them were teachers (one had just created an innovative staff development program) who were excited about the idea that we could provide some kind of collaboration that would be part of their doctoral program and relate more closely to their working lives. They worked during the day and somehow found the time to go to school at night and be doctoral fellows as well. This was a far cry from Mort's fellows who were full-time doctoral students.

Our first task was to gain the trust and respect of the nine districts still remaining in MSSC. They wanted a genuine connection to the college. In addition, it was clear that we also needed to *do something* to show that there was a real basis for collaboration. Because there was so much hostility toward research done at the college that school people felt was irrelevant to their problems, I decided to send the fellows to the schools to make friends, to find out how they could be useful, and to begin to gather information about what might be the form and content of activities that we might run. Several districts paid small sums that helped support doctoral students in this role. These students, who worked in their own school districts during the day, identified very much with the complaints that the MSSC schools had about the college. The students were most uncomfortable with their role as fellows and their exact function in the schools. Meanwhile, I had been heavily influenced by the theorists who spoke about action preceding goals (Weick, 1976). My teaching days had taught me that in spite of the most beautiful lesson plans, I always became clearer about what I was doing *after I did it*. In order to find a direction for MSSC, I thought that we all needed to know what *they* (the schools) were doing, what *they* were ready for, and how we could find ways to link to *their* problems. A moratorium was called on research. We were trying to build a relationship.

As a professor, I used the opportunity to teach a class to the fellows. The substance of the class was to be derived from their experience in the field. The sociology of educational change had a great deal of content, but the practical experiences of the fellows were to make it come alive. For example, concepts such as the "culture of the school" took on great meaning for the fellows who were observing firsthand what cultures looked like, what they allowed people to do, and what they prevented them from doing. In short, a laboratory was being created for the students while we were gathering information about how to proceed with MSSC. While we struggled together, learning intellectually, we were also building an informal set of ties that was far different from either their setting or mine.

## The Work Group and Conference

Teachers College had long been known for having work groups and work conferences. Some of them eventually produced books from papers given at the conferences (e.g., Passow, 1963).

As the students began to know their schools and districts, we began to build agendas for future work groups. In addition, I went to faculty who I knew would be attractive to the school people and asked if they would address a work group on a topic of their choice. In the process, several things were happening. Gradually school people were becoming convinced that the college really cared about them *and* that there were important ideas in the college and people there who had something to say to them. At the same time, we were finding people in the field who were expert in a variety of curricular areas. MSSC was a good vehicle to promote interdistrict sharing of expertise. We were beginning to build in a brokerage function as part of our work. By the end of the first year, we had held two very successful conferences, and a series of work groups had met at an old mansion owned by the college in Riverdale (a close-in suburb). The structure of activities and, to some extent, the place became associated with the rebirth of MSSC. Informally, other district personnel were hearing about the interesting activities run by MSSC, and new districts began to call our office to inquire about membership.

## Building an Agenda for MSSC

Students had gone out to the schools for a year and brought back much information on what was happening, what teachers and principals were doing, and, most important, what they defined as their most salient problems. We were building an agenda for future work, building trust between the college and the field, providing a mechanism for collaborative work, and, in so doing, providing a focus for MSSC. The focus was no longer the training ground for the superintendency, nor the question of what makes a "quality school"; the focus was on how to improve schools. School improvement was a large enough focus for the school people, and it could involve many college faculty members as well. School improvement projects abounded in all school districts, and new roles to facilitate new projects were proliferating. Students in C & T and other departments of the college saw these projects as legitimate foci for research. They could do their research in the schools, documenting the initiation, implementation, and institutionalization of these projects. Themes taken from the research, as well as from the literature on educational change, could then become subjects for work groups and conferences. Thus the content of school improvement efforts, along with the processes for implementing new ideas, began to undergird our work and to clarify the focus of the renewal of MSSC.

## The Changing Structure of MSSC

In 1977, there was enough money donated by the college to support the revived fellows program. In a two-year period, the 13 fellows helped to mount over 20 work groups on diverse topics and participated in several high-quality conferences. But by 1979, due to the college's financial problems, the number of fellows was severely reduced. In addition, I became ill and took a year's leave from the college. In that year no new programmatic thrusts were initiated, and some of the momentum that had been built waned somewhat. However, my replacement, a master of detail, used his time to order the many processes that had been growing for two years. Where I was strong on initiating activities, he was strong on evaluating and institutionalizing the formats. Thus, when I returned, there was a brochure describing the purposes of MSSC, an annual description of its activities with their evaluation, and a far more orderly operation. He had created a way of summarizing every activity, evaluating its worth, and writing an annual report that not only showed a record of the activities, but allowed us to assess who participated, what types of activities we were running, and the formats and people that were most attractive to the membership. These have remained to this day.

By 1979 there were more than 25 districts in MSSC, though the number of fellows had been reduced to four. It was becoming clear that if there was to be any assistance by doctoral students, it was going to have to be paid for by the membership dues of the districts themselves. By 1981 the structure had changed yet again. Now there was a program coordinator (a part-time doctoral student who organized the work groups, conferences, newsletter, and other activities of MSSC), and a project director (a part-time faculty member with strong ties to the field who served as an idea person and also helped integrate MSSC activities into college life). I was the executive secretary, whose job was to provide overall leadership while linking MSSC with the college faculty and national leaders and organizations. Four doctoral students were assigned specific jobs, such as leading urban activities or editing the newsletter. An executive board, made up of superintendents from New York, New Jersey, and Connecticut, and two school principals, advised the college staff and served as our link to the field.

Although MSSC had changed greatly since 1977, its changes, in some ways, represented one of the strengths of school-university partnerships. The flexibility with which we could adapt in terms of number of staff, roles, and activities was only possible because of our independent status vis-à-vis both the college and the schools. We had no significant office expenses, no important job titles, no activities that we could not change or drop. Although we had staff commitment to what we were doing, all of us were doing it part-time. Perhaps this may sound unstable and an example of poor administration to some, but it allowed us to shift and adapt to changing conditions, expanding when we had the resources and redirecting our energies when we didn't have them.

### Collaborative Research

Although there had been no formal research done in the first two years of the renewal of MSSC, by 1979 we were ready to begin the process. Several of us took the opportunity to do collaborative research. We went back to an earlier period at Teachers College when work known as "action research" had been carried on (see, e.g., Corey, 1953). This work had been renamed and expanded in 1975 by Tikunoff, Ward, and Griffin, who reasoned that one way to fill the gap between research done at the university and its eventual implementation in the field, was to do "interactive research." This meant that teachers and researchers would work together to define a research problem, collect evidence, interpret the evidence, and use either the process of deliberation or the product to intervene in the team's own professional development. By the late 1970s, there was increasing discussion about involving school people in looking systematically at their practices. This type of research, then, seemed well fitted to the needs of the time and the type of organization MSSC had become.

In 1980–1982, funded by the National Institute of Education, we

formed three teams, each team consisting of several teachers, a researcher, and a staff developer from MSSC. Our aim was to try to
understand the process and to see if we could do this type of inquiry in
different contexts. (For a complete discussion, see Griffin, Lieberman,
& Noto, 1983, and Lieberman, 1986.) We took the opportunity to do
collaborative research and, at the same time, to learn more about connecting the world of the university to the world of schools. We were
struck by the different attitudes and work styles of the team in the
suburbs and the team in the urban environment, one major difference
being that suburban teachers felt far more autonomous. We also realized that MSSC needed to make greater efforts to include urban districts. We saw that, although all three teams learned a great deal, only
the team that had *all* district people working on it was able to institutionalize the process for use after the project was over.

Although our intent was to facilitate interactive research with all
the school districts, MSSC had grown too large, and we did not have the
kind of resources to mount an effort of this size. We did, however, build
action research into the college curriculum while creating yet another
set of opportunities for both college faculty and school district personnel
to work together.

## The Consortia

By the early 1980s, the formats for the work groups and several
conferences a year, as well as daylong seminars on selected topics, had
been fairly well institutionalized. At this time, a new movement to
improve the teaching of writing was developing on both coasts (see, e.g.,
Calkins, 1986). Several of the MSSC districts were beginning to work
with teachers, essentially teaching them how to write in order to sensi-
tize them to the learning process of their students (see, e.g., Calkins,
1986). We took this opportunity to call together interested districts to see
if they wanted to meet together to teach each other what they were
learning. Out of a meeting of superintendents, principals, teachers, and
several staff developers, a writing consortium was formed. Districts
would pay a small fee to work together with other districts focusing on
writing. In this way, it was felt, district personnel would have a peer
group struggling with the same problems. They could visit one another's sites, share knowledge, and learn more about this new process. We
hired a research assistant who was expert in the area to work with the
consortium.

At the same time, several districts were just beginning to hire computer consultants to try to figure out how to use these new machines.

Again we called together a group of interested parties to see if this too wouldn't lend itself to a special group focusing on the computer. The meeting, like the one on writing, turned out to be very significant. Many of the people at the meeting were teachers who had become computer buffs. They were already trying to figure out how to get other teachers involved, how to get the districts to think through possible computer needs, and how to answer the big questions involved in computer use. (What is computer literacy? Does everyone need it? Is it a separate subject, or should it be integrated into the curriculum? Who will do this?)

In the beginning, both of these special interest groups fulfilled very specialized functions and became the leaders in the MSSC schools in both areas. In time, some of the people evolved into experts who taught others in the MSSC group. We had provided a forum for leadership groups to emerge by creating yet another form: special interest group consortia.

### The Urban Districts

Despite the fact that many of the MSSC districts were in the suburbs, they were increasingly having urban problems. Changing family structures, teenage suicide, drugs, apathy — all were becoming suburban problems too. Previously, we had tried to get urban districts back into MSSC without much success. Now all agreed that a concerted effort had to be made.

We found that with the pressure of a growing need for staff development, urban districts began to see MSSC as another possible resource. Initially, a friend from the United Federation of Teachers got us to our first urban superintendent. He had been a member of MSSC many years before and now reluctantly, at first, decided to rejoin. As an incentive we gave a half year's free dues to the urban districts to lure them to several of our events. (This particular superintendent's district was located where we held many of our workshops and conferences. In effect, he could send many of his people, and they had only to drive ten minutes.) Word of mouth let others know that the work groups were worthwhile. Our first urban superintendent then got us seven other urban districts. With the advent of these districts, the quality of many of the work groups changed. For the first time, urban school people were sharing their frustrations and their successes with suburban people. (In some cases, although the urban school people faced tremendous problems, they had become more resourceful and innovative than their suburban counterparts.) This expansion of MSSC then brought the need for an additional fellow who would focus on some of the urban areas. We needed to accommodate the needs and interests of an ever-expanding group that shared some common problems but had some very different ones as well.

MSSC had grown to be a large network of 48 school districts in three states, serving teachers, principals, and district office staff. Its service function was clear. It had become a legitimate link between Teachers College and schools. Its research focus was less clear. Although it was to legitimate dissertations for many students, it no longer had one focus that bound it together. School improvement, with all its complexities, had become its agenda.

## MSSC and the Future of School-University Collaboration

MSSC still exists as a living history of a school-university collaboration. While we have learned much from its existence, over the years some persistent problems and tensions have continued to the present time. As an organization that stands between two cultures, a school-university collaboration must create a culture of its own, one that is important to both institutions, but one that stands independently as something unique and different. This culture, because it is making demands on two systems, must be sensitive to both, yet it must weave its way around some obvious constraints and tensions as a result of its "organizational third world" quality (Clark, 1985). The collaboration requires an irreverence for the traditional rules and regulations of both cultures, somehow maintaining credibility while building new norms and new ways of working (Clark & Astuto, 1986; Lieberman, 1985).

Whereas the early years of MSSC were characterized by a clearer sense of mission, in later years the focus became far broader (Stirling, 1987). In its formative years there was an assumption that the university was the source of all knowledge to be received by the schools. In our era this idea has changed and become part of the challenge that must be negotiated in the new culture. The notion of a brokerage function as a part of the collaboration serves the purpose of organizing both the expertise of the university *and* the expertise in the schools; the collaboration builds an agenda that becomes mutually informing and mutually influential. This function has been performed by independent agencies and federal labs and centers for several decades. Colleges and universities, however, have not normally been known to perform these functions.

Given today's fiscal restraints on both colleges and school systems, financing school-university collaborations offers still another tension to be negotiated. In its renewal period, MSSC started with substantial funding for a fellows program that involved enough people to rebuild the organization and to socialize students to a new way of thinking about collaboration between school and university. In a short time, that money was no longer available, and our ability to be a physical presence in the college and schools was diminished. The quality of the programs that were offered continued to sustain great interest in MSSC, but there is no question that more money could have bought more time, more people, and greater involvement in more substantial efforts to effect change in the schools and the college. If school-university collaborations are intended to make serious constructive changes, then both the schools and the university will have to make serious financial commitments to them. Without such commitments, we will have new forms without the people, the resources, and the time to build them.

At its inception, MSSC had many institutes within the college that supported faculty work on educational problems. These forms helped provide normative conditions that allowed and encouraged faculty to work together with schools. MSSC was the laboratory, while other institutes within the college provided the structures for faculty to work with one another. During the renewal period, the students who worked in MSSC became a special group and formed tremendous loyalty to the ideas and thrust of the organization. Faculty made contributions but were never intimately involved. It seems clear that large numbers of faculty will probably never be involved in such collaborative activities because of their broad range of interests and concerns. Moreover, the reward system has limited the range and possibilities for greater faculty involvement. It is hard to get tenure in many universities for working with schools on collaborative projects. Short-term, quantitative research that yields quick results — and several papers — is more likely to be rewarded. Getting articles printed in refereed journals carries more weight than influential articles in journals read by school people. The norms of Teachers College during the renewal period were still supportive of this kind of work, yet few faculty felt they could risk the time or effort that might be involved in such efforts. This may have been a function of the complex and fast-paced world of Teachers College, but I suspect that the limited view of research and scholarship that has dominated most research universities in the last two decades was an underlying factor.

What can we learn from this reconstruction of the history and renewal of the oldest school-university collaboration about building future collaborations? To begin at the beginning, when school-university collaborations are first organized, the actual working out of the agenda marks the beginning of the relationship, the cornerstone of the trust and mutual respect being built between the two cultures. What issues, what forms, where the meetings are to be held, who is represented—all contribute to building the culture of collaboration. Doing something together is probably more important than big agreements about what should happen. From participation in activities, people in both cultures get a chance to face one another, shed their stereotypes of one another, and join in organizational learning together (Lieberman, 1985).

There seems to be no question that school-university collaborations should be organized and run by a person (or persons) who holds a large vision of constructive change in both school and university—an "idea champion." People who run these interorganizational arrangements need ideas, energy, and commitment to a vision that is larger than either school or university. How large their vision, how deep the changes attempted, and how much commitment they maintain depends upon the degree to which the interorganizational arrangement is supported by both cultures. Without this support, the vision shrinks, the changes attempted are shallow, and the commitment slowly fades away.

As a corollary to this, it seems imperative that the leadership be credible to and respected by both the school and university cultures. It is important that a leader be a person of status in the university who understands the life of schools and is perceived as such by school people. School people legitimately want to know that their participation will be taken seriously by the university. Who is chosen and how this person is supported tells them how serious the university is. The university faculty, on the other hand, need to respect the academic credentials of the leader as someone who has paid the same kind of academic dues that they have. They need to see that the collaboration offers a legitimate focus for their work and that the university both accepts and rewards this work. But how is this legitimacy to be gained? What kinds of work are respected in both cultures? This too is problematic.

The kind of work that school people see as legitimate is work that they define as dealing with their real problems; but this has not been the definition that has been used by the university in the past. Scholarship has been defined primarily as research that emanates from the academy and is published in particular journals. Describing problems, rather than bringing knowledge to bear to act on problems, has been seen as the work of the university. Working on problems in collaboration with school people has not usually been seen as respectable faculty work. (It has been legitimate to consult but not to get involved with schoolwide efforts at improvement or with new ways of working together.) It seems necessary, then, that the university perspective expand to a broader view of scholarly work and that rewards for faculty be linked to a variety of research *and* development opportunities mutually worked on by the collaboration. Faculty members know that collaborative work with schools is important when institutes, inquiry groups, and centers (forms that are familiar to them) become a part of the internal structure of the university. Such structures help provide the cultural norms necessary for university people to expand the nature of their work just as the network of schools provides those norms for school people.

It is probable that the loose, flexible, adaptive nature of the renewal years of MSSC is typical of many interorganizational arrangements. It stands in contrast to both schools and universities characterized more by stability than by change. It may be that these collaborative arrangements do indeed provide a choice of different ways to mobilize people, different forms and activities that allow for new norms to be built, and different means to facilitate the building of collaborative work. If this is so, this era may be an especially fruitful time for these collaborations to flourish. It may also be a time to make a real difference in the ways schools and universities function.

## References

Bentzen, M. M. (1974). *Changing schools: The magic feather principle*. New York: McGraw-Hill.

Berman, P., & McLaughlin, M. W. (1975). *Federal programs supporting educational change, Vol. IV: The findings in review*. Santa Monica, CA: Rand Corporation.

Calkins, L. M. (1986). *The art of teaching writing*. Portsmouth, NH: Heinemann.

Clark, D. (1985). Factors affecting the success of interorganizational arrangements for school improvement. Paper prepared for the Allerton Symposium on Illinois Educational Improvement.

Clark, D., & Astuto, T. (1986). *Paradoxical choice options in organizations*. Unpublished manuscript.

Corey, S. (1953). *Action research to improve school practices*. New York: Bureau of Publications, Teachers College, Columbia.

Cremin, L. B., Shannon, D. A., & Townsend, M. E. (1954). *A history of Teachers College*. New York: Columbia University Press.

Goodlad, J. I. (1975). *The dynamics of educational change*. New York: McGraw-Hill.

Griffin, G. A., Lieberman, A., & Noto, J. J. (1983). *Executive summary final report, Interactive research and development on schooling*. Washington, DC: National Institute of Education.

Hall, G. E., Wallace, R. C., & Dossett, W. A. (1973). *A developmental conceptualization of the adoption process within educational institutions*. Austin, TX: Research and Development Center for Teacher Education, University of Texas.

Havelock, R. G. (1981). *School-university collaboration supporting school improvement*, Vol. III. The Eastern Private University Case Prepared for the Research and Educational Practice Program, National Institute of Education.

Lieberman, A. (1985). Enhancing school improvement through collaboration. Paper prepared for the Allerton Symposium on Illinois Educational Improvement.

Lieberman, A. (1986). Collaborative research: Working with, not working on. *Educational Leadership, 43*, 28–32.

Lieberman, A., & Miller, L. (Eds.). (1978). *Staff development: New demands, new realities, new perspectives.* New York: Teachers College Press.

Lieberman, A., & Miller, L. (1984). *Teachers, their world and their work: Implications for school improvement.* Alexandria, VA: Association for Supervision and Curriculum Development.

Passow, A. H. (1967). *Toward creating a model urban school system: A study of the Washington, D.C., public schools.* District of Columbia Public Schools.

Passow, A. H. (1967). *Toward creating a model urban school system: A study of the Washington, D. C., public schools.* District of Columbia Public Schools.

Stirling, L. (1987). *Collaboration among school districts and a college of education: A case study of the Metropolitan School Study Council.* Unpublished doctoral dissertation, Teachers College, Columbia University.

Tikunoff, W. J., Ward, B., & Griffin, G. (1975). *Interactive research and development on teaching study.* San Francisco: Far West Laboratory.

Weick, K. (1976). Educational organizations as loosely coupled systems. *Administrative Science Quarterly, 21*, 1–19.

# CHAPTER FOUR

# A Partnership for Increasing Student Learning: The Massachusetts Coalition for School Improvement

ROBERT L. SINCLAIR and ANNE E. HARRISON

These are exciting yet unsettling times for professional educators. Like our colleagues across the country, Massachusetts educators are caught up in a swirl of challenges. For example, teachers and administrators in schools and universities are trying to make sense out of widespread criticism of school effectiveness, mounting dissatisfaction with teacher preparation programs, and imposed state legislation intended to restore excellence to public education (Massachusetts Legislature, 1985). School improvement is high on the priority list of increasing numbers of citizens, parents, policy makers, scholars, and others who recognize that the vitality of public education is central to the health of our society. There will be few chances like the present one to bring about reform of American education, and we are convinced it is necessary to rally educators from all parts of the enterprise to join together to create better schools for all children and youth.

One powerful approach to constructive reform is to gather interested leaders in colleges of education and elementary and secondary schools in a partnership committed to a common goal — increasing student learning. Ideally, such collaboration functions in a spirit of parity among participants who recognize that they can benefit from sharing knowledge, experiences, and insights about ways to help more students realize their potential. Collaboration that pays more than rhetorical attention to parity, however, will have to build a fresh, more unified approach to reform rather than merely bridge programs that already exist.

The Massachusetts Coalition for School Improvement is an example of a partnership built on parity and designed to increase the amount and quality of student learning. For us, renewal of curriculum, instruction, and organization of schools gets its direction from what students need to achieve to overcome academic, social, and physical deficiencies or to stretch their current strengths to even higher levels of excellence. This means that changes in the educational environment are made to assist all students in accomplishing desired objectives for learning, including those marginal students who are not succeeding in school. Collaborating to increase student learning does not mean joining forces only to boost grades and standardized achievement test scores, although such indicators of gains may be considered. Rather, the emphasis is on working together to create conditions that promote school success for all individuals and groups. Some examples of what students may do to increase learning include: improving oral and written communication skills, perfecting ability to solve problems, becoming more effective in working with others, developing positive attitudes toward individuals from different cultures, sharpening hand and eye coordination, gaining knowledge about the workings of a democratic government, analyzing associations between mathematics and music. Data about achieving these various kinds of learning go beyond the typical information collected in standardized tests. Samples of student work, teacher reports of changes in learning, observations of student behavior, self-evaluations by students, and interviews with parents about changes in their children are useful sources of data for determining progress schools and students are making in increasing learning. Creating environments to promote learning, then, is at the heart of collaboration for school renewal. Simply put, the Coalition strives for significant improvements that emerge from student needs and that are guided by student progress.

The Coalition joins public elementary and secondary schools and the University of Massachusetts. When schools were selected, considerable effort was made to create a microcosm of conditions and problems without sacrificing manageability. To this end, 26 diverse schools were selected (11 core schools and 15 affiliates), including a large inner-city high school fighting to keep students in school, a small rural elementary school where local farmers bring fresh vegetables for student lunches, a regional high school set amid picturesque hills, adjacent to the school tree farm, and an urban elementary school that doubles as a community center until 11:00 P.M. each night, set amid tenements, adjacent to the county jail.

In building the Coalition, educators from the different schools and the university recognize that they are entering a long-term, learn-as-we-go alliance to accomplish the following goals:

- To promote educational environments that increase learning for all students, particularly those who do not have a history of academic success.
- To provide opportunities for participants to share knowledge and

expertise relating to effective policies and practices in schools and the university.

- To promote increased community awareness and involvement in educational problems and issues.
- To provide opportunities for professional development and preparation for educational leadership.
- To foster collaboration among educators for researching persistent problems which exist in school and university settings.

These goals emerged during the planning and implementation of the Coalition. They are intended to guide further action, but are not thought to be impervious to change. The goals are open to modification to ensure consistency with shifts in school and university practice.[1]

We are optimistic about creating an effective partnership to pursue shared goals, and we are convinced that diverse settings and alternative approaches to improvement are an advantage, not a hindrance. Yet, there is a lingering concern that tugs at our efforts to provide leadership: the real possibility that the current educational reform movement will be ineffectual in realizing lasting improvements, just as past reform movements fell short in meeting challenges for better education. With history in mind, we are making haste slowly in order to avoid several persistent obstacles that have plagued educational reform in the past.

## Some Obstacles to Reform

The intention is not to suggest all the obstacles that must be avoided. The purpose here is to describe some obstacles that Coalition members are attempting to overcome in order to promote meaningful and lasting improvements in the learning environment.

First, participants in the Coalition try to shun the practice of relying on "experts" from the university to solve school problems. According

---

1. Goals and action are both important in the Coalition, and which comes first is not an issue. More important than the sequence is that goals accurately reflect the priorities of those who are engaged in action to improve education. We believe that although it is possible for educators from different institutions to come together by centering their efforts on activities, the necessary momentum for constructive change is more dependent on shared understanding of how people, particularly students, are benefiting from the activities. For example, an exciting seminar is more likely to generate long-lasting effects when its relationship to desired goals is clear. Activities for accomplishing change are important but are not enough. Similarly, goals are necessary but are not sufficient for accomplishing change.

to Sarason (1982), defining resources solely in terms of individuals with credentials attained through years of education and training may actually limit the school's capacity to solve problems. As teachers and principals come to rely heavily on outside forces for solving local problems, recognition of possible resources and existing abilities within individual schools is minimized. Yet, because of past associations with institutions of higher education, many school people may be conditioned to think that the role of the university in a partnership is to deliver services. As one high school teacher stated during planning of the Coalition, "We have problems in our school, and we are glad that you will be bringing us some solutions." The persistent expectation that the university will deliver services to solve school-based problems undermines the concept of parity among partners. Similarly, too often professors think they must have all the answers to all the questions. University faculty who are unwilling, unable, or unaccustomed to participating as equals with elementary and secondary school colleagues also contribute to the lack of parity.

A second obstacle the Coalition tries to avoid is the failure to acknowledge important school constituents, notably the teachers, as key decision makers in the reform process (Sarason, 1982). Changes initiated by academic experts, administrators, or legislators often fail to affect classroom practice in compelling ways. For example, curriculum projects in the wake of Sputnik produced science materials developed by scholars who were remote from life in schools. A team of researchers at the University of California at Los Angeles observed a sample of early childhood classrooms that professed to be implementing the science materials (Goodlad, Klein, & Associates, 1970). They discovered that the materials were not being used to promote scientific inquiry as the designers intended. Rather, teachers were continuing to use the new materials just as they had used the old—for students to memorize content. One finding of this research is that innovations conceived, planned, and developed without genuine teacher involvement are less likely to be implemented effectively when teachers lack understanding of the change or are not committed to making it succeed.

The tendency to ignore variation in individual schools and adopt trendy innovations based on generalized research and development is another obstacle to reform that the Coalition tries to clear. For example, programmed instruction received wide acclaim in the 1950s as a promising means to individualize instruction, ensure mastery of content, and increase class size without jeopardizing student learning (Tyler, 1976). When implemented in varied schools, however, it was ineffectual in achieving the improvements its developers envisioned. Programmed instruction was an imposed answer to problems that school staffs had not yet identified. There is wide variety in the characteristics and needs of American schools (Goodlad, 1984). It follows, then, that local school staffs should identify problems within their own settings and develop solutions based on their special conditions and available resources.

Also, we are attempting to set realistic expectations for school improvement, recognizing that past reform efforts failed in part because they were based on goals for which available resources were inadequate, including the major resource of time (Sarason, 1982). Too often, educators think that goals can be achieved without fundamental changes in daily practices. Both schools and universities need the capacity to examine practices with critical eyes and open minds. They need to become renewing institutions where educators identify problems unique to their setting, gather data, formulate solutions, implement a plan, and monitor results in an ongoing improvement process (Goodlad, 1984; Tyler, 1986). To achieve desired results, the process of renewal requires time, willingness to alter routines in how people behave, and ability to change regularities in how institutions function. According to Tyler (1986), significant improvement typically takes about seven years. During this time, educators committed to increasing learning for all students are challenged to examine old habits and replace ineffective practices with promising ones. Significant reform, then, requires time to build broad-based support for lasting results.

Interest in pursuing a collaborative approach developed gradually in western Massachusetts as superintendents, principals, teachers, and university faculty gathered in seminars to inquire into how a partnership might lead to accomplishing shared goals. In plain terms, the potential of collaboration caught the imagination of participants, and they became excited about working together to improve education. Critical awareness gained from dialogue about the obstacles described above led to agreement that the Coalition needed a set of working premises to help ensure that mistakes of past reform efforts were not repeated.

## Premises

Five interrelated premises give direction to the efforts of the Coalition. One premise is that *reform efforts should be directed toward correcting weaknesses in student learning and building on students' academic and personal strengths. Priorities for school improvement are best stated in terms of increasing the amount and quality of student learning.* Acting on this premise required some readjustment among Coalition participants, however. Claudius Mkangaza (1986), a researcher in the Center for Curriculum Studies at the University of Massachusetts, conducted a study to determine to what extent principals stated school priorities in terms of student learning. He asked all Coalition principals to describe their priorities for school improvement. Of the resulting 190 priority statements, only six were stated in terms of student learning. The vast majority of statements reflected an orientation toward means rather than ends—toward defining school improvement as changes in school services rather than as the relationship between student learning and such services. The distinction is an important one because the members of the Coalition are now discovering that the value of more or different services for students depends on how well they produce successful learning. As Seeley (1984) points out, "Reformers have always assumed that educational services would produce learning. But all too often they don't. Therefore, we must redirect our attention, make learning our primary goal, and recognize that the student—not the teacher or the school—is the prime producer of what we want" (p. 386).

To determine priorities for improving Coalition schools, administrators, teachers, and occasionally students and parents, discuss strengths and weaknesses in student learning. They gather data about perceived problems and use these data to refine and clarify priorities. In one urban elementary school, for example, the principal and teachers are concerned about the lack of communication skills of youngsters in the primary grades. Their third graders were lowest in the district on holistically scored writing samples, and teachers observed infrequent contributions to class discussions and awkward speech patterns when students expressed their ideas. In a rural secondary school, teachers express concern that students seldom read unless specifically assigned to do so . . . and then not carefully or critically. An inner-city high school is investigating reasons for deficiencies in science learning, a suburban elementary school is considering the causes behind disruptive student behavior, and so on. Again, the connecting pattern across all schools is that priorities for improvement are determined as the staff comes together to take a close look at strengths and weaknesses in student learning.

Another premise guiding Coalition practice is that *the individual school is a powerful unit for change.* Wide variation in school characteristics, even within a single school district, support the need for school-based improvement efforts. No single set of recommendations for renewal will connect in the same way to all schools. Rather, the unique conditions of an individual school demand that members of the school community come together to examine the specific learning needs of students, formulate plans to meet those needs, and monitor student progress as changes occur.

This is not to suggest that school districts are insignificant in the change process. Quite the contrary. In designating the single school as the unit for change, we recognize that schools are not independent of the complicated political pressures or crucial resource network which characterize school districts. As Goodlad has consistently advised, "Unless the district provides a protective umbrella, the possibilities for major innovation and change are limited. . . . Leave out the district and it will find a way to curtail change in the individual school."[2] With this in mind, we maintain high involvement of superintendents and school committee members in study teams, staff development seminars, and ongoing school-based activities. As we work together to solve problems in individual settings, the larger context of the district is often a guiding force and valuable resource.

Involving superintendents, principals, teachers, professors, and interested members of the community in school-based efforts to increase student learning can be challenging and rewarding. For example, preliminary meetings with the superintendent and a principal in one Coalition district included lively discussions about what priorities for increasing student learning should be. At the principal's urging, and with the superintendent's support, it was decided that priority setting should involve teachers' perceptions as well because they are closest to the learners and are likely to know most about students' academic and personal needs. The superintendent arranged release time for teachers to participate in a planning session in which the principal posed the question, "What do our students need to learn most?" The principal was met with a resounding "DISCIPLINE" from teachers. As a result, improving discipline became the starting point for school improvement efforts. Attempts to collect evidence about the discipline problem led the staff to discuss student motivation and work habits. A study team was set up at the university, and teachers and administrators from other interested Coalition schools joined with professors and graduate students to look carefully at the problem from a local and national perspective. Even further attempts to understand the problem resulted in teachers observing one another's classes to identify instructional practices that were effective with "difficult" students. University staff taught classes in the school to regain insights into elementary classroom teaching while releasing teachers to observe their colleagues in action. This in-depth examination of ways instruction motivates students to engage

---

2. J. I. Goodlad (personal communication), October 14, 1986.

productively in learning tasks encouraged some teachers to modify their behavior toward disruptive students. In turn, professors and graduate students who observed faculty meetings, led study teams, and served as substitute teachers were exposed to life in schools that cannot be realized in a university classroom.

A third premise guiding the Coalition is that *effective collaboration requires regular work in schools by professors, participation in the university by teachers and administrators, and engagement with each other to inquire into common problems*. Unfortunately, too often people in the university are not used to studying learning in the complex school environment or actually entering the school to help students learn. While professors may research the dynamics and impact of schooling, it is but from a distance. In-depth classroom observations and direct interventions for helping learners are indeed rare.

By contrast, experienced teachers usually take courses at the university, choosing from a catalog published each semester. While this may be helpful to teachers, the practice of simply picking from what is offered is quite different from systematically working together to increase student learning. It lacks joint decision-making in determining courses that may help solve persistent problems in curriculum and instruction or may challenge teachers to alter habits in their thinking or behavior that hinder student learning.

In the Coalition, participants come together to identify problems that are relevant to improving student learning, and they assume different roles in how problems are explored and solved. Professors, for example, may share research findings about increasing student motivation, teachers may demonstrate techniques for individualizing instruction, or principals may inquire into the impact of morale on teacher effectiveness. The point is that when the team assembles for dialogue about helping more students learn, they bring different experiences, resources, and insights to a common problem identified in the spirit of parity. If there is hierarchy in the Coalition, it is a changing one: teachers learn from professors and vice versa; principals learn from teachers and vice versa. The possible combinations are many and varied.

An additional premise is that *teacher involvement is crucial throughout all phases of the change process*. Traditionally, the process of educational innovation is characterized by a linear progression of discrete parts: research, development, dissemination, implementation. It seems that teachers are considered passive consumers in this process, simply receivers of decisions made by others. They are often isolated from research and development activities and given answers to questions they never ask and solutions to problems they never experience (Tikunoff & Ward, 1983).

Teacher involvement in conducting educational research is a logical extension of this premise, and collaborative research linking schools and the university is important to the Coalition. John Dewey (1929) offers early guidance for the development of collaborative research paradigms. He states, "It is impossible to see how there can be an adequate flow of subject matter to set and control the problems investigators deal with, unless there is active participation on the part of those directly engaged in teaching" (p. 48). Current writers, including Lieberman (1986), and Oakes, Hare, and Sirotnik (1986) offer the consistent message that collaborative research has a greater likelihood of affecting practice and encouraging further inquiry because it involves from the beginning the people who will implement improvements in the learning environment. It also tends to reflect realistically the complexity of the classroom and shorten the time between the study and use of its findings (Tikunoff & Ward, 1983). An almost serendipitous advantage of collaborative research is the shared sense of professionalism among teachers, school administrators, and professors actively engaged in critical inquiry. The process fosters collegiality among participants working in common, and it generates knowledge intended to improve learning for all students.

Finally, participants in the Coalition recognize that *lasting institutional change requires sustained effort over several years.* Initially, participants asked for a three-year commitment. This was subsequently revised to five years. Ideally, however, collaboration among schools and universities should be ongoing and not constrained by even long-term time designations.

These premises, then, guide planning and action as we work toward increasing student learning by making schools more effective, improving the education of educators, and promoting useful research. Several ongoing program components help the Coalition achieve its goals.

## How the Coalition is Organized

Each school in the Coalition has put together an *Improvement Team* consisting of the principal and at least four to six teachers. Often, the total school staff makes up the team. The team members work together to identify compelling priorities for action within their educational setting. These priorities center on improvements in curriculum, instruction, and other school conditions that are likely to influence student learning.

Each school in the Coalition determines its own project for school improvement, determined by that school's team under the leadership of the principal.

Teachers and administrators from member schools and persons from the School of Education also form a *Study Team* when there is a need to develop guidelines or generate information central to the improvements in several schools or in the university. A study team, for example, might work on guidelines for involving teachers in curriculum decision making. Another team might analyze the impact of ability grouping upon student learning. Yet another team might suggest changes needed in the clinical aspect of the teacher preparation program. Two or three study teams operate at the same time, lasting as long as necessary to determine a clear direction for using the results of their inquiry to improve practice. While increasing the knowledge of individual members, the study teams provide practical, relevant information to assist Coalition partners in accomplishing their priorities for educational improvement.

The School of Education, through the Center for Curriculum Studies, joins with member district and school staffs to implement *Staff Development Seminars* for all members of the Coalition and for interested teachers and administrators from school districts throughout Massachusetts and beyond. These seminars are on topics identified by Coalition members as important in designing and implementing innovations that meet the academic and personal needs of students. The seminars are also designed to stimulate thought about crucial issues in American education such as creating equal educational opportunities for all students. This emphasis on a national viewpoint is complemented by attention to pertinent research findings of interest to practicing educators. The seminar participants also consider problems that suggest a direction for further research.

The *Schools' Council* consists of superintendents from member school districts and principals and teachers from participating schools. The director of the Center for Curriculum Studies, the dean of the School of Education, and the chancellor or a designee represent the University of Massachusetts. Formed during the first year, the Schools' Council meets periodically to create policies that will assist the Coalition in accomplishing its goals and to encourage schools and the university to reach their priorities for improvement. The Schools' Council is responsible for facilitating collaboration among members of the Coalition.

Advanced graduate students and professors in the Center for Curriculum Studies serve as the *Coalition Staff*. They provide technical and human resources to initiate and sustain lasting educational improvements in the schools and the university. Reflecting Sarason's (1982) suggestion that it is important for each partner to understand the other, the Coalition staff is a valuable liaison between school and university cultures. Virtually all members of the Coalition staff have taught at the elementary or secondary level. Their collective teaching experience covers diverse schools — public and private, large and small, urban and rural — in various locations in the United States and several foreign countries, including Kenya, Zambia, and India.

Staffing the Coalition with teachers is helpful in several ways. First, it contributes to credibility with teachers in the schools. Second, it provides some common ground for discussions about the complexities of teaching. Third, the teachers in the Coalition staff draw on their own classroom experiences in relating theory and practice and in proposing directions for improving the preparation of teachers.

Through frequent contact with schools, the Coalition staff strives to maintain awareness of common concerns shared by schools and attempts to tailor its actions to connect resources within and outside the Coalition to the needs of each individual setting. Examples of technical support provided by the Coalition staff include collecting evaluation data, assisting in instruction, observing classes, locating curriculum materials, reviewing school plans, and drafting documents for school approval. The staff also coordinates the ongoing activities of the Coalition, including identifying crucial topics for study teams, planning seminars, and recruiting faculty from the School of Education when there is a match between faculty abilities and school needs.

The *Evaluation Team* is responsible for devising evaluation procedures and overseeing activities to determine the effectiveness of the Coalition. Team members include Coalition staff, superintendents, principals, and teachers. The evaluation data are used to revise action plans, support greater institutional acceptance of successful innovations, and increase understanding of why some changes were not effective.

Teachers, administrators, professors, and graduate students also form *Inquiry Teams* around issues of mutual interest that demand systematic investigation. Working as equal contributors, participants identify research questions, collect data, and examine and interpret results. Equal involvement in research is important, but it does not mean that everyone does the same thing at the same time and in the same way. As Oakes et al. (1986) suggest, there are often "circumstantial inequalities" inherent in collaborative inquiry projects, including salary, status, and release time from other job responsibilities. For example, Inquiry Teams depend heavily on Coalition staff for coordination of activities and for maintaining effective communication among researchers. In this role, Coalition staff makes an effort to keep projects moving, without taking the directing role away from the group.

The Coalition for School Improvement, then, makes possible continuing dialogue among its members, critical review of decisions, and some division of labor in trying out constructive ways of restructuring educational environments so that more students gain access to quality learning. The work of the Coalition is largely done through coordinated efforts of helping each school plan and implement desired improvements. The key is that when the local school staff decides what needs to be done to improve the learning environment, support comes from different places, including resources from within the school, the community, other schools, and the university.

Participants in the Coalition are learning many things about the process of collaborating for educational renewal. Here are some of the major lessons that we hope will strengthen our partnership and prove useful to others planning or implementing partnerships.

## Lessons from Collaboration

Focusing school improvement efforts on needs and characteristics of learners presented a major challenge from the start. As described earlier, there was a tendency for principals to set priorities for improving services rather than increasing student learning (Mkangaza, 1986). The advantage of monitoring student progress to determine if services are effective is reinforced many times in the Coalition. It seems that careful attention to student progress is useful in identifying problems and evaluating solutions to problems. We also find that gathering information about student progress can help clarify or validate the perceptions of administrators, teachers, and parents about shortcomings and strengths of students.

For example, in one Coalition elementary school, observations of students in class as well as reported incidents of disruptive or unsocial behavior on the playground led teachers to decide that students working cooperatively with peers and adults was a priority for improvement. Numerous activities took place in the school to address this priority, but one activity is particularly relevant in illustrating the importance of monitoring student progress. At the faculty's suggestion, a Coalition staff member observed class and nonclass time periods to help identify when disruptive behavior or rudeness occurred. The observations suggested a supportive, friendly learning environment, with only a few disruptions during transitions from one class to another or between the classroom and the playground. The observations were discussed with the principal and several staff members who then targeted these transitional times for focused effort. In a later assessment, teachers reported that students who were disruptive in the past were showing marked improvement in their behavior. At the request of the school's Improvement Team, a Coalition staff member administered a classroom climate survey of student attitudes towards teachers and other students. Survey responses indicated, for the most part, positive relations between students and teachers as well as constructive interactions among classmates. In this example, information about student progress helped to accomplish three things. First, it framed the problem in terms of a few students rather than the entire school population. Second, it focused the solution on specific problematic time periods rather than the entire school day. Third, it provided evidence that, in general, the school has a positive climate in which problems can be identified and overcome.

Another lesson about collaborating to meet pressing challenges for reform extends from the first lesson. We are learning that the process of bringing together administrators, teachers, and occasionally parents and students to identify problems and pursue solutions can be an invigorating, empowering process. It is a common thread running through all Coalition schools. The process of inquiry leads to teachers discussing important educational issues, professors listening to teachers' ideas, principals asking teachers and parents for their perceptions, and a general feeling that if at first we don't know, together we can eventually find out. We are discovering that when principals and teachers commit themselves to solving a problem they consider crucial, they can be persistent, and they can indeed succeed. We have much to do before this partnership matures and major changes occur, but we are optimistic. Leadership through the power of ideas is becoming a norm in the Coalition.

This persistence and leadership is particularly evident in a Coalition elementary school where half of the students are bused from the inner city. Addressing the school's priority for improvement involved strengthening the relationship between home and school as one means to help students work cooperatively to solve academic and personal problems they were experiencing in school. Involving parents from both the inner city and the local neighborhood in parent workshops and other events proved to be a significant challenge because only a few people showed up for the initial meetings. Yet, under the leadership of the principal, the school staff extended personal invitations to parents, offered transportation, provided child care, and most important, conveyed their concern for helping all children become more productive in school. Each meeting saw an increased number of parents, culminating in a family supper at the school that exceeded all attendance expectations.

Another lesson from the Coalition's efforts has numerous interrelated dimensions, all of which are less than satisfactory. This lesson relates to our premise that educational change depends on parity among participants and reciprocity between schools and universities. We are discovering that the university is comfortably couched in the security of its traditional roles and responsibilities, and collaboration seems to mean that the other partner will be doing the changing. For example, the foundation for educational improvement that has been built by the Coalition rests solidly in the public schools with administrators and teachers who are willing to examine existing conditions critically in order to make necessary improvements. We are learning that for the most part, however, colleges of education are slow to engage in critical inquiry into the appropriateness of their own practices. They are even less enamored with the possibility of involving public school people in deciding priorities for improvement of the university.

Even the best profile of the university partner is a bit blurred when it comes to considering the effectiveness of present conditions. A large research-oriented university is simply not geared toward the same introspection that is starting to characterize Coalition schools. Nor is the university setting conducive to involvement with colleagues in elementary and secondary schools. One pressing reason for this latter condition is the lack of institutional rewards for professors working with public schools. Involvement in public schools is not a deciding factor leading to a positive decision for tenure or promotion, nor is it recognized as a viable alternative to teaching or other academic responsibilities. As a result, professors who might otherwise be interested in maintaining ties with schools are reluctant to make a commitment because they think it will take them away from teaching and publishing. As one professor whom we tried to recruit for the Coalition told us, "I'm looking for a new job and my chances are not as good if I work with the schools. I have to do research and write articles."

Traditional boundaries between schools and universities are persistent, but they must be overcome if collaboration is to succeed (Maeroff, 1983). This suggests that university faculty engage in action to increase learning as well as study learning. It means finding better ways to educate teachers as well as better ways to study them. It involves finding the means to connect schools and communities as well as studying the gaps between them.

Our work in the Coalition indicates that involvement with public schools need not preclude professional success in a college or university. Over 50 years ago, John Dewey (1929) stressed that researchers need the context of the school for strengthening insights about the learning of young people. He states:

> [Educational practice] comes first and last; it is the beginning and the close: the beginning, because it sets the problems which alone give to investigators educational point and quality; the close, because practice alone can test, verify, modify and develop the conclusions of these investigations. (p. 34)

With careful attention to practice, research is no longer the exclusive province of the university. Yet, it seems that university educators often see research as their exclusive responsibility. They view public schools as laboratories for experiments and see teachers as consumers of findings. This persistent notion that university people conduct research for public school people to use is a powerful force creating and maintaining barriers between institutions. In the Coalition, we are attempting to broaden research to include teachers and administrators who are working in public schools.[3] We are discovering that researchers at the elementary, secondary, and college level can work in concert to identify questions that, when answered through careful study, may contribute to helping more students reach higher levels of learning. According to Eisner (1984), "Educational research ought to take its lead from the practices that pervade school programs. That is, those engaged in educational research should have an intimate acquaintance with life in classrooms" (p. 450). We think that only when university and school-based researchers collaborate to forge meaningful inquiry that is informed by what goes on in schools will it be possible for research to become a more constructive means for renewal.

The preparation of teachers is also viewed as a traditional province of education professors. Unfortunately, teacher education is often out of joint with the reality existing in public schools, and this disconnection results in a problem that for too long has had no name. Simply put, the

---

3. Often participants who collaborate to inquire into problems are labeled as "university researchers and school practitioners." We have avoided this terminology because we think it emphasizes traditional producer/consumer roles that are inconsistent with the concept of equal contributions from partners.

problem is that student learning will not increase if the quality of teaching does not improve, and teaching will not get better unless there are dramatic improvements in teacher education. It is not surprising, then, that criticism once limited to elementary and secondary schools is ricocheting to institutions of higher education that prepare teachers. Separate reports by the Holmes Group (1986) and the Carnegie Forum on Education and the Economy (1986) recommend fundamental changes in how colleges and universities educate teachers. Both reports propose changes in how teachers enter the profession, gain access to opportunities for professional growth, and advance in job responsibilities. The reports leave little doubt that reform in the teaching profession is necessary and that collaboration between public schools and the university may be a viable means to this crucial end. However, the willingness of education professors to share the responsibility of preparing teachers with the public schools remains to be seen.

Improving the education of teachers is a long-range goal of the Coalition for School Improvement, one that we are only now starting to consider. We are already discovering that extending our collaboration to include improving the practicum experience of "student teaching" is of foremost importance. We are finding that when principals, teachers, and professors work together in an ongoing relationship, all participants on the team are in a better position to advise student teachers about placement decisions and monitor students' progress toward becoming effective teachers. Too often these decisions are made in a haphazard manner with convenience winning out over rigor. Although student teaching is a crucial part of teacher preparation, the university may place interns with practicing teachers almost by chance — because teachers simply volunteer or feel obligated to take a turn. It seems that precious little effort is made systematically to match future teachers with truly outstanding practicing teachers so that the practicum experience is likely to be positive and meaningful. Student-teacher placement is one major part of teacher education that could be improved through collaboration.

The tough lesson, then, is that too often the sense of parity in collaboration among educators in the public schools and the university goes begging when it comes to improving the university, conducting research, and preparing teachers. It seems that the university rhetoric of parity and collaboration becomes hollow when traditional responsibilities are examined and professors are called on to change the ways they relate with the public schools.

The premise advanced earlier that teacher involvement is crucial throughout the reform process leads to another lesson about making a partnership work. It is no accident that many of the examples in this chapter focus on improving student behavior in school. Whether described as "discipline" or "problem solving" or "cooperation," concerns about student behavior frequently surface. Improving student behavior is a priority in half of the core Coalition schools.

We are learning that teachers' views about school problems are important considerations for starting the improvement process. Asking teachers what concerns them about their students' learning involves them from the beginning in the process of school reform. Teachers' perceptions are a legitimate entry for priority setting, especially when there is wide agreement among teachers about student needs. We are also finding that as evidence is gathered to document problems, the need for fundamental changes in conditions for learning often emerge. Usually, it does not take long for discussions about proper student behavior to turn to desired changes in school organization, curriculum, and instruction. In other words, it becomes clear that reasons for deficiencies in student behavior go beyond what is inside the learner to include school conditions that might be contributing to the very behavior teachers desire to change.

This lesson was especially apparent in a study team on "understanding student behavior." Thirteen teachers and three administrators from nine school districts participated in the study team, along with three representatives from the university. The group worked under the leadership of a professor in the School of Education who reported:

> At the first session, it became clear that our dialogue had to relate to both theory and practice and that isolating the issue of student behavior from the larger social and political contexts of school and community would be impossible. Participants decided to focus on three areas for the remaining meetings: parent involvement, early identification of potential problems, and relating Study Team findings to actual work in the participants' schools. Thus, while teachers were anxious to share short term concrete suggestions related to student behavior, they also saw the need to address the question of the structures of schools and classrooms as a source of student misbehavior. (Nieto, 1986, p. 3)

Study Team participants pushed toward factors that may be causes of problematic student behavior rather than only sharing strategies for dealing with the symptoms. They reported gaining a broader insight into early identification of potential problems, positive parent-teacher and home-school relationships, and effective curriculum and instruction that engage all students productively.

These lessons suggest that the Coalition is making progress. The efforts of participants are supported, in part, by opportunities to get together with colleagues from other schools and the university to discuss important educational issues, by the process of inquiry within individual settings, and by knowledge and insights gained from research and practice. The Massachusetts Coalition for School Improvement can take only modest credit for putting things in motion. The compelling force for making schools better places for students to learn is the teachers, working systematically for school improvement with the support and leadership of principals and superintendents. From this reality in the practice of school reform may come the direction for making partnerships between schools and universities a powerful means for improving American education. From these partnerships may come the leadership for educators to meet the challenges of these times — challenges which can lead to an increase in the quality of learning for all students.

## References

Carnegie Forum on Education and the Economy. (1986). *A nation prepared: Teachers for the 21st century.* New York: Carnegie Forum.

Dewey, J. (1929). *The sources of a science of education.* New York: Liveright.

Eisner, E. W. (1984). Can educational research inform educational practice? *Phi Delta Kappan, 65,* 447–452.

Goodlad, J. I. (1984). *A place called school.* New York: McGraw-Hill.

Goodlad, J. I. (1986). *School renewal and the education of educators: The partnership concept.* Amherst, MA: Center for Curriculum Studies, University of Massachusetts.

Goodlad, J. I., Klein, M. F., & Associates. (1970). *Behind the classroom door.* Worthington, Ohio: Charles A. Jones Publishing Company.

Holmes Group. (1986). *Tomorrow's teachers: A report of the Holmes Group.* East Lansing, MI: Holmes Group, Inc.

Lieberman, A. (1986). Collaborative research: Working with, not working on. *Educational Leadership, 43,* 28–32.

Maeroff, G. I. (1983). *School and college partnerships in education.* Princeton, NJ: Carnegie Foundation for the Advancement of Teaching.

Massachusetts Legislature, Joint Committee on Education. (1985). Public School Improvement Law, Chapter 188.

Mkangaza, C. (1986). *Determining priorities for school improvement: A school-based inquiry into deciding directions for increasing school effectiveness.* Unpublished doctoral dissertation. Center for Curriculum Studies, University of Massachusetts.

Nieto, S. (1986). *Final report: Study team on student behavior.* Unpublished report of the Coalition for School Improvement. Amherst, MA: University of Massachusetts.

Oakes, J., Hare, S., & Sirotnik, K. (1986). Collaborative inquiry: A congenial paradigm in a cantankerous world. *Teachers College Record, 87,* 545–561.

Sarason, S. B. (1982). *The culture of the school and the problem of change,* 2nd. ed. Boston: Allyn and Bacon.

Seeley, D. S. (1984). Educational partnership and the dilemmas of school reform. *Phi Delta Kappan, 65,* 383–388.

Tikunoff, W. J., & Ward, B. A. (1983). Collaborative research on teaching. *The Elementary School Journal, 83,* 453–468.

Tyler, R. W. (1976). *Perspectives on American education.* Chicago: Science Research Associates.

Tyler, R. W. (1986). *The role of the principal in promoting learning.* Amherst, MA: Center for Curriculum Studies, University of Massachusetts.

# CHAPTER FIVE

# The Southern California Partnership: A Retrospective Analysis

PAUL E. HECKMAN

Having just introduced John Goodlad to 320 educators from the South-ern Maine Partnership, I had the distinct feeling of having "been there" before. This time, Goodlad had come to visit one of more than a dozen school-university consortia that have become members of the National Network for Educational Renewal (NNER), and to explain the purposes of the NNER, its values, and its hopes for real collaboration between schools and universities.

Six years earlier, the faces were similar, but the place was on the opposite side of the continent. Instead of in a Portland, Maine, hotel, over 100 superintendents, board members, teachers, and principals had gathered in a southern California conference center to hear Goodlad explore the purposes and possibilities of The Partnership, a new collabo-ration at that time between the University of California at Los Angeles (UCLA) and local school districts that would eventually come to serve as a prototype for the concepts and practices discussed here in Chapter 1 of this volume.

Many of my "I've been here before" experiences have been accom-panied by considerable apprehension. This time, however, the feeling was one of excitement and anticipation. For although my work as the Executive Coordinator for the first five years of The Partnership — since renamed the Southern California Partnership (SCP) — was not without trials, it was not without successful experiences as well. On the threshold of beginning a new partnership in southern Maine, therefore, I was eager to build upon the SCP experience, to avoid or at least anticipate some of the pitfalls, and to realize much of the promise that I knew was possible in this type of collaboration.

In what follows, I will focus on a number of conflicts and dilemmas that arose with respect to the underlying principles guiding the SCP and the ensuing activities. Although my analysis of the lessons learned will draw heavily upon the SCP for examples, my more recent experiences in Maine have also enhanced my understanding regarding many of the issues to be addressed.

A number of very specific conflicts and dilemmas could probably be enumerated, but several classes of these concerns will suffice.[1] In particular, problems arose over conflicting views of school change, the connection of research to practice, and the meeting of self-interests between and within the institutions making up the partnership. Since these issues cut across many of the SCP activities, it will be convenient to discuss them as they arose in these several key features of collaborative effort:

- getting the partnership organized and "off the ground"
- beginning and sustaining activities at the building level
- involving university faculty in school-based inquiries

First, however, it is important to provide a descriptive overview of the principles and practices of the Southern California Partnership as they emerged over a five-year period during 1980–1985.

## Overview

The SCP was, in essence, conceived by John Goodlad over six years ago as the next logical step following what was learned from two previous studies, the Study of Educational Change and School Improvement (and the League of Cooperating Schools) and the Study of Schooling. (See Goodlad, 1975 and 1984.) Goodlad, who served as the dean of the Graduate School of Education at UCLA, convened a group of southern California school district superintendents, community college presidents, and county school office superintendents to discuss the creation of a collaborative venture designed to improve education in the public schools and in institutions of higher education, particularly at the points of interface between colleges of education and the schools.

In proposing this idea for *equal* partnership between educational institutions, Goodlad emphasized that there was indeed some business at hand, a set of persistent problems of the time, that was simply not being attended to in any significant way. These problems included such concerns as a declining faith in our major social institutions, a withering sense of community, an increasing diversity of school clientele, confu-

---

1. Many successes can also be reported (see Occasional Paper No. 1 by the Laboratory in School and Community Education Staff, 1985). In the interest of best serving the reader, given the intent of this book, a more problem-focused approach will be taken here.

sion regarding the scope and limits of decentralizing power, and a crisis of instructional leadership (particularly at the school building level). The argument put forth was that these problems, although appearing intractable, were actually quite amenable to working solutions. What was needed, however, was an approach to school improvement and change other than the usual research, development, and diffusion paradigm.

More specifically, instead of viewing change as a process of intervention and installation, Goodlad viewed the school as the unit of change and school staffs as the source of renewal and improvement. Instead of imposing an alien paradigm of generating and using knowledge onto the schools, he advocated the idea of involving people in their own knowledge-generating process, in the cultural context of their work. (See Heckman, 1987, and Sarason, 1982.) School renewal, then, was proposed as a process for altering dominant world views by encouraging discussions among staff about existing school conditions, identifying critical problems, trying out alternative practices that might be suggested through literature reviews and interactions with district and university resource staff having common interests, and continually re-evaluating and modifying (if necessary) these practices. (Examples of these activities are noted below.)

Bridging the proverbial gap between research and practice, therefore, was a prevalent theme for this school-university partnership effort. Obviously, in order for the school culture to rise above some of its more unproductive schooling regularities (Sarason, 1982), extant knowledge must be brought to bear upon extant practice. The SCP, consequently, would create activities designed to challenge many educational beliefs underlying traditional school practices with the ideas and possible practices inherent in more current lines of educational research.

Even more important, was the idea that theory and practice would share a common source — the real world of schooling. Although Dewey (1929) argued convincingly nearly 60 years ago that the sources of a science of education are the problems and practices of the schools, this notion has not often guided the reward structures or research styles in many universities, and the schools, colleges, or departments of education within them. The SCP, therefore, would eschew the separation of thinking and doing, and encourage the idea of reflective practice (Schon, 1983). Certainly, teachers and administrators do not have a great deal of time to read, design research studies, collect and analyze data, write reports, and so forth. The challenge for the partnership, therefore, would be to find ways to capitalize on the time available to university researchers and faculty, to gain more release time for district- and school-based educators, and to bring together these groups to inquire over the long term into the circumstances, beliefs, and practices of schooling.

Embedded unavoidably in these operating principles were the seeds of conflict, sowed particularly in the furrows of individual and group self-interests between and within the educational institutions forming the partnership. Teachers are accustomed to closing the classroom door and carrying on business as usual; administrators are accustomed to making sure that all can be adequately accounted for; and university faculty are accustomed to publishing and not perishing. Many educators in schools and universities have spent too little time identifying what they can do in common while still achieving what they need to accomplish in their respective places of work. Meanwhile, the common ground is considerable; for example, universities prepare many of the educators that work in public schools, and these educators, in turn, prepare many students for postsecondary schooling.

To break through the cultural regularities that tend to perpetuate the anticollaborative tendencies in both educational institutions, a number of activities were proposed, but many simply emerged over the course of the SCP effort. One major set of activities used meetings of job-alike groups to bring new ideas and practices to the attention of the participants, to provide the simple but rare opportunity for participants to share their thinking and experiences with one another, and to develop peer support groups with members willing to experiment with alternative educational practices. The primary job-alike groups were the SCP Council (chief executive officers of the participating institutions), the Leadership Development Group (primarily building-level administrators), and various workshops focused mostly on teachers and issues concerning curriculum, instruction, and school improvement strategies.

A second major set of activities was aimed directly at involving teachers, principals, district staff, and university researchers and faculty in collaborative inquiry and research. For example, a curriculum task force convened over a period of a year to engage in an intensive study of curriculum theory and practice, interact with curriculum scholars, and prepare a monograph-length report that served to guide other SCP projects and to articulate the SCP curricular perspective. Several collaborative research projects emerged which involved university- and school-based educators in the long-term study of cooperative learning strategies, computer courseware authoring for teachers, comprehensive information systems for school and classroom planning, alternative approaches to the teaching of reading, and alternative math and science curricula over the K–12 spectrum.

Focused mainly on outreach to the educational community at large, a third set of activities included a number of major, statewide public forums involving nationally respected educators speaking on issues of particular concern to the state (e.g., future of the reform movement; conditions and circumstances of teaching; science and technology; and uses and abuses of testing).

Rather than continuing to elaborate upon these three sets of activities, however, I wish now to turn to the analyses promised regarding conflicts and dilemmas, using, when appropriate, some of the above activities for illustrative purposes.

## Analysis

As noted above, many of the problems faced by the SCP revolved around the tensions inherent in alternative change paradigms, bridging research and practice, and meeting the self-interests of individuals and organizations. These concerns will be discussed as they emerged in several major phases of partnership activity.

### Getting The Partnership Off the Ground

Early on, the chief executive officers of the participating institutions formed the council for governing the activities of the SCP and elected a subgroup, the Executive Committee, to bring action items to the attention of the full council. The ten district superintendents, four community college presidents, four county superintendents, and the dean of the Graduate School of Education at UCLA served as equal voting members of the council. The dean, two school superintendents, one county superintendent, and one community college president served as members of the Executive Committee.

During the first year, a chronic set of questions occupied the discussions of the SCP Council and Executive Committee: What is this "partnership?" What activities will be in place? What products will it produce? To help deal with these questions, the Executive Committee created agenda items for the entire council to wrestle with during their monthly meetings. First, a great deal of time centered around how to organize the partnership. In many ways, the executive officers had real expertise in organizing and managing, and these were logical foci for their talents. They did not, however, have as much experience with working through the specific features of substantive agenda concerning curriculum, instruction, change strategies, and so forth. As they struggled with substantive issues, it became particularly troublesome and frustrating for a number of members that they could not immediately resolve major issues and develop programs to address them.

Second, council members decided to have speakers join their meetings to provide input on a variety of issues of interest. A demographer, for example, presented data regarding major shifts in the racial/ethnic composition of the population of southern California. But while these meetings generated much discussion and excitement about issues and possibilities, nothing much appeared to happen afterward. Council members returning to their districts did not seriously confront these issues, and it was nearly impossible to carry a discussion begun at one meeting over to the next.

These events annoyed many of the members as well as those of us serving as resources to the SCP Council. It became evident that many of the members expected something to happen after a single meeting — something tangible, concrete, and specific that they could "sell" to those to whom they were accountable (school boards, for example). In effect, the administrators wanted quick results and they wanted them yesterday. This was, of course, understandable considering their position.

Those of us attempting to coordinate SCP activities, on the other hand, although heeding one important lesson learned from a previous partnership effort (the League of Cooperating Schools), had lost sight of another one. We had learned that collaboration with schools could not be sustained unless significant groundwork was accomplished at the district level. We had forgotten, but soon remembered, that the action, ultimately, is in schools, and that "payoffs" are unlikely to be recognized until significant numbers of educators become involved in work-related activities.

Consequently, a parallel activity arose. We asked superintendents to identify principals and schools that might willingly and readily engage in renewal activities at the building level. Some superintendents responded immediately to this idea and identified several such places; others were unable either to select likely candidates or even to relate to the concept of renewal itself. Rather than force the issue, we chose to work with those districts and schools that were open to the possibilities of involving staff directly in change-related activities. Moreover, significant school-based effort required significant resources and support. We had some of both, but not enough for every school in every district of the

SCP.[2] It was fortuitous, therefore, that we worked initially with only a few receptive districts and schools. As it turned out, this strategy created something of a counterculture to the more common, one-shot, in-service change strategies, and it began to suggest some answers to the questions, "What is this partnership about and what will it produce?"

Two superintendents, whose districts happened to share a common boundary, responded quite favorably to our proposal. Their geographical proximity facilitated initial progress in identifying a common agenda. We arranged a weekend retreat so that selected superintendents, principals, and teachers could actually meet together for hours at a time to hammer out a common set of interests and some ways to collaborate across districts. Our strategy here was to identify key school people who demonstrated an eagerness to get involved in new ideas. Thus, we had a group of highly enthusiastic and interested educators working together in a climate of positive expectation.

At the conclusion of the weekend, enthusiasm ran high for continuing the discussions, particularly around issues pertaining to ways and means for grouping students for instruction and organizing the curriculum. The group made arrangements for involving more educators in the districts, including school-board members, in the ensuing discussions and meetings with university-based researchers. A number of the aforementioned collaborative research projects eventually became centered in these schools and districts.

Not all such efforts to get things going were successful. Another superintendent took us up on our offer and suggested that we work with several elementary schools in his district. However, he had a specific agenda in mind — namely, implementing the characteristics of "effective schools" that had been recently identified in the new school-effectiveness literature. He had already developed and conducted several workshops and offered other incentives to encourage key administrators (principals and central office staff) to transform their schools in accordance with the principles gleaned from this literature. Among the incentives, for example, was a differential reward system that would provide discretionary money to schools in his district in proportion to their rankings on standardized tests.

Our approach with this superintendent and his staff was frank; we

2. Primary support for coordinating the SCP came from a grant by the Charles Stewart Mott Foundation to the Graduate School of Education, UCLA. These funds were used to support whatever activities we thought could ultimately stimulate and support change at the school level. Additional funds were contributed in the form of SCP member assessments which helped support general coordinating efforts, task group meetings, and partnershipwide events like public forums.

discussed openly our concerns regarding coercive intervention strategies of this nature and the commitments made ostensibly by SCP members to alternative orientations of school improvement and change. Nonetheless, the superintendent encouraged us to work, as we saw fit, with one school staff in particular. Instead of immediately in-servicing the staff on principal leadership, academic emphasis, time on task, and the like, we held several exploratory discussions with the principal, a few teachers, and then the entire staff. These discussions were intended only secondarily to deal with school effectiveness formulas; primarily, they focused on problems of immediate importance to the staff, concerns that quite clearly revolved around cultural clashes between an 80% Anglo staff serving an 80% Mexican and Chicano community. It soon became clear that our approach and the superintendent's agenda simply did not mix, and we parted company on a friendly but understanding note. The superintendent eventually left the SCP during its second year; for him, the partnership simply did not match his expectations or his philosophy on changing schools.

## Getting Something Going at the Building Level

The above example illustrates a failure at getting something of a substantive nature started with teachers and principals in schools. In fact, the first two years registered few successes in beginning work at the building level. The work with large groups of teachers, principals, and superintendents created excitement for change, but little actual change occurred. Even when a principal and school were identified as a high potential site, not much happened in the building. Although we do not have adequate data to explain this outcome, my working hypothesis, in reflecting back on these first two years, is that we failed to mobilize sufficient commitment and support structures among district and school administrators to push for the kind of quality release time necessary to launch school-based improvement efforts. Several involvement strategies, which emerged rather serendipitously, tend to support this hypothesis.[3]

For example, one of the superintendents had become acquainted with the Harvard Principals' Academy, and he suggested that a similar activity be considered by the Executive Committee. The committee enlisted an interested county office superintendent to sponsor the idea and propose it to the entire SCP Council. The council endorsed the plan

---

3. I have since used these strategies successfully in my more recent efforts in the Southern Maine Partnership.

and most of the members encouraged and supported several principals from each of their districts to participate in what became known as the Leadership Development Group. Principals (and a few central office staff) began to meet approximately every month for at least a half day and continued in this activity over the entire period of this analysis. (In fact, it was this group that was primarily responsible for holding together and renewing SCP connections after those of us who "championed" the collaboration moved on to other professional involvements around the country.)

The primary focus of the Leadership Development Group was on building-based change. Participants were encouraged to share with one another their frustrations, worries, successes, and problems as they considered and, in some cases, tried out alternative practices in their schools. Many of the initial meetings, therefore, became focused as much on developing trust and communication as on school renewal activities.

But as with the council members, not all of the principals were ready to move in their schools, that is, to promote inquiry and innovative activities among willing groups of teachers. Once again, we capitalized on interests of the "front runners" in the group and formed subgroups that met at breakfast and dinner meetings in between the regular monthly meetings. The "breakfast group," for example, consisted of six elementary school principals, all of whom had similar interests and problems and were close to one another geographically. During each of these gatherings, the participants would discuss how they were doing and highlight a particular problem that they were facing. They might share similar problems and the ways that they tackled them; many times problems were acknowledged but unresolved. These issues provided the agenda for the next meeting, and, over several months, many of these issues came to be the concerns of the Leadership Development Group as a whole. Discussions focused on such issues as securing enough release time and resources from districts; short-term expectations as opposed to the reality of long-term change; pressures from what were seen as superficial accountability demands from districts and the state; managing individual differences in classrooms; discontinuity in K–12 curriculum; behavioral versus cognitive conceptions of student learning.

Goodlad (1975) has referred to the important role of the "alternative drummer" for promoting school renewal. This role often characterized my contributions to these meetings and group discussions. In effect, the alternative drummer has the luxury of being sufficiently disconnected from the daily detail and exigencies of the school building so as to raise more general questions, suggest alternative paradigms and sources of knowledge, and provide support for further inquiry into these alternatives.

The role is also one of constructive critique. Many times, for example, teachers and principals would come back from a recent workshop or in-service activity where the latest educational panacea had been promoted. Sometimes they were excited by what they had heard; always they were frustrated with being unable to install the ideas into their school and classrooms. Without negating the impact of the good ideas, I would often ask: "What particular problem was being addressed in the workshop?" "Were there fundamental educational issues at the root of this particular problem?" "Have teachers really identified with these issues in the context of their own school?" "Do all teachers have to change practices overnight, or can several interested staff begin seriously experimenting with some alternative ideas?" "How are you going to get the resources and time to do some of this?" These questions were usually followed by the imperative: "Let's get on with it!"

A number of principals and groups of teachers did just that. We had begun to establish a norm within the SCP for the importance of alternative educational ideas and the value of quality time to engage in reflective practice—to bring together knowledge, inquiry, and action right at the school level (Sirotnik & Oakes, 1986). For example, several schools and a few teachers and administrators within them became particularly interested in the detrimental effects of tracking students and in alternative ways for dealing effectively with individual differences in heterogeneous classes. One of our research colleagues had thoroughly investigated the tracking problem and had explored alternatives such as cooperative learning practices (Oakes, 1985). Instead of conducting an in-service program on cooperative learning, however, she began to work with the several teachers and administrators who were interested in trying something out over an entire academic year. Together, the group explored the literature available on grouping practices and the several alternatives being advocated. They did this not with an eye toward picking one and implementing it; rather, they explored the problem in the context of their own school and classroom practices and developed a modified version of cooperative learning that suited their styles and school conditions. This activity extended over a two-year period during which several other schools became involved: a Graduate School faculty member with similar research interests joined the project, a dissertation was done based upon collaborative research in one of the schools (Farivar, 1985), and a cooperative learning network involving over a dozen schools was formed.

Other projects of an equally important nature were now ongoing in

SCP schools. As a way of celebrating and affirming this work, the two-day retreat idea became an annual event. This activity provided a way to integrate the many diverse activities under way at individual schools and in the various support groups. August weekends at the Lake Arrowhead University of California Conference Center were beautiful and the price was right, but not all was fun and games. Teachers, principals, district and university staff came to work; substantial time was set aside for individual school staffs to take stock of where they were and where they were going. Additional time was invested by the entire group in discussions that identified the common problems and themes that held the SCP together. Superintendents used the retreat to enculturate new principals and staff into SCP activities, to inform board members and garner support for continuing these activities, and to become more involved as instructional leaders along with their school-based staff. In effect, we all used these retreats as a way of charging our batteries, refocusing on purpose, and establishing directions and expectations for the coming year.

In sum, school-focused activities of the SCP began slowly and, at times, infrequently, until a number of parallel support group activities got under way. These included a leadership development group, subgroups meeting around common interests, alternative drummers gently pushing alternative change strategies, collaborative research projects, and annual ceremonies to reaffirm commitments and share both the pitfalls and possibilities in collaborative work. Without these kinds of support structures and deliberate attempts to challenge much of the prevailing wisdom regarding school improvement, the beat of alternative drummers would simply fall on deaf ears. People need substantial opportunities to share their own problems and concerns, examine their own norms and world views, and come to understand alternative views and knowledge in the context of their own practices.

### Getting University Faculty Involved

The previous two sections have been relatively easy to write in the sense that the analysis, at least in retrospect, seems to square with the events that occurred. Although the going was not always easy in building support structures and getting things going at district and school levels, much occurred that could be accounted for in terms of participant satisfaction and substantive outcome. This section will be more difficult: the analysis is less clear, the going was always rough, and the successes were few. Indeed, the "university" did become involved significantly in SCP activities, but the connections were made primarily through a Graduate School unit developed for this purpose and staffed by nontenure line researchers.

It is true that the tough going was somewhat predictable. After all, the partnership idea was conceived precisely because of the growing disjuncture between the basic research interests and publish-or-perish reward systems of major research universities on the one hand, and, on the other hand, the increasing need for practical knowledge and long-term inquiry into the problems facing educators in schools. (See the analyses of Judge, 1982, and Boyer, 1987.) Certainly there are numbers of faculty who connect with the schools during the course of conducting research projects, paid and/or unpaid (service) consultation, in-service programs, and so forth. But rarely is there any significant *institutional* commitment and pooling of resources to coordinate major collaborative activities.

Goodlad's intention, therefore, was to create an institutional structure designed to support this kind of commitment and to shake loose some of the traditional barriers between and within schools and universities that inhibit the exploration of common interests. He convened a committee of faculty and administrators from the Graduate School of Education to examine ways of pursuing the idea of a symbiotic partnership between themselves and local school districts. A design calling for the creation of the Laboratory in School and Community Education was proposed as an institutional vehicle for doing this with a major part of its funding to be secured by extramural grants. The committee endorsed the proposal, the faculty approved it, and a five-year grant from the Charles Stewart Mott Foundation was obtained by Goodlad as Principal Investigator.

The Laboratory in School and Community Education began initially with two major subunits: the coordinating function for the Southern California Partnership and the Corrine A. Seeds University Elementary School—the UCLA laboratory school with a long and distinguished record as an innovative demonstration school. Connecting with the laboratory school seemed to be a made-to-order way to speed up the involvement process. Goodlad had directed the UCLA laboratory school for over 15 years, during which time a number of exemplary programs had been developed and demonstrated, most notably, nongraded organizational structures and techniques for addressing individual differences and Madeline Hunter's instructional theory-into-practice techniques. It seemed possible that the school was ready, now, to demonstrate how teachers could engage in long-term inquiry in collaboration with research faculty around crucial problems faced by the public schools.

In retrospect, we probably could not have picked a more difficult time, place, and structural arrangement within which to experiment with symbiotic relationships. For example, UCLA recently had received national attention for having a top-rated, research-oriented, graduate school of education; at the same time, the dean of the Graduate School was suggesting that faculty were not sufficiently involved in the problems of school practice. The staff of the laboratory school, somewhat shaken by the retirement of Madeline Hunter, considered the school an exemplary demonstration school; at the same time, the director was suggesting that the staff consider investigations into alternative practices.

These examples do not by any means constitute a complete explanation of the tensions and problems on the university side of the SCP effort. They are merely illustrative of the very complicated politics and organizational ambiguity that tend to characterize institutions of higher education (Baldridge, 1971; March & Olsen, 1976; Weick, 1976). In the earliest meetings of the SCP Council, for example, a number of faculty were indeed present and active; yet soon after, many of these same faculty seemed to be unaware of what the SCP was about, and they ceased to attend the meetings. In general, it appeared that many faculty perceived the creation of the Laboratory in School and Community Education as a power play on the part of the dean rather than as a structure for institutional and individual involvement with the schools. It thus became an uphill battle for me and my research colleagues (nontenure line staff members) to attract faculty into collaborative activities.

The battle, however, was waged on a broken front. As we had recognized in our work with districts and schools, although institutional structures were important, getting something started on which to focus collaborative activity was essential. At the university elementary school, for example, a team of teachers had been involved with a faculty member in a study of intrinsic motivation for student learning. Towards the end of this study, the teachers, in collaboration with a laboratory staff member, began to look into the literature on cooperative learning as a strategy to promote motivation. This inquiry blossomed over the subsequent year and developed into a full-scale research project. During the second year, one of the SCP high schools joined the inquiry; eventually, as described in a previous section above, a cooperative learning network emerged and attracted at least one Graduate School faculty member to contribute significantly to the inquiry activities.

The world of research and inquiry in schools is a messy one: the time frame extends considerably, and conventional methodology is not always possible or even appropriate. Even in the best of circumstances, it takes unique individuals from the university to brave the practical conditions of schooling. Tenure, as it is typically awarded in research universities, would be hard to come by for assistant professors engaging in long-term, unpredictable, research projects. In fact, all the faculty who became involved in SCP activities were associate or full professors. It therefore becomes of utmost importance that those who coordinate partnership efforts keep a constant lookout — much like a stockbroker — for opportunities to match up the interests of educators in the university and schools.

In one instance, a superintendent literally offered a high school in his district as a testing ground for any innovative ideas that people in the university thought might be appropriate to improve education in a suburban, lower-middle-class, secondary setting. One of the issues the district was dealing with involved comprehensive information systems and how to make them more useful to principals and teachers. This happened to correspond to an interest of one of the members of the laboratory's research staff who also had a joint appointment with the Center for the Study of Evaluation, another major unit of the Graduate School of Education. This interest also matched a research focus of a faculty member working part-time in the center. Together, these researchers secured additional grant money from the National Institute of Education (through the center) and developed a two-year investigation of the contents, uses, and abuses of information systems in schools.

This study, however, was conducted collaboratively with approximately half a dozen teachers, two administrators, and a counselor in the aforementioned high school, and several district office staff including the head of data processing. A number of work meetings were held requiring significant amounts of release time for teachers wherein the study was designed, instruments were constructed, data were interpreted, reporting devices were created, and so forth. (See Sirotnik & Burstein, 1987.) Through the SCP, the district, the Laboratory in School and Community Education, and the Center for the Study of Evaluation were able to bring the pieces of this project together.

The several successful involvements of university faculty in SCP activities followed the same pattern: common interests, associations with key research staff, and a willingness to "hang loose" as the inquiry unfolded. Other attempts to involve faculty either failed outright or dissipated over the short term. One professor, for example, expressed an interest in studying the perceptions of teachers regarding achievement testing and their use of test-score data. We arranged a joint meeting between this faculty member and one of the SCP districts likely to be interested in this problem. It was agreed that the study had merit, a school was identified, and arrangements were made for the first phase of the project—interviewing teachers and administrators. Subsequently, the interviews were conducted and tape-recorded, and secretarial services in the laboratory were provided for transcribing these interviews. That was the last we or the school ever saw of the data or any results therefrom.

Other cases resembled this one, but the fact remains that the individuals involved all had good intentions. They wanted to help and to relate to the schools. The issue was not the desirability of intentions but the understanding of what it meant to collaborate and how to proceed over the long haul. The research staff in the laboratory had the advantage of a shared philosophy of change and a culture of corresponding rewards and expectations. When school people referred to the "university" in SCP activities, it was usually the laboratory that was the referent in addition to the several faculty members associated with it.

A postscript to this account should be of interest to readers. At the end of the 1984–1985 academic year, Goodlad, myself, and the rest of the senior staff of the Laboratory in School and Community Education left UCLA, and, for all intents and purposes, the laboratory ceased to exist. This event was a difficult one for all of us, particularly in view of our commitment to the local schools and our knowledge of the growing recognition in the literature on educational change of the importance of "idea champions" and what their departure can mean to innovative programs.

We were pleasantly surprised to discover that we were not indispensable. The work we had been involved with over the years in developing and nurturing a culture of collaborative inquiry and change turned out to be embodied strongly in the membership of the Leadership Development Group. These principals, largely on their own time, kept the idea of partnership alive. Together with several key superintendents, they pursued a renewed relationship with the Graduate School of Education at UCLA. Unfortunately, however, it became clear to these administrators that those representing the Graduate School were willing to support nothing more than a consulting/service arrangement, and the partnership was therefore officially dissolved.

Notwithstanding this outcome, these administrators remained undaunted. Six of the original twelve district members of the SCP, with the urging of the Leadership Development Group, began to seek relationships with several other universities and graduate schools of education in the southern California area. At the time of this writing, negotiations have been completed with one of these institutions, the Claremont Graduate School, to continue and further develop this school-university partnership effort.

## Summary and Conclusions

I have tried to provide a frank account of the events and circumstances surrounding the first five years of the Southern California Partnership. As noted at the beginning of this chapter, I have viewed the experience as a rewarding one, personally, and have built upon it successfully in beginning a new school-university partnership elsewhere. This may seem a bit odd to readers, particularly those who have just read the last section. But I wish to remind readers that I chose deliberately to highlight conflicts and dilemmas, perhaps at the expense of de-emphasizing successes, in order to help others involved in similar endeavors anticipate some of the problems.

Many of the tensions arose around conflicts between worldviews regarding how schools change and improve what they do. The prevalent view is a linear one, based upon conventional research and development strategies and top-down, bureaucratic structures to implement change. The philosophy of change driving the SCP was quite different and consistent with the school improvement literature suggesting more time for inquiry, the empowerment of teachers in the inquiry process, and collaborative work between educators in both universities and schools (Heckman, Oakes, & Sirotnik, 1983).

The first major dilemma we faced, therefore, was the need to institutionalize the partnership concept through the creation of legitimating structures (the Laboratory in School and Community Education, in the university, and the SCP Council and Executive Committee) while at the same time trying to cut through "administrivia" and begin collaborative work with principals and teachers. In effect, getting the partnership off the ground conflicted with getting something going at the building level. The trick is to get to the school level as soon as possible. In my recent efforts at building a school-university partnership, I have found that working all levels (university, college of education, districts, and schools) simultaneously (or nearly so) from the very beginning has avoided many of the start-up problems we faced in the SCP.

Of course the size of the effort in southern Maine is considerably smaller in scale; nevertheless, this lesson may be well worth considering in any case. For it is clear that not until we developed support groups for administrators and teachers did anything of substance begin to emerge. Subsequently, instead of trying to determine specific goals and plan agenda, the council was able to endorse each support group and trust the processes that were occurring. Activities and collaborative inquiry projects "bubbled up" from these groups; commonalities in interests among support groups, schools, and the university became evident; and yearly retreats that began initially as chief executive planning sessions became working parties for educators at all levels for celebrating substantive changes in schools.

Another major set of conflicts was set in motion around the involvement of university faculty in SCP activities. Here, the issue of basic versus applied research, the competing interests of faculty and institutions, and the politics of university life conspired against such involvement. It turned out, in other words, that the cultural regularities promoting the status quo in a major research university were much tougher nuts to crack than those in the local districts and schools.

Hindsight is wonderful but, at best, speculative. Perhaps we should have better anticipated faculty reaction to the ideas proposed for partnership with schools. For example, notwithstanding the best of intentions, the dean might have been better off to have institutionalized the partnership activity within the Graduate School, to be directed by a tenured faculty member or a person recruited into a tenured position for this purpose. Such an individual would, however, have to be committed to the partnership concept and able to walk comfortably both sides of the "fence" between university research and school practice.

Yet structure alone is never the answer. It takes people and activities to begin the cycle of involvement and to attract the support and participation required to sustain the efforts. Throughout the five-year experience, I was aware of my function as a broker of ideas and people— putting people in touch with one another around issues of common concern. No matter how smooth or rough the intra- and interinstitutional dynamics, there must be one or more tenacious organizers and alternative drummers that take this function seriously on a daily basis— people who have a high tolerance for ambiguity and frustration. Moreover, it is the responsibility of these people, together with the entire membership of the partnership, to build a culture of commitment and action that does not depend on any one handful of participants.

I have the sense that although partnerships have been around for a long time, the type we are trying to foster here between schools and universities is in its infant stage of development. We have much to learn from past attempts, but even more to learn from future efforts. I look forward to this continuing education.

# References

Baldridge, J. V. (1971). *Power and conflict in the university*. New York: Wiley.

Boyer, E. L. (1987). *College: The undergraduate experience in America*. New York: Harper & Row.

Dewey, J. (1929). *The sources of a science of education*. New York: Liveright.

Farivar, S. H. (1985). *Developing and implementing a cooperative learning program in a middle elementary classroom: A comparative study of innovative and traditional teaching and learning strategies*. Unpublished doctoral dissertation, University of California, Los Angeles.

Goodlad, J. I. (1975). *The dynamics of educational change*. New York: McGraw-Hill.

Goodlad, J. I. (1984). *A place called school*. New York: McGraw-Hill.

Heckman, P. E. (1987). Changing school cultures. In J. I. Goodlad (Ed.), *The ecology of school renewal*. 86th yearbook of the National Society for the Study of Education, Part I. Chicago: University of Chicago Press.

Heckman, P. E., Oakes, J., & Sirotnik, K. A. (1983). Expanding the concepts of renewal and change. *Educational Leadership, 40*, 26–32.

Judge, H. (1982). *American graduate schools of education: A view from abroad*. New York: Ford Foundation.

Laboratory in School and Community Education Staff. (1985). *Linking educational theory and school practice: The Laboratory in School and Community Education*. Occasional Paper No. 1. Los Angeles: The Laboratory in School and Community Education, University of California at Los Angeles.

March, J. G., & Olsen, J. P. (1976). *Ambiguity and choice in organizations*. Bergen, Norway: Universitetsforlaget.

Oakes, J. (1985). *Keeping track: How schools structure inequality*. New Haven: Yale University Press.

Sarason, S. B. (1982). *The culture of the school and the problem of change*. Boston: Allyn and Bacon.

Schon, D. A. (1983). *The reflective practitioner: How professionals think in action*. New York: Basic Books.

Sirotnik, K. A., & Burstein, L. (1987). Making sense out of comprehensive school-based information systems: An exploratory study. In A. Bank & R. C. Williams (Eds.), *Inventing the future: The development of educational information systems*. New York: Teachers College Press.

Sirotnik, K. A., & Oakes, J. (1986). Critical inquiry for school renewal: Liberating theory and practice. In K. A. Sirotnik & J. Oakes (Eds.), *Critical perspectives on the organization and improvement of schooling*. Boston: Kluwer-Nijhoff.

Weick, K. E. (1976). Educational organizations as loosely coupled systems. *Administrative Science Quarterly, 21*, 1–19.

# CHAPTER SIX

# The Brigham Young University–Public School Partnership

DAVID D. WILLIAMS

Although universities depend on schools to place their student teachers, schools depend on universities to provide newly prepared educators, and efforts have been made over the years to improve the quality of cooperation between these institutions, true unity has been absent. The public schools and the universities have proceeded with schooling quite independently of one another within boundaries intentionally drawn by both institutions. Critics of the partnership notion (Barth, 1984; Schlechty, 1985) identify a variety of barriers which may have prevented (and they believe will continue to prevent) successful cooperation between schools and universities.

However, in response to the recent barrage of criticism of schools and the preparation of teachers and other educators, several educators (e.g., Dansenberger & Usdan, 1984; Goodlad, 1984; Martin & Wood, 1984; Tyler, 1983) have realized that integral, significant improvement of schooling will *require* a team effort. Seeley (1984) summarized the need for more serious collaboration between schools and universities thus:

> The partnership model enables us to talk constructively about how we have failed in the past and how we can work together in the future. There is no need to waste time and energy assigning blame. We all share responsibility for maintaining an approach that hasn't worked adequately and we can all work together to fashion a new collaborative approach that has a better chance to succeed. (p. 386)

Through a variety of circumstances, a partnership involving Brigham Young University (BYU) and five public school districts (Alpine, Jordan, Nebo, Provo, and Wasatch) was formed in April 1984.

The author wishes to thank participants in a symposium for the American Educational Research Association in April 1986 from which this chapter was conceived: Clark Cox, Bonnie Dahl, John Goodlad, Lillian Heil, Joyce Nelson, Ralph Smith, and Del Wasden.

This chapter provides an overview of historical relationships among these participating institutions, the national and local conditions leading to the cooperative alliance, a description of the partnership itself, and a summary of collaborative activities conducted to date as preamble to a discussion of lessons learned so far by participants in this partnership.

## Historical Relationships

Prior to the BYU–Public School Partnership, the relationships between the five participating school districts and BYU were typical of most schools and universities in the United States: almost mutually exclusive. The five districts represent approximately one-third (100,000 + ) of the rapidly growing total student enrollment in Utah and include one rural, one urban, and three suburban districts. The districts are contiguous and adjoin the private university. BYU is the largest teacher education institution in Utah, preparing over one-half of all teachers graduated in the state.

Notwithstanding an emphasis on preparation of school professionals, BYU faculty have followed the convention of using the schools as settings for training their students without seriously cooperating with teachers and school administrators to define those experiences jointly so that the mutual benefits could be more effectively reached. Also, except for a few exceptions, instead of joining the BYU faculty in joint research ventures, the schools have set policies which essentially prevent university faculty and students from overwhelming the schooling process with their requests to install student teachers and interns in buildings and to "do research on the schools and the students in them."

Although the relationships have not been antagonistic, perhaps because the BYU faculty have focused more on preparation of educators than on research, neither have they been especially beneficial. These five districts and the university have essentially coexisted for many years; but recent developments in conditions have led to a change in the status quo.

## National and Local Conditions

Since 1982, national, state, and local public attention has focused heavily on public education and the preparation of educators. National reports from a variety of sources (e.g., Adler, 1982; Carnegie Foundation, n.d.; Goodlad, 1984; National Commission on Excellence in Education, 1983; Sizer, 1983; Task Force on Education for Economic Growth, 1983; 20th Century Fund Task Force, 1983) have warned public school personnel and schools of education which prepare educators that they need to improve the system and quality of education.

In Utah, which has one of the fastest growing public school student populations in the country (enrollments growing by 4–6% per year), the same public pressure has been mounting. The following recommendations from the Utah Education Reform Steering Committee's November 1983 report (*Education in Utah: A Call to Action*) are both representative and indicative of this public pressure:

> The Board of Regents, the State Board of Education, colleges and schools of education, and academic departments should reform their methods, procedures, and curriculum for educating teachers and administrators. Reforms should include increased cooperation and coordination with school districts in student teaching and in evaluation of prospective teachers. That cooperative relationship should extend to support the professional development of newly employed teachers. The academic preparation of teachers should be substantially improved, especially in subjects they will teach. Other college and university departments should be more active partners with the departments of education in the preparation of teachers. Practice teaching should be given heavier emphasis. (p. 17)

Locally, the pressure for improvement from national and state sources was reinforced by several well-attended public meetings as well as by increased attention in the news. The central BYU administration specifically charged the College of Education to serve the public schools' interests more appropriately through research and the preparation of educators.

In response, the dean of the College of Education initiated dialogue with the superintendents of some of the local school districts to discuss possible ways to respond to the many calls for reform. He also arranged to have John Goodlad fill a visiting scholar's chair at BYU to encourage the faculty and public school representatives to respond to the public outcry for change.

## An Outside Catalyst

John Goodlad and his associates (1984) had recently published the findings of a series of studies of schooling in *A Place Called School* when he came to BYU as a visiting scholar. He met with BYU faculty in a variety of settings to discuss the status of teacher and administrator preparation programs in the college and requests from the central administration to increase scholarly productivity while focusing on ways to improve the public schools. He met with representatives of the public schools to discuss the needs for reform there and to ascertain some of their concerns about working with the BYU College of Education.

After several such discussions, Goodlad identified a set of common interests shared by the university and public schools which might serve as a basis for cooperation. In April 1984, he met jointly with the superintendents of the school districts and the deans of the college to outline those common interests and to propose a collaborative means of addressing related concerns. As a result, the BYU–Public School Partnership (BYU-PSP) was formalized.

The five common interests of the cooperating institutions were stated as objectives or goals:

1. Improve educator preparation and in-service programs.
2. Develop ways to make educational practice more congruent with what is known about learners, the learning process, and teaching effectiveness.
3. Explore the use of key schools to address the most pressing educational problems.
4. Develop strategies for attracting highly capable students into the education profession.
5. Coordinate research activities and the evaluation of programs in the member institutions so that common interests are properly addressed.

## The BYU–Public School Partnership

At that same meeting a very simple organization was agreed upon. First, there was to be a Governing Board consisting of the chief executive officers from the districts and the BYU College of Education who would meet monthly to identify and determine how to address common interests, make policy decisions, and oversee financial affairs. A member of the board was elected chairman and made responsible for convening the board, setting the agenda for board meetings, and managing the affairs of the BYU-PSP.

Second, others in the schools and university would contribute their perspectives by participating on task forces consisting of faculty, teachers, and administrators from the member institutions assigned to work on specific challenges as requested via "charges" issued by the Governing Board. Projects could be initiated by faculty and administrators other than those on the Governing Board; but before receiving official endorsement of the BYU-PSP, these activities would need the approval of the board.

Third, an executive secretary was appointed by the Governing Board to assist the chairman of the board in coordinating all the activities of these groups, representing the BYU-PSP to outside agencies, facilitating communication within the BYU-PSP as well as with other interested parties, encouraging research, evaluation, and development projects, seeking funding, and documenting the evolution of the BYU-PSP.

During the first two years of the partnership, the executive secretary was a BYU faculty member nominated by the dean and appointed by the Governing Board. He was assigned to spend a quarter of his time on this project with no secretarial support other than what the dean's secretary could contribute. Because he was housed in the same building at BYU as the dean, this executive secretary consulted more with the dean than with the superintendent who was the chairman of the Governing Board.

In the spring of 1986, a new executive secretary was hired and several changes were instituted to enhance this position. The title was changed to Executive Director, and this became the only assignment at the university for this person. BYU continues to pay the director's salary and provides an office. The school districts pay for a half-time secretary/assistant and share expenses such as travel, office equipment, and so forth with BYU. The director has made a concerted effort to work more closely with the superintendent chairing the Governing Board than with the dean or anyone else on the board.

In September 1986, another group, the Coordinating Council, was organized consisting of assistants to the Governing Board members from each of the participating institutions (the associate dean of BYU's College of Education, assistant superintendents, and other district office personnel from the districts). This council was formed to generate (and communicate from the individual institutions) salient issues for the Governing Board's consideration, to help operationalize policies mandated by the Governing Board, to facilitate the introduction of approved projects and programs into member institutions, to monitor BYU-PSP projects, to keep the Governing Board members apprised of project progress, to stimulate the flow of information within the BYU-PSP, and to motivate others in the pursuit of educational renewal. The executive director links the council to the board as secretary to the Governing Board and chair of the Coordinating Council.

## Collaborative Activities

Throughout the first three years of the BYU-PSP, a variety of collaborative efforts have been initiated. These will be summarized briefly to set the stage for the analysis of lessons that have been learned over the course of partnership activities.

### Administrative Preparation Task Force

During the first meeting of the Governing Board in April 1984, a task force was proposed to begin addressing ways to improve the preparation of school administrators. The Governing Board prepared a written "charge" to ten school principals assigned from the districts, four faculty from the college of education, and a representative from the State Office of Education who formed this task force. The charge stated the philosophy that "the education of administrators should be a joint responsibility of the university and local school districts" and proposed that the task-force members review the efforts of an earlier group (organized by BYU's Department of Educational Administration) which had met for six months to review the current BYU program for preparing school principals. The board also urged this new task force to "feel free to think creatively and without concern for traditional preparation programs or current state certification standards" as they began to "develop a model program for the preparation of school principals."

A co-chairperson from the school districts was elected by the members of the task force to help organize the group. The BYU dean appointed a faculty member who was *not* a member of the Department of Educational Administration to be the other co-chairperson of this group, reasoning that the chair should not have too much at stake to function properly as a chair. Subsequently, the chairman of the Department of Educational Administration was assigned to replace the BYU co-chair on the task force as the task-force members began to apply the suggestions from the group to a new program to be implemented by the Department of Educational Administration.

Although the charge requested a progress report within six months and a complete proposal within eight months, the members of the new task force began meeting rather cautiously on a monthly basis. They spent the first few months reviewing a long list of principal competencies while establishing ownership for the task and a working relationship among themselves. Then after considerable conflict, accommodation, and study spanning nearly two years (rather than the six to eight months anticipated by the board), this task force produced a plan for a new program to prepare "educational leaders."

This new Principal Preparation Program was the first "child" of the BYU-PSP. The Governing Board was both proud of the birth and insistent that the program be considered a pilot and that evaluative information on it be gathered. The 15 master's students (mostly classroom teachers from the five BYU-PSP school districts) selected to participate were carefully screened jointly through a rigorous process by the superintendents, the BYU faculty, and "mentor principals" selected from the five districts to supervise the students in intensive full-time internships during the school year.

The students entered the program as a cohort group in the summer of 1986 to participate in skill and knowledge assessments and begin a program of seminars on the BYU campus. They then began the first of three internship experiences paired with a mentor principal in that principal's school for four days per week. One day per week was reserved for a campus seminar in which BYU faculty led the students in an analysis of the experiences they were having in the schools and prepared them in several foundation topics. The districts and university have cooperated to provide the students with partial salary, benefits, tuition, and books so that they can dedicate their full time to this program. There is no guarantee that graduates will be hired in vacant positions in the BYU-PSP school districts when they finish; but the BYU faculty and superintendents anticipate that the graduates will be competitive.

## Teacher Preparation Task Force

At the same April 1984 meeting, the Governing Board also proposed that a task force be established consisting of elementary and secondary school teachers and principals from the five school districts as well as elementary and secondary education faculty from the college. In their charge to this group, the board stated, "Teacher education by its very nature is a joint responsibility of colleges of education, university-wide academic departments, and local school districts" spanning from the first year of college "through the first two years of teaching service." The board requested that the task force develop a model for teacher education based on these assumptions which would clarify the relative roles of the school district and college personnel in preparing and evaluating new teachers. This group was also urged to "think creatively without concern for traditional preparation programs or current state standards [and to] take a fresh look at teacher education in light of current knowledge about teaching as a profession and the professional preparation of teachers." A co-chairperson from BYU was appointed by the dean, and one co-chairperson from the schools was elected by the task-force members to organize the group.

The members of this task force were also given six to eight months to fulfill their "charge." They spent that time building trust among themselves and clarifying the purposes of the task force, discussing the characteristics of a good teacher and a program to prepare such teachers, and identifying problems with the existing preparation program that would need attention. However, the task-force members stopped short of proposing a new preparation program or process. They prepared a document outlining several concerns and recommendations for further study and then stopped meeting. Standing committees within the College of Education were asked by the dean's office to review this document and begin to plan teacher preparation program revisions. These committees invited a few representatives from the school districts in the BYU-PSP and from other departments across the BYU campus to participate with them to consider and develop selection, admission, and evaluation criteria, curriculum content, and practical instructional experiences needed to prepare teachers more effectively.

Although a new teacher-preparation program has not yet evolved from these many deliberations, people associated with the teacher preparation task force and subsequent college committees have encouraged the formation of four "partner" schools at the elementary level within three of the BYU-PSP districts. Inspired by Goodlad's (1984) notion of "key" schools, partner schools are intended to foster a working relationship between public school teachers, school administrators, college educators, students, and other community members to improve both teacher preparation programs and schooling. The principal of each school and a faculty member from BYU assigned as a college coordinator are supposed to cooperate to develop a program unique to that school and to organize the efforts of classroom teachers, school and district resource personnel, BYU personnel, and university students assigned to that school as they address four major functions: designing educational content and practices that lead learners to master fundamental learning outcomes, improving the teacher preparation program, designing and implementing effective in-service training, and conducting research and evaluation studies to solve problems mutually agreed upon by representatives of the BYU-PSP institutions assembled in the partner schools.

## Counseling and Guidance Task Force

Upon seeing the progress being made by the administrative and teacher-preparation task forces, faculty in BYU's Counseling and Guidance program and the dean talked about creating a similar group to review and revise that program to make it more effective and "mainstreamed" with the most recent research. The dean presented this idea to the other Governing Board members during the fall of 1984 and found that they agreed that the role of guidance counselors in the schools was vague and that most counselors were frustrated because they believed they were misused and misunderstood in the schools and could not spend their time doing the kinds of counseling they were trained to do.

After some deliberation and consultation with the BYU representatives about what they wanted to accomplish, the board members prepared a charge similar to the charges issued to the other task forces. They also appointed counselors and school principals (to enhance collaboration between these frequently conflicting parties) from the five districts to work with the BYU faculty, and this task force began meeting in January 1985. Like the other task forces, the Counseling and Guidance Task Force had two co-chairs: one representative of the schools and one from BYU. The BYU chair was assigned by the dean; the school representative was elected by the task-force members.

Although the first few months of activity produced several proposals for study of the literature, review of other programs, and conduct of surveys within the BYU-PSP schools, there was also some discussion among the members of the task force about using their combined influence to lobby for policy changes in one or two of the individual districts. The Governing Board responded negatively, reminding the group to focus only on the agenda embodied in the charge. From then on, the board doubted the intents and actions of this task force.

The task-force members focused on the items in the charge; but the members also requested resources from the board which the other task forces had not requested to conduct their assignment, and they let the board know they were unhappy when the requested resources were not forthcoming. They had difficulty establishing a healthy working relationship with the board and after about a year and a half the BYU co-chairman resigned and the group adjourned for the summer. Only recently have they begun to revive with new co-chairs. No new programs or modifications to the existing Counseling and Guidance program at BYU have been recommended by this group yet.

### Gifted and Talented Task Force

In the late spring and early summer of 1984, a small group of BYU faculty who had previously been active in advising teachers and parents on issues relevant to gifted and talented children initiated a special summer enrichment program (Bright Ideas) and invited children from several school districts near BYU to participate. As the BYU-PSP formed, this group approached the board through the dean and requested advice and assistance from the schools in planning this summer activity and in considering other programs for children with special interests, gifts, and talents. The superintendents responded by appointing persons from their district offices and schools who were especially interested in this topic or were already involved with the BYU faculty. During the 1984–1985 school year the committee organized workshops for parents and teachers to discuss ways they could provide opportunities to their children at home and at school to develop academic and other talents. BYU sponsored visits by national figures in this field who made presentations to parents and teachers. The group also planned another summer program for 1985.

All during this first year, the committee kept the Governing Board informed of its activities, requested endorsement of its programs, and sought funding to offset the tuition costs to the summer program for financially needy children. During the summer of 1985, the board members decided that this group was so active and involved in concerns relevant to the BYU-PSP that they prepared a charge and made the group an official task force. The charge requested that the group continue to "develop a comprehensive, systematic gifted and talented educational plan that will help insure that students with distinctively high intellectual, creative, or skill capabilities will have individual and group learning programs designed to best meet their unique needs." The board also noted that "it is important that the [task force] establish a means whereby both prospective teachers and practicing teachers can develop a sound philosophy and needed skills to insure that the needs of gifted and talented youth are met."

The charge further cautioned that recommended plans should include supportive research, information on the cost efficiency of the delivery plan, and a "comprehensive evaluation plan." The Governing Board was especially anxious that it have an opportunity to review and approve any gifted and talented programs or activities held in the name of the BYU-PSP (because the committee had referred to the partnership in some of the committee's publicity during the previous year without specific approval of the board).

During the 1985–1986 school year the task force was heavily involved in preparing materials and making presentations to schoolchildren throughout Utah to encourage them to visit the *Ramses II* exhibit which was on exclusive display at BYU during part of the year. Although the display and the materials that the task force prepared appealed to all children in the schools, not just the gifted and talented subpopulation, these efforts were applauded by the Governing Board as extremely helpful and relevant. The members of this group are currently writing curriculum materials for the schools to use in celebration of the United States's Constitutional Bicentennial. They continue to plan the summer enrichment program and a series of "super Saturday" activities for gifted and talented children and their parents. No suggestions for the teacher-preparation programs have appeared.

### Regional Language Planning Group

In October 1984 a BYU Russian language professor learned of the BYU-PSP and talked to the executive secretary about the possibility of forming a partnership group to explore interest among the schools and the logistics of expanding foreign language offerings in the schools. He made a presentation to the Governing Board and pointed out that several critical languages such as Russian, Japanese, Chinese, and Arabic were not being offered in the schools. He proposed that each district provide a representative to meet with him and other BYU foreign language faculty to discuss this problem and propose solutions.

The board was hesitant, concerned that the schools did not have the resources to offer new courses and hire new faculty in new language areas which might not be attractive to students. After several months of deliberation, however, the superintendents assigned representatives, the dean of the College of Education assigned a representative from the Department of Secondary Education, and the committee held its first meeting in April of 1985. Interestingly, the members of the board did not develop a charge for this group, nor did they consider it a formal task force which they had sponsored.

The group met a few times during the following year, conducted a needs assessment throughout the five districts to see how much interest there was in each of the target languages, and endorsed a pilot program in Japanese in one school. The group also drafted a letter for the Governing Board to sign, voicing concern that the State Office of Education seriously consider foreign language as an optional way of meeting the fine arts requirement in the new core curriculum sponsored by the State Office. It has been interesting to note that although the Gifted and Talented Task Force has been including instruction in Japanese, Chinese, and Russian in its Bright Ideas summer program, it has not coordinated efforts with this group.

## Special Education Task Force

During the fall of 1985, there was a change of superintendents in one of the BYU-PSP school districts. The new superintendent had a long-term interest in special education and almost immediately began to discuss the need for a task force in that area to help prepare teachers to deal more appropriately with students in special education. The other board members agreed and soon drew up a charge requesting this new group to review seriously the existing special education program at BYU and to "develop a model for the training and supervision of [special education] teachers which spans the university experience and at least the first two years of professional service." As with the other task forces, the board members identified representatives from their institutions to participate and the dean appointed one of his representatives to be the BYU co-chairperson. At the first meeting of the group in January 1986, the school representatives elected their co-chair representative.

Unlike the other groups, this task force began meeting bimonthly and continued doing so for the first six months (until the interruption of summer vacations). Moreover, the members seemed to require less time than those of other groups to establish rapport with one another. However, major proposals for new programs have not emerged from the group as yet. It resumed meeting (on a monthly basis) in the fall of 1986.

## Research and Evaluation Task Force

From the beginning of the BYU-PSP in 1984, the Governing Board discussed the value of conducting research and evaluation collaboratively across the five districts and the university. Nearly all the districts were interested in year-round schooling and various versions of career-ladder programs for teachers, and the superintendents shared data from studies in their districts on these and other topics. A temporary committee consisting of the research and evaluation directors for each of the districts and a BYU professor specializing in evaluation met two or three times to discuss funding opportunities for inquiry in the partnership and a possible research agenda for all the participants to consider. However, the board decided not to emphasize the inquiry interests during the first year or so, and this group ceased meeting.

During the second year, BYU created a Center for the Study of Education in the college to encourage research activity among the faculty. To facilitate inquiry in areas of relevance to the schools, the director of that center began meeting regularly with the district research and evaluation directors. Also during this time, the Governing Board members sensed the importance of evaluating the effectiveness of the programs being proposed by the various task forces. They also found that the task-force members needed technical assistance in the conducting of surveys and other data collection activities connected with their assignments. This combination of events led to the formalization of the Research and Evaluation Task Force in February 1986.

The charge to this group urged the participants to "promote research among partnership members, especially research aimed at solving immediate district and school problems; conduct evaluations of ongoing and new programs within the partnership; review and make recommendations on proposals for research intended for the partnership; cultivate a research and evaluation relationship among the members of the partnership; and report periodically to the Governing Board the status of all research and evaluation projects." The director of the BYU Center for the Study of Education was designated as the chairperson for this group with no school representative co-chairperson.

Just a month after their formalization as a task force, the chairperson met with the Governing Board to persuade the members that this group should not be used actually to conduct research and evaluation activities on behalf of the BYU-PSP or to help task forces develop instruments. Rather, because the members of the task force are administrators and serve many other functions, they would serve best as "shadow members" of the board who assess the relevance, cost, and priority of research and evaluation issues that come before the board, and then make recommendations for action. The actual role this group will play remains to be seen.

### Other Task Forces

At least two other task forces are in the planning stages. Provo School District has invited the other institutions to join it in exploring recent research and curriculum activities associated with the teaching of thinking. Personnel in Provo are reviewing new thinking programs and associated literature and are exploring the need for a program in Provo, which they may begin developing for the Provo schools, depending on the results of initial inquiry. A few faculty at BYU have joined Provo in these early activities, but the other school districts have declined to participate until they see what Provo and BYU learn. If the topic appears to be worth further exploration, they may join in by forming a task force on learning.

The superintendent of another partnership district has been heavily involved in the exploration of alternative instructional delivery systems, particularly as used in distance education. He is informing the other board members of some of these alternatives, and the executive director anticipates organizing a task force which would explore the topic in detail.

## Research and Evaluation of the Partnership

In addition to the task forces and other efforts to address problems of education through collaborative efforts of BYU Partnership members, the Governing Board has joined several collaborative efforts across the country in a network organized by John Goodlad: the National Network for Educational Renewal. Goodlad has urged the participating partnerships to document carefully the activities, successes, and problems faced in developing these consortia. In response, a BYU faculty member (the former executive secretary) with an interest in research and evaluation, and in the role of collaboration in the process of educational change, has initiated an extensive study of the BYU Partnership itself as a medium of educational change. Results from this ongoing study will also be used to provide formative feedback to each of the task forces, the Governing Board, the Coordinating Council, the executive directors, the network officials, and others regarding their activities.

A naturalistic inquiry approach is being used in this comprehensive study of the BYU-PSP from its inception and throughout its life. Because the partnership is quite large, a variety of sampling procedures are being used to focus attention on selected components of this huge "case." Purposive sampling predominates. For example, to describe relationships between school and university personnel, meetings and communications between members of various task forces are observed (as are less formal interactions as they are discovered). Similarly, snowball samples are used as participants suggest other sources of information.

The principal instruments are the researchers who employ interview schedules, questionnaires, participant observations, systematic observations, and document analyses in gathering data. A team of researchers is coordinating its efforts so that, whenever possible, parallel forms of data are collected to facilitate aggregation of results across settings and sites. The researchers maintain records of data collection procedures and findings, documenting how the instrumentation develops. Records of researchers' emotional and personal reactions to the informants and the objects of study are also kept. The resulting data record contains transcripts of interviews, extensive observation notes, ongoing analyses and syntheses of results, and narrative portrayals of the context in which the study is taking place.

Analysis of fieldnotes occurs throughout the data collection phases (which will continue throughout the life of the BYU-PSP). Researchers are analyzing data descriptively and theoretically, seeking grounded theory. Extensive reports are being written to provide the reader with plenty of raw description so that alternative interpretations of the data are facilitated and the reader can vicariously experience some of the impressions and perceptions of the researchers. Briefer articles are also being prepared for dissemination to participants in the partnership, to members of the network of partnerships, and to the general reader. These ongoing analyses are also used to modify collection activities in response to emphases discovered in the data.

This research and evaluation method will allow the inquirers to understand how BYU-PSP members interact and perform their functions as they naturally do so. Some of the inquiry questions being addressed are:

1. How did the BYU–Public School Partnership form and begin operation? How and why do operations change over time?
2. What were and are various participating organizations' needs and their members' motives for joining forces in this way and continuing to cooperate?
3. How do relationships among participants (particularly those from the university with those from the schools) develop and impact on outcomes?
4. What are the different roles played by each of the participants? How do university personnels' teaching, scholarship, and service roles change? How do school personnels' teaching and scholarship roles change?
5. How are policies made and enacted?
6. What are the most likely outcomes to be associated with the partnership for the BYU programs and faculty and for the school personnel and students?
7. Does participation in the BYU-PSP encourage faculty and school reforms? If so, how and what kinds? If not, why?
8. What are the communication patterns within the BYU-PSP and what are the implications for education and learning generally?
9. What problems are encountered and how are they addressed?

That this inquiry is not being sponsored by the partnership itself (but by BYU currently and by other outside agencies in the future) provides the inquirers with considerable autonomy; but it also complicates the formative evaluation role that can be played. The inquirers are struggling to decide the best ways to identify evaluation audiences and their questions and how much of the time available to dedicate to addressing those concerns versus the basic research interests associated with the processes of change manifested by this collaborative effort. How this inquiry effort evolves and is perceived by participants will be an interesting aspect of the partnership to be studied as well.

## Patterns Discovered and Lessons Learned

Although the research and evaluation of the BYU–Public School Partnership began formally only in the spring of 1986, the project director gathered data during his participation as the executive secretary as well. Based on the data collected to date and on the reflections of several participants on their experiences (Williams et al., 1986), participants who have studied the partnership have discovered some patterns and identified some lessons learned. These are summarized in this section of the chapter.

### Building Trust

"We didn't realize how different we really were!" This comment by the BYU College of Education dean, as he reflected on the evolving relationship of the university with the schools in the partnership, reveals one of the biggest hurdles this collaborative effort has faced and continues to struggle with after nearly three years. To symbiotically realize mutual self-interests, the participating parties have to trust one another; but universities and schools have plenty of reasons *not* to trust their partners.

During the first few months of existence, members of all the task forces spent hours defending their ideas, clarifying their purpose in meeting, learning to listen to perspectives they disliked, worrying that they would be overrun by "the other side," expressing skepticism, feeling as though they were wasting time because they were not addressing the official agenda, and in many other ways building a group rapport and identity. No one predicted that so many pent-up fears and doubts due to previous experiences would have to be overcome before the intended collaborative work could even begin.

The Administrative Preparation Task Force, which eventually produced the highly touted Principal Preparation Program, provides an excellent sample. During the first three or four meetings, principals were overheard to say, "I don't think BYU really cares what I think about how it prepares principals. This is all just a facade — a public relations act to make us think BYU might change." Others complained, "I can't keep leaving my school to listen to all this; I don't think it is going to make any difference." BYU representatives didn't complain much, but they dominated the dialogue and often all participants sat and listened to the university professors arguing their pet theories about esoteric skills none of the practicing principals found relevant to their jobs.

Attendance declined, and eventually the co-chairperson from BYU instructed the secretary to include a note in the minutes telling the group that the task force was to be dissolved because he didn't really believe they were making any progress. When the other co-chairperson read these minutes, she called group members and found that no one else had understood that the group was through. This threat of abolishment united the participants to overcome their many differences long enough to keep meeting and to address the official agenda.

Thus, the BYU faculty realized that the school representatives were interested in contributing to a new program and that they had valid concerns to share. When the people from the schools saw that this was a chance to express themselves and realized they would just have to trust the BYU faculty to do something meaningful with their input, the group got serious about reviewing and revising the principal-training curriculum. But even now that a program is being piloted, all parties are still skeptical. Members of the Governing Board are insisting that in addition to internal formative evaluation of the program, external summative evaluation is needed to see how well BYU is implementing the program which the task force designed.

### Developing Collegiality

Related to the above concern has been the challenge of developing a sense of collegiality and mutual respect among the members of the partnership. The dean and the superintendents work well as peers; but many of the teachers and principals working with the university faculty on task forces took their degrees under these same persons and struggle to feel like true colleagues. Also, because most of the task forces have been formed to develop recommendations for improving the university's programs in light of real world concerns, the college faculty realize they are rusty, and some feel inferior to the school representatives.

Even "small" details contribute to the problem. For example, when the "field programs" university committee members began meeting to follow up on recommendations of the first Teacher Preparation Task Force, they met on the BYU campus. They invited several representatives from the schools to meet with them but forgot to provide parking passes for the "visitors." As a result, the school representatives were late and received the message that they were not being welcomed as equals. When people are afraid of pending changes, new time demands, and the threat of losing what autonomy they believe they have, it is even harder to establish confidence in their ability to cooperate as colleagues with the people they believe are threatening them.

## True Symbiosis?

A quick review of the task forces indicates that the first two were created when the BYU-PSP was formed (Administrative and Teacher Preparation) with the goal of improving university programs. Only one of the existing groups was initiated by the public schools (Special Education by one of the superintendents) while two others are still being considered (Thinking and Learning Strategies). All the other task forces have come about at the request of personnel from the university. Even more fundamentally, the BYU-PSP itself began at the suggestion of the university and its quasi representative, John Goodlad, who had been hired to advise the university about how to do something useful for educational renewal. For the first two years of the consortium, the dean of the college and the faculty member acting as executive secretary essentially controlled the agenda of the Governing Board. In addition, the university provided nearly all the financial support for the enterprise during the first two years, except for a small grant from the Utah State Office of Education.

It could be argued that in a truly symbiotic relationship, whatever is good for one partner is good for the other. But this imbalance in the initiation of task forces and other activities and the financing of activities suggests that perhaps the university's self-interests were being emphasized much more than those of the schools. The superintendents, however, have frequently claimed that they anticipate benefiting from the expertise of college faculty, improved academic programs, and financial resources of the university in improving their schools. Perhaps they will have their interests met if they can help the university personnel meet *their* interests which would also enhance the quality of those resources. This remains to be seen.

*Authoritarian Governing Board*

Although most of the school district and university personnel approve of the BYU-PSP in principle, many acknowledge that the Governing Board formed the consortium as a formal organization and then imposed it on their respective institutions. The superintendents, dean, and department chairpersons did not poll their constituents as democratic representatives to see if they were interested. They assumed that they could sell their school boards, central administrators, and the faculty and staff who would do much of the collaborating on the idea once the relationship was confirmed. The accuracy of this perception is confirmed by the way members of the task forces have been selected. Rather than invite volunteers to nominate themselves to serve, the dean and superintendents have assigned their representatives to the task forces. Similarly, superintendents took the central role in selecting the schools that became partner schools, in spite of the Teacher Preparation Task Force's recommendation that school staffs should have the opportunity to discuss the concept and apply for consideration.

A related issue the Governing Board faces is deciding how much and what responsibilities to delegate to others. Thus far, there has been a general feeling of anxiety among board members about people doing things in the name of the BYU-PSP without review and approval of the board. Although they have assigned task forces to discuss issues and present opinions to them, they have reserved ultimate decision-making power to themselves, making the task force members hesitant to consider some alternative recommendations because they lack the authority to enact them. The members of the board have tended to want to review all proposals, make all assignments, and make all decisions; but too much is going on for them to continue to do so. Now, after two years, the board has established a Coordinating Council to share some of this burden, although it remains to be seen how the board will use this group.

All this suggests that the authoritarian role the board has taken may have been useful in getting the partnership off the ground quickly; but for true collaboration to take place at the school and individual participant level, it may be necessary for board members to delegate much more responsibility for initiating collaborative activities and making decisions to these lower levels.

*Funding Inequity*

Unlike several other partnerships that are forming, BYU-PSP members have been slow to discuss the matter of financial support for the partnership. A small grant from the Utah State Office of Education has provided sufficient support for initial efforts. The school districts have employed substitute teachers to replace school representatives who participate on task forces, while the university has provided faculty and graduate student time to support the partnership. However, BYU has also paid for the executive officers, their offices, travel, and other expenses. Insofar as the amount of money an institution is willing to contribute is an indicator of that institution's commitment to a cause, this pattern of inequity between university and school-district funding is cause for some concern.

One problem is that the schools in Utah are severely strapped financially. For example, using the dollars spent per year per pupil in 1985–1986 as an index, one finds that Utah is the lowest in the United States (mean of $2,100 per student compared to the national average of $3,200), and the Alpine School District is the lowest in Utah ($1,870 per student). Pressure to increase educational productivity at the same or lower cost levels is intense throughout the BYU-PSP school districts. The superintendents have hesitated to petition their school boards for funding to participate more equitably in the partnership. And perhaps the schools are already paying their share if the percentage of funds available is used as the index instead of the absolute contribution. But, if all are to be equal partners, it seems critical to find ways for all participants to contribute a reasonable proportion of the operating expenses.

## Communication

A continual problem is lack of communication. Even after two years, many people in the schools and university know very little about the BYU-PSP and what they can do with it to help improve the schools. Task-force members are unaware of what other task forces are doing (e.g., the Gifted and Talented Task Force and the Regional Language Planning Group were both promoting Japanese language instruction independently). In spite of fairly regular reports by co-chairpersons, the Governing Board remains often uninformed or misinformed about the activities of the task forces. At the same time, the task-force members spend much of their meeting time debating the intent and interests of the Governing Board because they do not have clear information from that body.

Lack of communication not only hinders formal collaboration efforts, it prevents the informal networking among the individuals in the participating organizations who could otherwise mushroom cooperative efforts in unanticipated ways. A brochure has been produced, and a newsletter is in the planning stages. These tools may alleviate the problem, but other ways to inform and involve members of the participating organizations need to be explored. The executive director and the Coordinating Council are exploring ways to connect people throughout the five districts and the entire university who have similar interests.

### Institution Versus Individual

Institutional and individual self-interests are diverse and often divergent. Notwithstanding the claim that collaboration can facilitate the achievement of common self-interests of institutions, the individuals who must cooperate to meet those goals have their own self-interests which must be met before or as they work for the common good. There is some indication that the organizations participating in the BYU-PSP are not oriented to reward individuals for their efforts to satisfy the institutions' self-interests.

For example, in the university, publications in journals are the major requirement for advancement and reward. It is in the self-interest of faculty to spend their time doing research and publishing that work. Thus far, the activities of the task forces, the Coordinating Council, and the partner schools have focused on committee discussion, curriculum development, and the beginnings of evaluation design. Faculty who have participated have had less time to conduct research and publish. The university reward system is not set up to promote them for the efforts they have made to meet the university's "self-interests" via the partnership. Arrangements may change so that such effort is rewarded or so that faculty can conduct research that is publishable through the partnership; but until then, the institutional and individual self-interests appear to be in conflict.

In the schools, principals and teachers are rewarded for the services they provide their constituents. Although participation on task forces and other partnership bodies may eventually help them and other principals and teachers to serve the public better, the rewards associated with those impacts will be long in coming. Unless there are more immediate rewards for collaborative efforts, the individual self-interests of school personnel will remain unmet while they are addressing the institutions' interests.

### Kingpins

Key individuals play important roles in the activities and progress of the BYU-PSP. These roles can be both positive and negative. As these individuals take new assignments, move, or change their focus, entire components of the collaborative effort are modified. As summarized earlier, John Goodlad played a critical role in getting this partnership started. He was able to meet separately with the potential members of the collaboration and identify common interests which could cement the relationship. He continued to visit Utah and meet with task forces and the Governing Board for several months. But those contacts have diminished and others have taken the leadership and facilitating roles.

The BYU dean of the College of Education who first invited Goodlad to visit the university made a significant contribution but was replaced before Goodlad made his very first visit. The succeeding dean has spearheaded the formation of many of the task forces by inviting the schools to help him and his associates review and revise BYU's programs.

The first chairman of the Governing Board was a strong leader who set the tone for the first six months until he took another superintendency. There was then a brief period when some participants nervously watched to see if the schools would maintain their interest and continue participating actively. They did, but the new chairman took a much more authoritative role, changing the board's role slightly.

Two new superintendents to the board have recommended new task forces, whereas none of the original board members took that initiative. An associate dean has actively promoted the formalization of the partner school concept and the selection of some initial schools to test the idea empirically. If it weren't for him, nothing might have been done in this area. Also, the BYU faculty who had requested the formation of the several task forces have been kingpins in forming the BYU-PSP into the configuration it has taken.

## Evaluation

Finally, there is the issue of how best to evaluate progress. A series of naturalistic studies has been initiated to describe and facilitate the assessment of how the partnership generally is functioning. Moreover, the Governing Board has requested that all individual programs and projects sponsored by the BYU-PSP (like the Principal Preparation Program) be evaluated formatively and summatively. The Research and Evaluation Task Force has been appointed to advise the Governing Board on how to do this appropriately. The Coordinating Council members have divided up the task forces among themselves so that each person is responsible for monitoring the efforts of one to two task forces and reporting on progress to the Council and the Governing Board. A task force has been formed in the National Network for Educational Renewal to address these issues as well. People are anxious to make sure all this effort is worth the costs.

Ideally, all partnership participants should be interested in critically reviewing what they are doing and what they can learn from the experience. But most of the evaluation plans appear to be externally imposed. The Governing Board wants to know how the task forces and the programs it produces are doing, but it has no plans for evaluating its own performance. Very few of the task forces have systematically planned evaluations of their efforts. Unless there is interest in self-evaluation, participants will not learn all they could from this innovative experiment.

## Conclusion

It should be clear from this overview that the BYU–Public School Partnership has been born and is growing through its infancy and well into its toddler phase. The focus has been on getting things done that will improve education; but the partners recognize that they may need to pay more attention to maintenance and development of the mechanism as well. They anticipate collaborating with other partnerships in the National Network for Educational Renewal to attack the truly difficult problems faced by educators and to learn more about how cooperation affects educational change.

## References

Adler, M. J. (1982). *Paideia proposal*. New York: Macmillan.

Barth, R. S. (1984). Can we make a match of schools and universities? *Education Week, 24*, 16.

Carnegie Foundation. (n.d.). *High school — A report on secondary education in America*. Scranton, PA: Keystone Industrial Park.

Dansenberger, J., & Usdan, M. D. (1984). Building partnerships: The Atlanta experience. *Phi Delta Kappan, 65*(6), 393–396.

Goodlad, J. I. (1984). *A place called school*. New York: McGraw-Hill.

Martin, R. E., Jr., & Wood, G. H. (1984). Early field experiences: Unification of cooperating teachers' and teacher education students' diverse perspectives. An unpublished paper presented at the annual meeting of the American Educational Research Association, New Orleans, Louisiana.

National Commission on Excellence in Education. (1983). *A nation at risk*. Washington, DC: Government Printing Office.

Seeley, D. S. (1984). Educational partnership and the dilemmas of school reform. *Phi Delta Kappan, 65*(6), 383–388.

Schlechty, P. C. (1985). Reconstructing the teaching occupation: A proposal. Unpublished manuscript.

Sizer, T. (1984). *Horace's compromise: A dilemma of the American high schools*. Palo Alto, CA: Houghton Mifflin.

Task Force on Education for Economic Growth. (1983). *Action for Excellence: A comprehensive plan to improve our nation's schools*. Denver, CO: Education Commission.

20th Century Fund Task Force. (1983). *Making the grade*. New York: 20th Century Fund.

Tyler, R. W. (1983). Studies of schooling: A place called school. *Phi Delta Kappan, 64*(7), 462–464.

Utah Education Reform Steering Committee. (1983). *Education in Utah: A call to action*. Salt Lake City: State of Utah.

Williams, D. D., Cox, C., Dahl, B., Heil, L., Nelson, J., Smith, R., & Wasden, D. (1986). Improving Education Through a Public School–University Partnership. In *Resources in Education*. ERIC Clearinghouse on Teacher Education. ID# ED267063 (SP027385).

# CHAPTER SEVEN

# Accent on Leadership: The Puget Sound Educational Consortium

PAMELA J. KEATING and RICHARD W. CLARK

On August 2, 1985, nine urban and suburban school districts joined with the University of Washington College of Education to create the Puget Sound Educational Consortium (PSEC). This event grew out of informal interactions over a year and a half, developing educational leadership around emerging issues and ideas. Since the founding of the PSEC, the number of school districts involved has increased, but the central focus of the partnership has remained on leadership for educational renewal.

Havelock, Huberman, and their colleagues (see Chapter 2) have suggested a general model for studying interorganizational arrangements such as school-university partnerships. Essentially, these authors argue the importance of what they describe as "antecedent coupling": the history of previous collaboration, the number of formal and informal links, the degree of coupling, the centrality of the university service function, and the goal congruence of the institutions involved. In other words, they are convinced that it is necessary to understand what has gone before in order properly to describe the present. We share their sense of the significance of previous experience and mutual values and effort, and we describe here the current work of the PSEC in the context of prior collaboration. Our interest in these historical roots is not so much the events themselves as the insights they yield in understanding the evolution of the consortium and the fragility of such interorganizational relationships.

Subsequent to this discussion of origins, we will turn to matters of structure and substance: the way in which the PSEC is organized for collaboration and the kinds of activities that have characterized the collaboration. Finally, we will outline some issues and concerns that have already become apparent during the relatively young life — barely a year and a half at the time of this writing — of this school-university partnership.

## Historical Context

Exactly a year prior to the formal PSEC agreement, administrators and other educators from nine large neighboring school districts, the College of Education, and the Office of the State Superintendent of Public Instruction came together in an Educational Leadership Seminar designed to promote dialogue on fundamental issues in school reform and renewal. Several aspects of the development of the seminar helped to shape the subsequent focus of the consortium on thoughtful leadership and educational excellence. These features included perceived mutuality of interest, interpersonal trust developed out of prior association, shared commitment to quality, and belief in the power of ideas to stimulate educational change and school improvement.

The Educational Leadership Seminar was created out of concern about how best to respond to the public rhetoric regarding educational reform and renewal. Two deputy school superintendents from neighboring districts approached their former graduate professor, the head of the administrative training program in the College of Education, about university assistance in addressing ideas emerging from the plethora of reform reports then circulating around the country. Internally, the Institute for the Study of Educational Policy within the College of Education had also identified an interest in playing a leadership role in raising the level of conversation about educational improvement, perhaps by providing forums for focusing on more substantive and timely examinations of educational issues.

These meetings to develop the Educational Leadership Seminar signaled a new, potentially powerful, relationship between school administrators and representatives of the College of Education. Unlike some previous associations, it was an interaction of *peers*. To appreciate fully the significance of this change, we must look back past the seminar to some 30 years of various and sundry relationships between the College of Education and the schools.

### Prior Origins

During this previous era, relationships between the college and the schools fluctuated between active cooperation and passing interest. Beginning with a small fund in the early 1950s, the Bureau of School Service and Research was established by the University of Washington to help schools solve problems. The bureau was given added attention when a new dean, who came from Teachers College, arrived in the early 1960s and attempted to apply the lessons he had learned from the successes of the Metropolitan School Study Council. While the bureau provided a typical, noblesse oblige relationship between the College of Education and the field, it also provided a base for graduate field work and a common gathering place for administration professors and school administrators — some of the same administrators who would years later approach the college to collaborate in the reform era of the 1980s.

Relationships that began strong and then weakened were not limited to the bureau. Teacher education, curriculum, guidance, and other fields within the college alternately developed strong relationships with the schools and then withdrew as funding or faculty or school district interests seemed to shift. During this period, several advisory groups were established for specific programs at the University of Washington, for the Bureau of School Service and Research, and for different areas within the College of Education. Essentially, the university invited former graduates to listen to faculty members describe programs that were being developed and to offer their reactions. State and regional accrediting requirements also called for school personnel advisory groups to the college, although participation was largely superficial.

In the late 1970s, the university faced severe funding problems, which, by the early 1980s, threatened the very existence of the College of Education. On the one hand, school district advisory groups were telling the college that it needed to be more attuned to the field of professional practice, while the university's message to the college was a challenge to justify its existence in a major research institution. Partly as a response to internal demands for research, and partly as a reaction to a teacher surplus, the college drastically reduced its teacher preparation program, opting for "quality rather than quantity." In redirecting internal resources to primary research, the college scaled back, then eliminated support for the Bureau of School Service and Research, forcing it to survive from fees charged for services. Without support for faculty positions, the bureau lacked the personnel and the products necessary for generating substantial fees. The general withdrawal of the college from interaction with local school districts was perceived by local administrators as a lack of interest in the public schools by a very vulnerable college program.

Some faculty members doubted the College of Education could survive if it removed itself from the field. Their sensitivity to the richness of a relationship with local schools resulted in a special collaborative arrangement with the Seattle School District for the study of indicators of effective schools. Just as the college and the local school districts needed each other's help in the 1960s in order to train and place new teachers, an urban school system undergoing stress and a college in transition needed each other now, in an ongoing collaboration centered on identifying and measuring characteristics of schools where students were learning successfully regardless of race or economic status.

Another group of faculty members began a series of discussions around the role of educational policy in the improvement of public schooling. This group was instrumental in the creation of the Institute for the Study of Educational Policy which was ultimately to become the institutional base for the PSEC Consortium. And when the flurry of educational reform reports hit in the early 1980s, they provided the perfect opportunity for educators in both the university and the schools to raise their level of conversation about educational reform and renewal.

It was at this point that the institute's interest in shaping public discourse and previous administrative relationships with local school leaders came together. Representatives from both institutions sat down to plan a program for local school leaders to hear and discuss the ideas and issues of the reform initiatives. John Goodlad, a visiting professor in the College of Education at this time, was invited to join these discussions. His previous experience with the Southern California Partnership contributed to these initial conversations and the subsequent formation of the Puget Sound Educational Consortium.

This was the context, then, for a dialogue between peers that would develop into a central theme of leadership in the consortium. And while it was a dialogue that would grow in trust, it was one founded on years of on-again, off-again relations between the college and the schools — relations that will always influence the level of trust among partnership participants.

### The Educational Leadership Seminar

Initially, individual interest was piqued by the possibility that educators thinking together might be able to plan a program about emerging ideas in education for senior school administrators that was tailored to their actual professional concerns and settings. The seminar could provide the professional challenge most conferences stopped short of offering; that is, the seminar's agenda could go beyond the formal presentation of information and ideas to a less structured interchange among participants, which would allow for a real exploration of challenging ideas. Planners were eager to avoid conferences where information was disseminated piecemeal with little opportunity for discussion. Neither did they wish to replicate professional meetings that talked about the latest trend without linking new ideas to timeless principles and evolving understandings.

During the early stages of the planning for this initial seminar, decisions were made which significantly affected the subsequent composition of the PSEC. First, faculty members and representatives of the districts who had initiated the planning meeting identified colleagues in other districts who might be interested in seminar types of discussions. Participants were identified based on the initiators' perception of their interest in engaging in serious deliberations about school renewal.

Selection and exclusion are delicate issues in collaborative activity. In developing the Educational Leadership Seminar dialogue and the subsequent PSEC partnership, the planners invited geographically contiguous districts of similar size in the Puget Sound area to participate. Implicit in the districts' interest in this shared activity was the perception on the part of their administrators that they ought to serve in leadership roles, given the size and complexity of their districts. The level of professional preparation and opportunities available for continuing professional development distinguished most of these administrators, who were perceived among their peers as effective educational leaders.

The coincidental publication of a number of books on educational reform by such scholars as Mortimer Adler, Ernest Boyer, John Goodlad, Sara Lawrence Lightfoot, Seymour Sarason, and Theodore Sizer provided sufficient substance for the initial dialogue and formed the reading list for the first Educational Leadership Seminar. Each speaker gave one presentation; all other discussions occurred in various small group configurations with blocks of time provided both for role-group exchanges and informal discussions with each guest educator.

Some participants reported that it was their first extended experience discussing ideas with other professionals. Others noted the rarity of simply relaxing with a distinguished guest and discussing important schooling issues. Seminar planners, elated but cautious about the long-term effects of this exchange, immediately focused on follow-up. An expressed desire by participants to continue the dialogue led to planning for two additional days during the year to continue the conceptual exchange. The shared interest in being proactive in a period of public examination of education was sufficient motivation for continuing attention to key ideas underlying the popular discussion of schooling. During the school year, for example, seminar participants joined in additional sessions focusing on reforms needed in secondary education and the implications of changing demographics for educational change.

Some very practical discussion seemed warranted as well. Throughout the fall and winter, 1984–1985, a series of extended brown bag lunch discussions were arranged with high school principals from the Educational Leadership Seminar districts. The principals got together in groups of 10 to 15 to discuss issues related to reforming the high school, with special attention given to the particular problems of building administrators. These principals initially were wary of this work, and they had had little opportunity to discuss these issues and ideas with each other, either within or across districts. But when the series ended, the principals were enthusiastic about the need to continue to meet and talk further about the issues.

Midway through the year, seminar planners began developing a second year's Educational Leadership Seminar dialogue. After considerable discussion, they chose to move beyond the reform literature and focus on change itself: how to push further, how to initiate change, how to prepare people for change, and how best to engage educators in renewing processes predicated on change. School culture was a recurrent theme as the internal and structural patterns in schooling and the constraints that shape institutional behavior were being considered.

Adapting the title of a Sarason book as an organizing theme for the second year's work, planners developed a seminar focused on "School Culture and Change." Experts invited to the seminar included organizational consultants, anthropologists, political scientists, and educators whose studies focused on both public and private school cultures and the larger political context of schooling. Follow-up sessions related to the overall theme were again conducted during the school year. Moreover, eight five-hour clinics were developed during the year for high school principals in participating districts to explore issues of special concern articulated in the earlier series of brown bag lunch discussions. Clinic sessions were organized around issues of core curriculum and tracking; staff selection and evaluation; and district-school relations, authority and responsibility. Thus, while the PSEC was formally organizing during this 1985–1986 academic year, the seminar from which it had sprung was contributing to the growth of the leaders in the districts involved.

The third year of the Educational Leadership Seminar followed suit. This time, planners focused on the theme of "Core Curriculum": they designed activities exploring how to create a shared culture of the diversity we acknowledge and claim to prize, examining what curriculum "counts" and for whom, addressing how seriously we take common learnings in the common schools, discussing what to do about vocational education and the problem of tracking, and so forth. Again, outstanding scholars and school leaders were gathered for summer and school-year seminars. This pattern of identifying crucial themes, inviting distinguished speakers, engaging in serious dialogue, and following up with periodic seminars is currently continuing into its fourth year of operation.

## The PSEC: Form and Function

Clearly, some very potent ideas have shaped the development of the Puget Sound Educational Consortium. The Educational Leadership Seminar exchanges have challenged participating administrators to consider the roots and purposes of American public education and to hold themselves accountable for the failure to realize genuinely common learnings in the common schools. All good theory impels to practice, and, in this instance, good ideas have been the impetus for formalizing conceptual exchanges into a collaboration focused on specific problems and actual change activities in consortium districts.

### Organization and Structure

Conceptualizing the PSEC was primarily a matter of exploring commitments to working together, listening to dominant concerns, identifying points of mutual interest, and suggesting several possible directions for development. The organization and substantive development of this practical partnership among Puget Sound educators occupied the consortium throughout 1985–1986.

The PSEC was formally created with a memorandum of understanding, signed by all nine school district superintendents and the dean of the College of Education at the University of Washington. (The institutional link to the university's College of Education has been the Institute for the Study of Educational Policy.) An important feature of this level of governance is that the principal individuals involved in consortium development have never had to obtain a higher level "buy-in" for the consortium's processes or programs, since superintendents and their deputies have been the primary agents of its development.

Parity was (and continues to be) a major concern of the participants in the PSEC. The Coordinating Council consists of voting and ex officio members, with the dean of the College of Education and superintendents each representing a single vote. Selected university faculty and district administrators, who have been instrumental in consortium organization, serve in a nonvoting membership capacity.

Given this governance structure, the Coordinating Council members readily assumed shared authority and took care of the business of their new organization. Direct appeals for agenda-setting included expressions of the need for help with local boards, identification of the long-term value of this association, and concern about how to get moving with the real work of educational improvement. One bit of business dispensed with at the formative meeting of the PSEC was the cost of partnership participation. It was agreed that each district would contribute $17,500 annually plus ten cents per pupil. This meant that consortium districts would contribute between $18,500 and $22,000 per year for basic membership. Districts also agreed to a five-year commitment to the consortium. Since its creation, three districts have been added, so that the partnership now operates with an annual cash budget of about $250,000. In addition, the University of Washington provides substantial in-kind contributions of office space, secretarial service, and faculty time which exceed in dollar value the individual contributions of any of the participating school districts. (Districts absorb additional costs for major activities like the Education Leadership Seminar and more recent events designed to develop leadership at the instructional level, the latter resulting in considerable teacher-release-time costs.)

During the initial meeting of the PSEC, the Coordinating Council members had made it clear that one reason for a substantial budget was to enable them to seek an effective executive director. At that first meeting of the consortium, members appointed an Executive Committee and initiated a nationwide recruiting effort for an individual who could "walk both sides of the street"—that is, someone able to interact effectively in the university environment as well as in school settings and provide substantial leadership to the PSEC. It is instructive to consider this search process in more detail since it illustrates well the problems likely to arise when disparate organizational cultures attempt to collaborate in more than superficial ways.

At the outset, the search committee clearly symbolized the equal partnership of the university and the school districts. Both institutions were represented, with the latter's representatives slightly outnumbering the former: three university faculty members, three superintendents (one being chair of the committee), and a deputy superintendent. The committee foresaw that the desired director might come from any number of quite different institutions and backgrounds and might or might not qualify for, or be interested in, a university faculty position. The salary was to be paid entirely from the PSEC budget, however, whether or not the individual chosen would perform some university duties such as teaching and committee work. In turn, the university was willing to guarantee continued employment should a person be selected for a tenured position and the partnership cease to operate. The position was established as an 11-month appointment likely to be attractive to both academics and experienced school administrators such as superintendents, since the individual ultimately chosen would also be working primarily with superintendents as peers and colleagues.

The broad, national advertising for the position and the attractive salary associated with it brought over 250 applications. As the screening process moved forward, certain differences between university culture and school-district culture emerged. University faculty are used to being deeply and personally involved in all elements of the review for appointment; school district administrators are accustomed to delegating initial stages of the hiring process to personnel specialists, and then entering the process at the time of decision and selection. Thus, misunderstanding developed when school administrators on the search committee asked personnel specialists from several districts to do some initial screening of candidates. This prescreening upset some faculty members who thought that the lack of university experience by the personnel specialists made them unqualified for their screening task.

Direct conversation among members of the search committee clarified the process which then moved forward according to criteria mutually agreed upon by the participating district and faculty members. The selection committee eventually identified a consensus candidate for executive director who had many years of experience as a faculty member in a graduate school of education and as a coordinator of collaborative work between universities and schools. The Coordinating Council of the PSEC, in turn, approved the appointment.

It was not known until the end of the search process, however, whether the person chosen by the PSEC as executive director, would receive a faculty appointment in the college as well. Only the faculty of the College of Education can recommend to the dean the appointment of a professor. Although professional educators are sometimes appointed to courtesy participation in university programs, instances of involving people from the field in the actual appointment processes of university professors are rare. Strong pressure for scholarly research productivity had been exerted on the College of Education faculty during the preceding years under an administrator appointed to strengthen the college. When one aspect of performance is being emphasized, less significance is often attached to others.

Thus, as the selection process moved forward, some faculty members concluded that their professional attention was being shifted again: collaboration, not research, seemed to be the new emphasis. Those who had just begun to adjust to the relatively new emphasis on research became concerned with what this change would mean for them. Faculty members active in earlier eras of closer association with the schools were hurt that their previous associations had been devalued by increased expectations for research; and although now that associations with schools were recognized as an important relationship for the college, they had not been included in this new, high-profile thrust.

Moreover, the recruitment process differed from the familiar search processes for faculty positions. Some faculty members resented the relatively high salary for the executive director, competitive among participating district superintendents, but higher than that of most College of Education faculty members. Coming as it did in the midst of a financial retrenchment at the college, and during a period of insignificant salary increases for college faculty, these faculty reactions were normal and predictable but they also opened old wounds and incurred new ones. In addition, PSEC activity was viewed as another instance of entrepreneurial initiative in an essentially conservative institution.

Early faculty resistance to a tenured, academic appointment for the executive director was defused through area meetings and numerous conversations with individual faculty members. Eventually, the faculty approved the new executive director's appointment. What could have been a major break between field and college became a unifying action.

## Agenda-Building and PSEC Activities

The recruitment of an executive director was an important activity for the PSEC Consortium during the 1985–1986 school year. More important, however, was building an agenda and developing specific activities. In addition to the previously described seminar activities, a series of task-force explorations designed to develop an agenda for the newly formed consortium was initiated under the leadership of the Executive Committee and an acting director. Nonetheless, given the amount of business associated with a new organization of this kind, as well as the managerial background of the Coordinating Council members, much of the first year's work was organizational and administrative. Several small group and executive committee meetings were devoted to assessing and evaluating consortium development and suggesting strategic assistance in its continual growth.

Most decisions, however, were choices acted upon rather than concepts explored, with one notable exception — the recurrent concern for setting a consortium agenda. After considerable discussion over several successive meetings, council members decided to develop six themes described in an original concept paper: professional preparation, continuing education, interorganizational exchange, collaborative research, technological exchange, and advocacy. The College of Education and each school district identified one person to serve on each of six task forces, co-chaired by Coordinating Council members. Task forces met regularly over a period of three months identifying issues of concern, possibilities for collaboration, and future directions, which were then shared at a spring "hearing," a culminating meeting of all task forces with the PSEC Coordinating Council. Seventy representatives from participating districts and the University of Washington met at this hearing to consider how the consortium might best use its time and resources.

At the conclusion of the event, the Coordinating Council agreed to support several major directions for the PSEC. In a subsequent meeting, council members approved a budget for funding specific, long-term efforts including such projects as an administrative leadership academy, an equity and excellence task force, an educational development center for experimentation in curriculum and instruction, and an educational finance study.

The approval of this budget and specific agenda took place just prior to the hiring of the new executive director, Ann Lieberman, formerly the director of the Metropolitan School Study Council (see Chapter 3). In other words, although the council members deliberately set out to recruit a strong leader who would serve both as an instigator of action and as a manager, they formed a fairly explicit agenda beforehand. One might predict the possible friction ahead. Indeed, the new executive director arrived with a high-priority item of her own, namely, expanding the base of leadership to include *teachers* as well as administrators. Shortly after her arrival, she involved representatives from several districts in a workshop involving science teaching with Bank Street College. On a larger scale, she initiated a full day, consortium-wide conference on teacher leadership, an activity which was well received by participants and supported by leaders in the state education association whom she had sought out in creating the conference. Thus, while she was taking risks with the Coordinating Council in that it had not formally approved the activity, her political experience was evident as she assured herself of sufficient support to carry off the activity.

Several major activities can be seen to characterize current PSEC efforts. First, continuing with the original theme of administrator leadership, a Leadership Academy has been designed with the expressed intent of bridging the proverbial gap between theory and practice. The academy program combines presentations of current educational research and theory with actual application of these concepts through peer observations and practical building-based activities. Most of the 250 academy enrollees are principals and assistant principals who are linked for site-based work and who are in a peer-coaching relationship to provide long-term collegial support among building administrators. Participants were able to choose from three strands of their work in the first year, specializing either in collaboration, visioning, or instructional leadership. The Leadership Academy is effectively establishing a network among school administrators for sharing ideas and developing professional collegiality. Administrators become resources for each other and together try out new strategies and discuss adaptation of ideas to particular building settings through nearly 30 collegial teams of five to seven principals each.

The normative alignment of college and district values is being developed in a research dimension of the academy, linked to these training programs. A cadre of principals, some identified by collegial team facilitators, others by using criteria developed in the effective schools project in Seattle, are brought together from throughout the Pacific Northwest. Not only do the principals serve as a subject pool for studying exemplary practice, but through the academy they are available to other administrators as role models and practical mentors. Principals are being provided with specially tailored opportunities for professional development, even as they are serving as visible examples of administrative success. Presumably, these same administrators will represent building leadership in creating the conditions for the schools we seek. The reshaping of administrative practice is being developed in the Leadership Academy, then, as an explicit strategy for change.

A second direction being pursued is support for a large task force on equity and excellence, incorporating the previous data-collection task force and highlighting the PSEC's commitment to equity and excellence in education. The current group of 30 educators — district and school administrators and teachers and university faculty — is struggling to identify indicators of quality and comprehensive ways to assess equality, to explore the implications of equity and excellence for curriculum and instruction, and to identify ways of providing leadership at all levels to achieve these ends.

Third, the PSEC has initiated a finance project, staffed by a former neighboring superintendent and a graduate-student assistant, to focus on adequate funding for quality education in public schools and higher education in the state. The project is responsible for reviewing funding formulas, analyzing any disparities between districts in their support and expenditures, and meeting with educational funding experts to document the need for more ample financial support and to suggest ways to improve educational funding. The project is also charged with building the cooperation needed among groups in the state whose influence is required to develop acceptable solutions to funding problems.

For example, a State Department of Education report to the State Board predicted no imminent teacher shortage in Washington. The PSEC's funding project staff reanalyzed the data and, with different assumptions and analytic techniques, found just the opposite: the state was due for a significant teacher shortage. The issue became how to handle, politically, the informed dissent. The Coordinating Council discussed several possibilities: a direct release to the media of the alternative interpretation, a formal rebuttal to the state office report and communication with the State Board, approaches to legislators and the governor's staff, as well as a low-key discussion with the report's authors. The last of these was seen as the best way to "flex the muscle" of this new entity, the PSEC. The subsequent discussion with state office personnel resulted in a mixed report to the State Board, taking into account the consortium research and alternative analysis. Thus, members of the Coordinating Council have had an opportunity to act together in ways other than merely shared administration of the partnership.

A fourth major and long-term investment of the PSEC is in the development of a demonstration center for curriculum and instruction for use in clinical training. Shaping a center for the pre-service and continuing education of teachers and administrators, of course, meets both district and college interests in exemplary training sites and well-prepared instructional staffs. The initial focus of the demonstration center's activities has been on creating specific projects concerned with interdisciplinary learning in heterogeneous classes and groups.

The College Board–sponsored Project Equality constitutes a fifth focus of the PSEC. In this activity, a group of secondary and postsecondary English teachers are engaged in an ongoing dialogue concerned with excellence, interinstitutional cooperation, and program collaboration. They have shared information about differences in district and departmental practice in teaching literature and writing, and they have examined projects that link schools and colleges in improving English instruction. Although these planning processes have been marked at times by indecisiveness, teachers are just now beginning to believe that decision-making has been decentralized and that they are being trusted to develop meaningful programs for their own use.

Finally, although there have been quiet and gradual pushes all along from within the PSEC to involve teachers — with some payoffs as noted above — the opportunities for genuine involvement during the first years of the Educational Leadership Seminar and the consortium have been few. However, as noted previously, the new executive director has made teacher leadership an explicit focus of consortium activities. Initially, a small group of PSEC teachers with two administrators were selected to work with the Bank Street interdisciplinary science education project in New York. Follow-up activities have since been conducted in the Seattle area involving a growing number of teachers. A large teacher leadership conference in the fall of 1986 signaled more intense activities: with a modest grant from a local foundation and some research assistance, information is now being collected on the various expanded roles that teachers currently play in the consortium districts, and follow-up conferences are being planned.

Much work lies ahead in broadening the base of leadership in schools; issues have yet to be resolved concerning selecting teacher leaders, releasing time and juggling daily class schedules, differentiating between the leadership responsibilities of teacher leaders and administrators, and so forth. Yet it is clear that a partnership that had its roots in a seminar for top-level administrators is now moving rapidly into developing leadership at all levels.

## Problems and Prospects

If partnership efforts of the type described here (and elsewhere in this book) were not problematic, they would likely be commonplace in educational improvement programs. Considering the variety of actors, human interests, and institutional cultures involved in the Puget Sound Educational Consortium, problems can be expected to surface in virtually all aspects of the collaborative endeavor: structure, funding, management styles, agenda setting, scheduling, involvement of university faculty and schoolteachers, mutual trust, and so forth. In the remaining pages, we will focus on a few of the more salient issues that have emerged in the relatively young life of this partnership.

### Structure, Style, and Agenda

Clearly, the PSEC was organized and presently functions in a fairly top-down, managerial fashion. This arrangement has provided considerable strength and solidarity to the partnership at both the university and district levels. On the other hand, the going has been difficult in terms of generating the involvement of large numbers of college faculty or teachers in partnership schools. Predictably, when the new executive director arrived on the scene, organizational structure, management style, and agenda setting became problematic issues.

The Coordinating Council had usually operated by applying practices typical to a formal organization. The council identified major areas of interest, appointed task forces that provided reports, analyzed the results of the task-force efforts, established priorities, and assigned budget support after work plans had been drawn for each of the new priority areas. By way of contrast, the new executive director began with a related agenda built around teacher leadership and mobilized grass roots support for this agenda before formal approval by the council.

Fortunately, the agendas are not hidden, nor are they incompatible. Currently, it is possible to observe both methods of setting priorities. We anticipate more open lines of communication between the Coordinating Council and the executive director as well as a continuation of the broad-based agendas for developing leadership at all levels of schooling.

### When Is Enough Money Too Much?

A question closely related to agenda building for the PSEC is the determination of how much funding should be used to support the management and activities of the effort. Some participants are concerned that a budget of $100,000 to $250,000, while substantial in comparison with similar school-university partnerships, pales against the staff development budgets of many of the school districts involved in the consortium. They note that even this amount will not go far if there are not substantial additional contributions. Since there already has been a significant financial contribution, there may be an unwillingness to make greater contributions later. Moreover, concern is expressed about whether the superintendents who have made the commitment of funding to the PSEC would be compelled by the size of their commitment to push for hasty action in order to "get a score on the board." It is hypothesized that this investment may lead them to call for short-term, quick-fix activities instead of the deliberate, analytical, and nurturing activities that are a requisite for real and lasting change.

Others take a different view of the funding commitment of the PSEC. They observe that the total funding allocated by each of the districts to the consortium is quite small in relation to the overall budgets of the participants. It is unlikely that any school district is driven to major courses of action by a need to account for $18,000 to $20,000 in budgets that range from $50,000,000 to $150,000,000. They argue it is more likely that the concerted drive for immediate action on the part of some members reflects some of the characteristics of the culture of public schools in contrast to the characteristics of the more reflective university setting.

Since not all the superintendents seem to be calling for quick fixes, the matter may simply reflect the personalities of some of the members of the Coordinating Council, being, therefore, neither a reflection of the culture of the school systems nor a consequence of the budgetary strategy of the PSEC. The basic argument that led to the commitment of funding on the part of each of the participants of the consortium was that if the participants really intended to try to accomplish something significant in the way of educational renewal, they ought to be willing to put their money where their mouths were. Thus far, the fiscal structure of the consortium has proved quite useful in supporting various activities and coordinating functions.

## Involvement and Rewards

Throughout the existing literature on school-university partnerships (see Chapter 2), one finds the issue being raised as to whether there can be sufficient rewards in these partnerships to attract both school and university faculty to collaborative activities. It is too early to make conclusive statements in this regard for the PSEC, although there are nearly a dozen faculty members from the University of Washington who have become involved in partnership activities and who view positively the potential for professional advancement through these efforts. The current dean, the provost, and the university president have all acknowledged, in various meetings involving consortium participants, that inquiry by faculty members working with the partnership needs to be recognized and legitimated on the same basis as is the more typical scholarly research of university professors. Nonetheless, many faculty continue to engage primarily in research that emulates the methodological and substantive subject matters of the academic disciplines, rather than creating and adapting methodologies appropriate to education itself. And of course, the reward system of the university and the culture of "publish or perish" is quite compatible with this behavior.

Recognition, involvement, and reward have been problematic as well for those in districts and schools. On the one hand, one need spend only a short time in any of the various seminars or conferences sponsored by the PSEC to know that the individual administrators or teachers have welcomed the opportunity to be selected and involved. On the other hand, there is little evidence that such participation has led directly to promotion or other kinds of recognition. For both university faculty and school and district educators, the issues of involvement and rewards are far from settled.

## Coordination, Time, Effort, and Responsibility

Given the magnitude of district participation in PSEC development, the leadership contributed by such an array of educators, and the capacity to invest in several directions simultaneously, it should not be surprising that consortium activities seem to have proliferated in the past twelve months. With this substantial activity, however, comes the appearance of multiple agendas due to diverse developmental directions, varying degrees of involvement, and a fragmentation of attention for the group as a whole.

Time—finding it and scheduling it—has become a common problem, particularly on the school and district side of the partnership. Planning programs, engaging in genuine dialogue, participating in multi-day activities, and undertaking renewal initiatives all require a tremendous amount of professional attention. More striking than the financial support of the consortium, perhaps, has been the commitment of personnel to its development. Literally hundreds of staff members—tens of thousands of staff-hours—have been given to consortium activities.

For all of this individual involvement, only a handful of "chief worriers" are actually responsible for attending to the collaboration as a whole. Several key university representatives meet irregularly and informally to assess progress in developing this new organization. The Executive Committee of the Coordinating Council has been delegated responsibility for negotiations with the executive director, approval of the PSEC agenda, and recommendations for funding priorities. Graduate-student assistants are assigned to particular project activities, and the executive director regularly brings project coordinators and assistants together to maintain a sense of common purpose and encourage cross-project communication. Again, it remains to be seen whether this interplay of tight and loose coupling in organization and coordination will serve well the guiding purposes of the consortium.

In Chapter 2, it was noted that a common figure in many successful partnerships was an individual whose ideas served as the central element in the evolution of the partnership. In the case studies that have preceded ours (Chapters 3 through 6), readers will find traces, if not outright examples, of the same phenomenon. The Puget Sound Educational Consortium has clearly benefited from the leadership of key figures since its inception. Notwithstanding the contributions of these idea champions, however, it can be argued that this partnership has gained its strength and momentum—historically and currently—from its broad base of governance and involvement. While some school-university partnerships may appear to be dependent on the energies of a single individual, this consortium appears to have spread leadership broadly enough so that its continuation probably will not be dependent on the continued participation of any single individual.

## Is There a Symbiotic Relationship?

We interpret Goodlad's argument for symbiosis in Chapter 1 not as a state to be reached, but as a condition to be approximated. There is ample evidence to suggest that the PSEC is making considerable progress in this direction. Indeed, the mutual satisfaction of self-interests can be seen for both the university and the schools.

The College of Education has received positive internal response from the university administration about the value of this link to K–12 education. The college is currently enjoying favorable recognition from legislators and staff in the governor's office who have noted its close relationship to the field. The college is also benefiting from the recruitment of strong graduate students to PSEC projects, thereby strengthening the quality of the pre-service preparation programs. School districts are benefiting from increased collegial exchange, from specific clinical activities for the continuing education of key administrators and teachers, and from opportunities to explore crucial ideas and issues that will shape the future of public schooling.

Yet, questions of benefit still remain: Can exemplary districts really influence the program of pre-service education of educators? Can clinical training sites in fact be developed that are closely aligned with course work and exemplify the best available knowledge for both district and college benefit? Can the PSEC challenge miseducation and redirect emphases toward equity and excellence? Can the partners even reach agreement on what constitutes equity and excellence? Clearly, many more extended exchanges are necessary.

From thinking together and working together for several years, the active members of the PSEC are developing increasing levels of trust and more open and candid discussions in shaping consortium development. Together, the participants are critically examining education. In an atmosphere of collegiality, they have agreed to work together to satisfy the self-interests of their separate spheres while tackling the tough educational problems that they have in common. To the extent that self-interest is rooted in the status quo and protected by time-honored ideas and techniques, however, the people involved will be limited in their ability to conceptualize alternatives and initiate change. How, then, can one challenge prevailing assumptions about current practice? The mutual self-interest in high-quality, equitable and accessible, relevant and responsive education is the common ground on which members hope to build a better educational foundation for the future.

What began as largely an involvement of central office administrators and faculty representatives has begun to evolve into a deeper partnership including many more educators in both the university and the schools. Some years ago, participants in another major school-university partnership were asked how much they valued their participation. They responded that they found the meetings of the partnership very stimulating, but they admitted that it would probably make little difference in the lives of their organizations if the partnership disappeared the next day. The challenge for the Puget Sound Educational Consortium is whether members will one day answer the same question the same way, or whether they can show a real difference in the preparation of educators and the renewal of the common schools in the greater Puget Sound area.

# Part III
# CONCERNS

# CHAPTER EIGHT

# The Meaning and Conduct of Inquiry in School-University Partnerships

KENNETH A. SIROTNIK

Even a cursory reading of the school-university partnerships (SUPs) reviewed in Part II should support the observation that "a SUP is not a SUP is not a SUP." Given the politics, personalities, extant relationships, and other features of the local context, there simply is no way of uniformly doing business when developing and sustaining significant relationships between schools and universities.

Similarly, it is clear that these SUPs are not (nor were they intended to be) *controlled* social experiments — that is, clearly defined social treatments or manipulations that are amenable presumably to traditional study using "objective" research and evaluation methods. Quite the contrary, these SUPs are evolving social experiments by people, in the context of their own work, ideologies, and interests, struggling with alternative ideas and organizational arrangements and activities for promoting collaboration between typically noncollaborative institutions. As I have argued elsewhere (Sirotnik, 1987), the traditional canons of research and evaluation are inadequate bases for an inquiry methodology under these kinds of conditions and circumstances.

The idea and practice of *collaborative inquiry* offers more promise. The phrase "collaborative inquiry" is intended to denote a process of self-study — of generating and acting upon knowledge, in context, by and for the people who use it. Knowledge will necessarily be developed through the use of quantitative, qualitative, and critical methods. Quantitative methods may include typical data-gathering techniques such as surveys, interviews, and observations wherein the data can be numerically coded and statistically analyzed. Qualitative methods include the variety of naturalistic/phenomenological approaches that ascertain knowledge through the interpretation of what is written, heard, and/or seen over the course of interviewing, observing, and reviewing archival documents. Critical methods are based upon conscious, systematic, and rigorous human discourse wherein (1) values, beliefs, interests, and ideologies in the educational setting are made explicit; (2)

the need for information is generated; and (3) actions are taken, critically reviewed, retaken, and so forth.

This process of collaborative inquiry can be seen as being at once descriptive, interpretive, judgmental, and decision- and action-oriented — all the ingredients of what many have referred to as evaluation, particularly formative evaluation. But the term *evaluation* carries with it a great deal of connotative baggage due to the climate created by the major, federally sponsored program evaluations begun in the early 1960s and the accountability movements in public education, generally. Much of this baggage is negative, conjuring up images of the "expert" (or handful of experts) judging the success or failure of individuals and programs based upon specified goals and outcome measures.

This negative connotation is the antithesis of the evaluative spirit intended by the principles and practices of collaborative inquiry, particularly in school-university partnerships. We have seen in the previous chapters that the very concept and assumptions of SUPs suggest a group of people struggling to overcome historically intractable interinstitutional relationships by using structures and processes based upon trust, communication, collaboration, reflection, and commitment to ongoing organizational and interorganizational improvement. The luxury of being able to inquire systematically — along with others in the same boat — into what is going on in the partnership and how to do it better should be embraced, not feared, by all involved. It is in this sense that the terms *evaluation* or *evaluative* will be used in this chapter.

In the next section, I present a brief interpretation of the history of program evaluation, with a particular focus of shifting "worldviews" on what constitutes appropriate research and evaluation theory and practice. Here, I argue for an emerging worldview that accommodates both research and evaluation under the rubric of collaborative inquiry. In the sections that follow, I explore the operational implications of collaborative inquiry — what it means to *do* it in real-life SUPs. This exploration is possible only if rooted in the actual principles and procedures of a given SUP effort. By way of example, therefore, I will use the partnership philosophy of the National Network for Educational Renewal (discussed at length in Chapter 1) and trace through the implications for collaborative inquiry in SUPs that make commitments and efforts in this direction.

## Historical Background and Emerging Concepts and Practice

The theory and practice of program evaluation have undergone several transformations — even paradigm shifts — over the last two decades or so. At its inception in the early 1960s on the heels of major federally funded program interventions, program evaluation was conceptualized as evaluation research conforming to the canons of traditional scientific method and good experimental design. "Program" was identified as a treatment or independent variable (i.e., program group versus control and/or other alternative program group[s]); based upon conceptual/ theoretical considerations of the program, hypotheses were deduced regarding expected programmatic outcomes; these outcomes were operationalized in measurable, quantitative terms; and data were collected, analyzed, and interpreted accordingly.[1]

But the world of social and behavioral research does not always conform neatly to this paradigm, especially when treatment variables are social or educational in nature and programs are implemented in nonlaboratory, field settings. Thus, programmatic contrasts with control groups (or other programs) were not always possible or feasible, nor was the random assignment of clients to alternative programs. In the face of mounting threats to the validity of causal interpretations and the generalizability of evaluation findings, quasi-experimental research designs were developed and advocated.[2]

Threats to the internal and external validity of evaluation research designs, however, were just technical glitches on the tip of an iceberg of messiness in the real world of planned social intervention. The idea that pre-post comparisons of a summative nature could enlighten action-oriented understandings of programmatic successes and failures began to give way to a more process-based and formative approach to evaluating program interventions.[3] Evaluators such as Stufflebeam et al. (1971) operationalized this shift in perspective by adapting a systems approach to the levels of decision making that occur over the course of the program intervention: needs assessment, program design, implementation process, and outcome analysis. This shift in perspective, however, still maintained a rather strong commitment to an objective, linear, input-process-output conception of program evaluation, as well as to essentially quantitative methods for assessing program impact.

The above evaluation research approaches are all rooted in classical scientific methodology or what has often been labeled as the empirical analytic tradition. In this tradition, knowledge is produced through the analytical associations between quantitatively measured variables that

1. For representative readings in this general evaluative tradition, see Boruch and Riecken (1975); Rossi and Freeman (1982); and Suchman (1967).
2. See the seminal work of Campbell and Stanley (1963) and, more recently, the work of Cook and Campbell (1979).
3. For example, see the discussions by Scriven (1967) and Stake (1967).

are presumed to operationalize theoretical constructs. Many, however, argue that analytically derived explanations alone provide little *understanding* of either the variables involved or the context in which they are being studied.[4]

For example, positive correlations between quantitative indices of "principal leadership" and average "student achievement" have been demonstrated in studies of school effectiveness. But what is principal leadership? Is it constant from setting to setting, or does it manifest itself differently depending upon contextual circumstances? Based upon knowledge of this type, for example, how do building-level administrators go about developing principal leadership? Do they try to change their behavior in accordance with images suggested by favorable responses to teacher survey items measuring principal leadership? Or, must building-level administrators begin to understand leadership as a complex array of interactions between different people, in different settings, during different times, and if this is true, what are the implications for developing leadership in a particular place, with particular people, during a particular time? Moreover, is the usual success criterion of student achievement (typically operationalized by scores on standardized tests) the same as student learning? The point here is that the correlation between $X$ and $Y$ is certainly a crude indicator of something, but understanding the nature of that something in the context of its occurrence requires considerably more in the way of inquiry.[5]

Those people who seek such understanding tend to gravitate more toward a distinctly different philosophical tradition of inquiry: phenomenology. This tradition gives rise to a number of similar (but not identical) naturalistic (mostly qualitative) methods of study such as ethnography, case study, and participant observation. In all these approaches, the central tenet is the grounding of understandings through long-term, firsthand experience with the phenomena under study: the situational context, the events, behaviors and activities, and the perceptions of people, including both the participants and observers (or observer-participants). Seeking insights into the questions posed above regarding leadership and student learning in schools, qualitatively oriented researchers would be inclined to "hang around" in schools (and their districts) for significant periods of time, to become part of the "woof and

---

4. A beginning list of critical readings suggesting alternative methodologies includes Blumer (1969); Cicourel (1964); Ericson and Ellett (1982); and Glaser and Strauss (1967).
5. An excellent discussion regarding the importance of contextual understanding can be found in Mishler (1979). Related discussions can be found in the work of Bronfenbrenner (1976); Goodlad (1975); and Sarason (1971).

warp" or the cultural regularities (Sarason, 1971) of these places. Through in-depth observation, interview, document/archival review, and the like, constructs such as leadership and student learning would be both recognized and understood as part of the entire tapestry of schooling.

It is not surprising, therefore, that the community of evaluation researchers developed a smaller but vocal contingent of advocates for more naturalistic methods of program evaluation.[6] The evaluators tended to be more concerned with understanding program goals and objectives as mutable constructs that are met in different degrees, in differing ways, at different times, with different program participants over the developmental course of the program.[7] Moreover, these understandings could not only be useful for general evaluative purposes, they could be used to inform the evolution of the program itself. This latter possibility, of course, represents a distinct shift in perspective from evaluation, not only as description and judgment but also as formative, action-oriented, critical inquiry (see below) and program renewal.

The nature of the program, therefore, can be seen to interact profoundly with the paradigmatic direction(s) taken by evaluators of the program. Highly structured, packaged program interventions with standardized, outcome-based implementation and assessment strategies may be reasonably consonant with the more empirical analytic evaluation approaches. Programmatic ideas resting on reasonably firm conceptual ground but, nevertheless, with fluid and emerging developmental processes will demand a more phenomenological perspective for evaluation and will profit greatly from an action-oriented, formative inquiry as an intrinsic part of the program itself. In this case, the program participants themselves are often in the best position to be constructive program evaluators. This is especially the case when evaluation is being conducted for internal program improvement and not as an accountability exercise demanded by external, controlling agencies.

---

6. Some examples are: Guba and Lincoln (1981); Patton (1980); Stake (1978); and Willis (1978).

7. Highly relevant to these changes in evaluation philosophy were corresponding shifts in organizational theory, particularly those viewing schools and universities as ambiguous, loosely coupled institutions (March & Olsen, 1976; Meyer & Rowan, 1978; Weick, 1976). The relevance, of course, becomes immediately apparent when one realizes that one's evaluative focus, the "program," must become institutionalized in order to be studied. For those who have worked in and/or spent considerable time with educational institutions, March's (1972, pp. 426–427) "playful" suggestions for reconceptualizing evaluation were most welcome, treating "goals as hypotheses . . . intuition as real . . . hypocrisy as a transition . . . memory as an enemy . . . [and] experience as a theory."

This shift toward nontrivial and participatory involvement of stake-holders in their own evaluative inquiries enjoys empirical support based on a parallel shift in methodological perspective found in research and development more generally. I am referring here to the movement away from research conducted *on* schools (and school staff) by outside re-searchers with their own agenda to research conducted by and with researchers and practitioners on a common agenda. This movement, rooted in the "action research" models introduced in the early 1940s (see, for example, Chein, Cook, & Harding, 1948) is well documented in the recent review by Tikunoff and Ward (1983) and the details will not be repeated here. However, the essential or ideal characteristics defining the emerging paradigms of "interactive" or "collaborative re-search," as summarized by these authors, should be noted:

> (1) researchers and practitioners work together at all phases of the inquiry process; (2) the research effort focuses on "real world" as well as theoretical problems; (3) mutual growth and respect occur among all participants; and (4) attention is given to both research and implementation issues from the beginning of the inquiry process. (p. 466)

The trend toward empowering educators — whether they are based in universities or in schools — to participate fully in the inquiry process should be clear in these characteristics of collaborative research. Else-where (Oakes, Hare, & Sirotnik, 1986) we have pushed the collab-orative research paradigm toward making explicit and operational the democratic features of participation and the more formative and phe-nomenological features of ongoing inquiry in the context of practice. In this chapter the paradigm is being pushed to its logical conclusion by making explicit and operational the inevitable evaluative nature of re-search in action in social settings.

We are talking, after all, not about decontextualized experiments (in the strict sense of the term) in laboratory or even quasi-laboratory conditions. Rather, we are talking about people joining together in the context of real working conditions to engage in ongoing experimenta-tion (in the loose sense of the term) with alternative ideas and the expressed intent of *improving* educational practice. Clearly, these people will necessarily confront the task of appraising the enterprises within which they are heavy stakeholders. It therefore becomes equally clear that values and human interests will bear heavily upon the process.

Given the root meaning of the term, it seems rather redundant to point out that evaluation is a *valuing* activity. Yet, it is only recently that a second major paradigmatic shift away from traditional method has received more than passing attention by concerned educators — namely, the recognition that evaluation in principle and practice is a process of critical inquiry.[8] The term *critical* is being used here in its constructive and positive sense in the same way that critical thinking has been advocated (at least in formal curriculum documents) as a valued goal for student learning. In this view, getting out the value of (*e*-valuating) a given phenomenon is the equivalent of producing and using *critical knowledge*: the consciousness raising and enlightenment gained through reflection on, and critique of, existing knowledge.

An emerging evaluative philosophy and practice, then, particularly well suited to dynamic and evolving school-university partnerships, rests on the notion of evaluation as the process of generating knowledge, by and for people who use it, enlightened by experiential data (both quantitative and qualitative), so long as a critical perspective is maintained throughout the process. I have briefly described this process as "collaborative inquiry" at the outset of this chapter, and I will do so again more specifically in the following section.

## Making Inquiry Critical: Collaborative Inquiry in Action

The "teeth" of collaborative inquiry are the act of making it critical — that is, the act of people confronting descriptive information and the knowledge they derive from it with the values base driving their programmatic efforts. It is for this reason that the assumptions, beliefs, and agenda forming the foundation of partnership efforts must, at every opportunity, be made as explicit as possible. This reservoir of values forms the basis for critique; moreover, the values are themselves subject to critique.

The process of making inquiry critical can be conveniently represented by a set of interdependent generic questions that guide the discourse between the stakeholders of a collaborative inquiry. These questions are:

- What is going on in the name of $X$?
- How did it come to be that way?
- Whose interests are (and are not) being served by the way things are?

---

8. Relevant positions have been outlined by writers such as Apple (1974); Coomer (1986); House (1977); Karier (1974); and MacDonald (1976).

- What information and knowledge do we have—or need to get—that bear upon the issues? (Get it and continue the discourse.)
- Is this the way we want things to be?
- What are we going to do about all this? (Get on with it.)

$X$ is a placeholder for the issue(s) in question. Examples are: school-university relationships; selection, education, and placement of educators; educational goals and schooling functions; curricular and instructional issues like integrating subject matter, the use of time, tracking students, testing students; organizational practices like leadership, decision making, communication, staff involvement; programmatic issues like gifted classes, remedial tutoring, marginal students; and so on.

I must emphasize that the above half-dozen questions are not just another organizational development (OD) kind of exercise in "needs assessment," "prioritizing," and the like. They are not capable of being "boxed and arrowed" in a linear flowchart. All of these questions can be relevant (and usually are) at any time during the collaborative (and critical) inquiry. The questions must be thought of as heuristics—much as probes are used in structured interviews—designed to keep the inquiry alive and productive. The first two questions are intended to remind participants that problems have a current and historical context, and that they must be situated in these contexts in order to be understood. The third question demands of participants that they confront (constructively) the political reality of significant educational issues, that they recognize and contend with embedded values and human interests. The fourth question demands of participants that the inquiry be informed, that knowledge of all types be brought to bear upon the issues. Finally, the last two questions are intended to remind participants that all is not talk; that, notwithstanding the omnipresent ambiguity in educational organizations, actions can and must be taken, reviewed, revised, retaken, and so forth.

Clearly, at the heart of collaborative inquiry is the willingness and ability of people to engage in competent discourse and communication. This is no mean undertaking, especially within and between places called schools, school districts, universities, and schools, colleges, or departments of education. Strong leadership that empowers rather than disenfranchises participants is required, as is leadership that can effectively facilitate group processes. Much work has been done in the area of group facilitation, and it will not be reviewed here. But I emphasize again that we are not talking about OD kinds of games that can be packaged and played out by some high-priced organizational consultant. We are talking about rigorous and sustained discourse wherein people have a good chance of being understood and trust one another as being sincere in their intentions; the discussion is infused with knowledge of all types, and values and human interests are legitimate issues in the dialogue. To come close to this kind of conversation, people must have real opportunities to enter into the discourse and challenge constructively what others have to say and the basis on which they say it; to say how they feel and what their own beliefs, values, and interests are; and to participate equally in controlling the discussion.[9]

How might this process unfold in partnership activities between schools and universities? I can only suggest some possibilities, based, in part, on experiences with several of the partnerships described in previous chapters. To do so, I will need to start with a case in point, with the working principles, structure, processes, and agenda of a school-university partnership. Then I will suggest some of the information likely to be useful as a catalyst for collaborative inquiry. Finally, I will simulate the kind of dialectic that needs to take place around the critical questions suggested by what the SUP professes to be about.

## School-University Partnership Commitments

No human effort is without initial concepts and driving assumptions that direct at least the beginnings of the endeavor. Traditional "evaluators" would have us specify goals and objectives in operational terms so that specific outcomes can be measured and, thereby, the program appraised. Others who have experienced the real worlds of organizations (especially of educational organizations) realize the messy and often ambiguous nature of such places. It is more common, in fact, for interesting goals to emerge from human activity rather than to direct these activities in the first place (Clark, 1980).

The trick, then, is to be explicit regarding the philosophy of any organizational or interorganizational effort (such as SUPs) while at the same time being open to modification and revision of initial assumptions. At any point in time, however, the operating philosophy will serve as an evaluative (in the sense we have come to use this term) screen by which people must judge their own efforts.

The easiest way to proceed for the purposes of this presentation is to

---

9. These principles of communicative competence come directly from the work of Habermas (1979). The work of Freire (1973) is equally relevant. The contributions of each of these authors has been integrated into an "epistemology of change" for school renewal by Sirotnik and Oakes (1986).

build upon the clear agenda set forth for SUPs by Goodlad in Chapter 1. This agenda, replete with suggested structures, processes, and substantive issues, is quite clear regarding the underlying philosophy of the partnership. I will briefly summarize these features first so as to make clear the connections with what will follow.

## Structural Considerations

Somehow SUPs have to have a way of doing business, of seeing to it that people get beyond the symbols of interinstitutional association and into actual activities designed to deal with fundamental educational issues. Structural features proposed by Goodlad can be summarized as follows:

- Recognizable and viable structures for making decisions, allocating resources, proposing and developing projects, keeping track of activities, etc.
- Organizational arrangements for addressing and doing something about significant educational problems with coordination between and within all levels of the partnership.
- Channels for the timely sharing of information and knowledge between and within all levels of the partnership.
- Mechanisms for the regular and systematic conduct of collaborative inquiry, including documentation of partnership activities and the collection, analysis, and interpretation of relevant information.

## Process

Consistent with these structural considerations and with the collaborative principles underlying SUPs, Goodlad has discussed a number of issues pertaining to the ways in which people engage one another in constructive, problem-solving behaviors. These process issues can be boiled down to the following five interrelated clusters within which many of the partnership beliefs and values can be seen to be embedded.

PARTNERSHIP. Districts, schools, and universities will work closely together with one another as equal partners towards satisfying mutually beneficial self-interests. Successful partnerships have at least three essential characteristics: (1) a moderate degree of dissimilarity between or among partners, (2) the potential for the mutual satisfaction of self-interests, and (3) sufficient selflessness on the part of each partner to assure the satisfaction of self-interests by all involved. Schools and universities can be seen to possess the first two characteristics. It is up to the members of the partnership to maximize the potential for maintaining the third ingredient of a successful, *symbiotic* relationship.

COMMUNICATION.   Partnerships must develop the means for efficient and effective sharing of information and knowledge produced by its members and/or coming from other sources. Districts, schools, and universities in collaboration for the improvement of schooling and education must maintain a commitment to quality information and knowledge *in context* — that is, in terms of relevant historical, current, and projected social, political, and economic circumstances and conditions at local, state, national, and international levels.

LEADERSHIP.   Leaders at all levels of the educational enterprise must possess, endorse, and communicate a clear, coherent set of fundamental educational values to which all participants in the enterprise can be committed. This set must be small enough to maximize near consensus of endorsement and yet permit maximum flexibility for local initiative and creative response. Leaders, therefore, must be willing and able to empower others with the necessary resources (e.g., time) and autonomy for inquiry and school renewal.

RENEWAL.   Although direction and support from all educational levels is necessary, the school is ultimately where students are taught and is, therefore, the primary unit of educational change. But educational change does not appear to come about and be sustained through intervention and installation techniques. Rather, it appears to require the ongoing involvement of the significant persons most affected by change (e.g., teachers, administrators, parents, students) in the development of innovative activities. Resources and time, therefore, must be provided at the building level for meaningful dialogue, decision making, action taking, and evaluation — in short, for the ongoing process of inquiry and school renewal.

ACCOUNTABILITY.   Accountability is best understood and acted upon as a system of shared responsibilities wisely distributed over the organizational pyramid of educational leadership. Clearly, the largest power base is at the bottom of this pyramid at the building level, including principals, teachers, students, and parents. Given the school as the unit of change, wisely distributed responsibility consists, in significant part, of providing the leadership and resources necessary for staff inquiry and renewal activities in schools.

*Substance*

The recent major studies of schooling have once again identified the same crucial set of problems that seem to recur over the history of the American educational "experiment" to provide a common education for all the nation's youth. In Chapter 1, Goodlad expresses his belief that these problems, although appearing intractable, can be significantly improved through genuine collaborative effort between concerned educators across relevant institutions. For our purposes here, we can take several thrusts of Goodlad's substantive agenda as exemplary problems around which the work of a SUP might be organized:

- Reconsidering what public schools are for and the implications for excellence in teaching and learning;
- Providing equal access to educational excellence for all students;
- Assuring long-term opportunities for educators to participate significantly in their own school improvement efforts;
- Reconstructing the education of educators in line with the above three issues.

*Fundamental Values and Educational Beliefs*

Implicit and explicit in the above arrays of structural, process, and substantive features are "shoulds," "oughts," and "musts," and assumptions of what might constitute better educational and schooling practices. Consistent with the argument here for collaborative inquiry, it is this body of values and beliefs that must be addressed critically in view of the commitments made by a school-university partnership effort.

In the structural array, for example, are values and beliefs pertaining to minimizing bureaucratic entanglements, maximizing understanding and communication among all stakeholders, recognizing and acting upon the need for organizational interdependency, and recognizing and acting upon the obligation to leave empirical and critical records of organizational activity.

The process summaries are explicitly organized around the values and beliefs under the rubrics of partnership, communication, leadership, renewal, and accountability. Here, for example, we see commitments to participatory democracy and collaborative activity both within and between organizations (districts, schools, universities, colleges within universities), responsible leadership that empowers stakeholders, and reflective practice at all educational levels.

Finally, implicit throughout the substantive agenda are values and beliefs pertaining to maximizing both educational equity and excellence in the education of public school students as well as in the education of those educators who are responsible for these young people. *Equity*, in this context, implies a commitment to excellent education for all students regardless of race, ethnicity, gender, family income, religion, eye color, or any other extraneous variable. *Excellence*, in turn, is taken to signify an operational commitment to the best that our knowledge base has to offer regarding teaching and learning *and* to the provision of the time necessary for reflective practice vis-à-vis this body of knowledge.

In sum, the specifics of the structures, processes, and substantive issues may differ from place to place, but the commitment to working through the implications of the underlying values and educational beliefs is expected to be common to all SUPs. Given this conception of a school-university partnership, then, it remains to sketch out what might go on in the process of collaborative inquiry. In so doing, I will focus on the two main aspects of the process: informing the inquiry and making it critical.

## Documenting and Describing Partnership Efforts

Pervasive throughout the foregoing discussion is the commitment to collaboration between responsible educators empowered to engage in reflective and transformative practice. This suggests at once both the primary process and a primary focus of collaborative inquiry; it suggests that partnership members be active participants in their own evaluation process, that the process be formative, and that the process itself be continually subjected to critical appraisal.

A high degree of awareness is required, therefore, regarding *what* is going on and *how* it is going on. This suggests the need to document and describe the structures, processes, and activities of partnerships: to trace the circumstances and conditions of partnerships as they develop and, it is hoped, as they move toward increased stability and productivity. This descriptive part of the evaluative endeavor is, by and large, what will inform an evaluative discourse (see below).

Documenting and describing the conditions and circumstances, the events and activities, and the attitudes and sentiments of participants require a sensitivity to information and a rigorous and systematic effort to collect, organize, and maintain an archive of this information. To be sure, some of this information must be deliberately created through surveys, interviews, and the like. Much of the valuable information, however, is (or should be) routinely generated via meeting minutes, task-group summaries, position papers, activity analyses, and so forth.

The following list is based primarily on only one five-year experience, namely with the partnership described in Chapter 5. As such, the list is intended to be a working outline to be modified and adapted by any given SUP effort as appropriate. With this in mind, the contents of an ongoing process-tracing and information system might include:

1.  Letters of agreement between SUP members (districts, county offices, universities/colleges) and/or other formal documents detailing the by-laws and mission of the SUP plus any updates or revisions of these agreements.
2.  Minutes of all the meetings of the governing structure for the SUP, i.e., the body of persons responsible for taking care of business with respect to general partnership issues.
3.  Operating budget as projected and as encumbered.
4.  Annotated bibliography of all reports, monographs, articles, transcribed speeches, etc. relating to and/or supported (all or in part) by the SUP. (Include actual copies of each document as well.)
5.  Set of all newsletters or newsletter type of communication documents.
6.  Calendar of all SUP-related activities, meetings, events, etc., including sponsorship and attendees.
7.  Annotated documentation of all significant educational events or activities relating to and/or supported (all or in part) by the SUP (e.g., ongoing projects, teacher workshops, task forces, principal leadership groups, school-university staff retreats, public forums, etc.). This documentation should include, at minimum, the minutes and substantive and interpretive summaries of these events or activities, detailing purposes, processes, and outcomes.
8.  Annotated list of unanticipated consequences of SUP efforts (e.g., development of a cooperative learning network, receiving additional funding from private or public agency, influencing local and/or state policy in schooling and/or the education of educators).
9.  Results of periodic evaluative survey and interview questionnaires ascertaining significant persons' perceptions[10] of what happened in the name of the SUP, what is happening, issues/problems, suc-

---

10. Significant persons would include the school district staff (e.g., superintendent, assistant superintendents, specialists), building-level staff (e.g., administrators, teachers, counselors, specialists), college/university staff (e.g., faculty, deans, involved students), administrative staff of the SUP, and participating community members (e.g., parents, school board members, nonformal and informal education agencies). Based on the literature reviewed in Chapter 2, only a few sources were found with explicit instrumentation for data gathering purposes. See, for example, Comer (1981) and Devaney (1982). Also, useful survey and interview questions can be deduced from the lists of issues and problems raised by Haberman (1971) and Hathaway (1985).

cesses/failures, future possibilities/directions, and so forth, with particular emphasis on the district/school-university/college collaboration. Is it really a partnership? If so, how? If not, why not? What needs to be done to further approach the ideal concept? Who is involved besides the superintendents, dean, and executive director? — administrators, teachers, faculty — and to what extent?

10. Journal/diary type of entry of critical incidents, events, activities, etc. that can support emerging understandings of school-university partnership dynamics (e.g., role of the "executive director," involving faculty, involving teachers and administrators, dealing with bureaucratic structures, etc.). Such journals could be kept by the executive director and any other "chief worrier" involved in significant, long-term work with partnership activities.

11. Yearly progress report (based upon the above information) describing the philosophy of the given SUP and the events and activities of the year, including pitfalls, problems, and possibilities in a form that best suits the conceptual and developmental features of the particular SUP effort.

Again, the items in this outline are intended as examples only. Each SUP will likely develop its own system of process tracing/documentation. Depending upon the resources available, some will be able to devote considerable effort to detailed data gathering in the form of ongoing interview, case study, survey, and other methodologies. Other SUPs may have to engage in more modest approaches. In all cases, however, it is expected that a sufficient commitment would be made to documentation and interpretation so that a reasonable reconstruction of the partnership experience could be shared with others. I will note only in passing that the descriptive analysis and interpretation of these materials can be quite rigorous and formal or less systematic and informal, depending upon the resources available and the specific uses of the information (e.g., research publication versus a descriptive summary for a group discussion). Many sources are available that outline ways to deal with survey and interview data and the content analysis of documents, field notes, and the like.[11]

At minimum, it would seem that a SUP would need to designate a "chief worrier" who would be responsible for seeing to it that the collabo-

---

11. Useful sources to consult for ideas on analyzing and displaying quantitative and qualitative data include Krippendorff (1980); Lofland and Lofland (1984); Miles and Huberman (1984); Schatzman and Strauss (1973); Sirotnik and Burstein (1987); and Tufte (1983).

rative inquiry process is carried out to the fullest, given the available resources. Ideally, this would be a half- to a full-time position. This person would need to become aware of, and often become intimately involved with, the structures, processes, and substantive activities going on in the SUP. It would be this person's responsibility to make sure that critical questions get generated, that quantitative and qualitative data are collected, that crucial documents are prepared and archived, and that interpretive summaries and progress reports get written. Depending upon the size of the SUP, the chief worrier may need a small staff consisting, for example, of one or two research assistants from the university and/or released staff from district offices; this, of course, implies a training function for the chief worrier as well. Whether the chief worrier function is embedded in the job description of existing SUP staff, taken on as a research project by university and/or district staff, or allocated through additional funding for new positions, it should be clear that this function represents real time and resources.

## Critically Examining Partnership Efforts

Earlier in this chapter, I proposed a set of six questions designed to generate and sustain a critical discourse aimed at actively improving collaborative efforts. The information suggested in the previous section is intended to act as a catalyst for ongoing inquiry guided by these questions; moreover, in reciprocal fashion, the discourse is intended to stimulate the need for relevant information. It is this dialectical process of continually questioning the knowledge accumulated over the experience of partnership activities that creates the "stuff" for evaluative activities, either for summative reports at any point in time or for formative inquiries to help promote change and improvement. Several examples, based upon partnerships as described above, should illustrate this process.

Consider, first, the *structural* features discussed above that SUPs might agree to work towards in reconfiguring relationships between schools and universities. Are task forces at work in developing substantive agenda that address significant educational problems? What is the composition of these groups? Are projects under way in the universities and the schools? Can the SUP governance structure bring university and school people together and fan sparks of substantive interest before they are blown out by bureaucratic red tape? Are there systematic procedures in place that promote the collaborative inquiry process suggested in this chapter? Is the SUP endeavoring to secure additional resources and funding both internally and externally? Are communication mechanisms in place for sharing information and experiences among members of the SUP (and with other members in other partnership efforts)? A careful examination of documents, especially those pertaining to budget and resource allocation, meeting minutes (with specific attention to who is in attendance), the general nature of formal agreements, and the character and range of participation in SUP activities, will inform a critical dialogue around the structures in place that facilitate/inhibit collaborative and productive relationships.

Second, consider the implications of the commitments made to the partnership *process* described above. Is there any evidence to suggest that a given school-university partnership is a functioning, symbiotic collaboration? Are districts, schools, and the university maintaining traditional boundaries (collaborating on paper and exchanging services in noblesse oblige fashion); or, are they each beginning to give up some turf, participate jointly in decisions around common interests, exchange staff and resources, bring pressures to bear as a consortium united around a common agenda for school and university improvement, etc.? How are issues brought to the attention of the members of the governing body and decisions made? Does the university control half the power, or is it one of $N$ (number of districts plus one) decision makers? To what extent are teachers, principals, and district staff involved in agenda-setting activities? Are they brought in every now and then in largely token needs assessment exercises; or, are they included routinely as valued participants in dialogue, decision making, action taking, and evaluation? How are educators involved in school improvement? Are results from educational research and school improvement technologies packaged and handed down to the staff at the building level; or, are "critical masses" of teachers and principals released and encouraged for significant periods of time to work collaboratively with district and university educators on crucial schooling issues in the context of educational practice? These questions (and a host of others) begin to suggest ways of sifting through the documents noted in the above list of information and of analyzing and interpreting additional data that might be gathered, particularly in surveys and interviews of the various constituencies in the partnership.

As a third example, consider the substantive agenda proposed for the consideration of SUPs, for example, the assurance of equal access of students to curricula. This is a good example of where critique will need to begin with the embedded belief system itself. What do we mean by *equitable*, and is that meaning compatible with what we mean by *excellence*? What are the competing interests in a meritocratic view of education versus a democratic perspective? What are the moral imperatives of a common education for all American children? Assuming that a SUP takes action on this agenda item, to what extent do partnership members make a concerted effort toward equal access? How are conventional (and pervasive) practices of sorting students—bluebirds and blackbirds at the elementary level, high and low tracks at the secondary level—reconceptualized and restructured? Is there any evidence of serious consideration of alternative ways to deal constructively with individual differences (e.g., cooperative learning strategies, peer tutoring, etc.)? Are vocational and career curricula oriented toward enriching the future lives of all students, or are they basically job preparation courses for the "academically untalented?" Again, the information above, particularly position papers, reports of projects in process, and task force summaries, would be most enlightening. Moreover, sustained critical discourse around these very issues should provoke the kind of grass-roots activities that can be further documented and interpreted.

Another substantive example, the education of educators, has the potential for generating an equally interesting body of discourse and activities. Implicit in these agenda items is the working assumption that nothing short of major reconceptualization and reconstruction of both teacher (and administrator) education in colleges and universities and the conditions and circumstances of educating in schools will suffice—unless we are content with the way things are and with tinkering here and there with educational features that leave matters mostly unchanged. Are the partnership council members taking a reconceptualist-reconstructionist position and considering and taking action on real alternative training configurations (e.g., key school training sites; tenured clinical staff in universities; long-term internship of trainees; fluid exchanges of staff members among districts, schools, and universities; collaborative research projects; etc.); or are members basically agreeing to agree on piecemeal alterations (e.g., raising admission standards, adding a year of training, changing the ratio of general to technical course requirements, instituting exit examinations, etc.)? Are school and university educators collaborating in a pedagogical curriculum that prepares educators for significantly altered school settings; or does the curriculum continue to socialize educators into the traditional regularities of schooling?

Again, these are merely examples of the kinds of questions that SUPs may wish to address. Many other bodies of equally crucial questions exist and may be the focus of SUP efforts. It may be useful, in fact, for each SUP periodically to generate the body of critical questions—in the structure, process, and substance domains—that it believes it will be addressing, share these questions within the partnership, and review and modify (if necessary) the list at least biannually with reference to what has actually taken place. The records of these kinds of inquiries, in the forms of position papers, discussion transcriptions, retreat summaries, and the like, will become important parts of the ongoing process-tracing system and will inform future analyses.

## Concluding Remarks

In this chapter, I have attempted to expand the boundaries of traditional educational research and evaluation concepts and practices with the express intent of developing a methodology more suitable for inquiry activities in school-university partnerships as described in Chapter 1. These partnerships can be seen as long-term, largely uncontrolled, social experiments involving multiple constituencies with diverse values, beliefs, and ideologies. Nonetheless, these constituencies profess a common commitment to some structural, process, and substantive ideas for improving public schooling through collaborative activities between the public schools and the colleges and universities preparing educators for these schools.

Based upon an argument that inquiry for social action is automatically evaluative, I have discussed both research and evaluation as a process of collaborative inquiry: a melding together of the principles and practices of interactive or collaborative research with an "epistemology of action" based upon critical inquiry. This is a process that demands the active and collaborative participation of all stakeholders in an ongoing inquiry wherein participants question current practices in light of extant knowledge and human interests, experiment with alternative ideas to improve current practice, and critically reflect upon their educational work in terms of the assumptions that guide their work and information that can describe that work.

I have no illusions that what has been described here as collaborative inquiry is a relatively easy and straightforward process. Those who have seriously invested their time and energy into activities of a related nature (e.g., Lieberman, 1986; Little, 1984; Oakes, Hare, & Sirotnik, 1986) know well the difficulties of making collaborative concepts practical in less than collaborative settings. But many who have made the investment have considered it well worth the effort.[12]

---

12. See, for example, the discussions in the February 1986 issue of *Educational Leadership*.

Clearly, the kinds of issues that partnerships are addressing are difficult educational concerns that have been with schools and universities for some time. For a school-university partnership to effect major educational reconstructions in a relatively short time frame, say five years, would be miraculous. For a SUP to make incremental and significant progress over this period of time would be remarkable; and documenting, informing, and stimulating that progress is what collaborative inquiry is all about. In the end, the inquiry participants should be satisfied from an evaluative standpoint if they have left a reasonably well-marked trail of trials and celebrations, successes and failures. This trail is not necessarily a trail for others to follow, but for others to scout as they proceed along the way of their own experiments with school-university partnerships.

## References

Apple, M. W. (1974). The process and ideology of valuing in educational settings. In M. W. Apple, M. J. Subkoviak, & H. S. Lufler (Eds.), *Educational evaluation: Analysis and responsibility*. Berkeley, CA: McCutchan.

Blumer, H. (1969). *Symbolic interactionism: Perspective and method*. Englewood Cliffs, NJ: Prentice-Hall.

Boruch, R. F., & Reicken, H. W. (Eds.). (1975). *Experimental testing of social policy*. Boulder, CO: Westview Press.

Bronfenbrenner, U. (1976). The experimental ecology of education. *Teachers College Record, 78*, 157–204.

Campbell, D. T., & Stanley, J. C. (1963). *Experimental and quasi-experimental designs for research*. Chicago: Rand McNally.

Chein, I., Cook, S. W., & Harding, J. (1948). The field of action research. *American Psychologist, 3*, 43–50.

Cicourel, A. V. (1964). *Method and measurement in sociology*. New York: The Free Press.

Clark, D. L. (1980). In consideration of goal-free planning: The failure of traditional planning systems in education. In D. L. Clark, S. McKibbin, & M. Malkas (Eds.), *New perspectives on planning in educational organizations*. San Francisco: Far West Laboratory for Educational Research and Development.

Comer, J. (1981). *Toward school improvement: A study of collaborative relationships between universities and public schools*. (Contract No. NIE-G80-0044). Washington, DC: National Institute of Education.

Cook, T. D., & Campbell, D. T. (1979). *Quasi-experimentation: Design and analysis issues for field settings*. Chicago: Rand McNally.

Coomer, D. L. (1986). Reformulating the evaluation process. In K. A. Sirotnik & J. Oakes (Eds.), *Critical perspectives on the organization and improvement of schooling*. Boston: Kluwer-Nijhoff.

Devaney, K. (1982). *Networking on purpose*. San Francisco: Far West Laboratory for Educational Research and Development.

Ericson, D. P., & Ellett, F. S. (1982). Interpretation, understanding, and educational research. *Teachers College Record, 83*, 497–513.

Freire, P. (1973). *Education for critical consciousness*. New York: Continuum (1982 reprint).

Glaser, B. G., & Strauss, A. L. (1967). *The discovery of grounded theory: Strategies for qualitative research*. Chicago: Aldine.

Goodlad, J. I. (1975). *The dynamics of educational change*. New York: McGraw-Hill.

Guba, E. G., & Lincoln, Y. S. (1981). *Effective evaluation*. San Francisco: Jossey-Bass.

Haberman, M. (1971). Twenty-three reasons why universities can't educate teachers. *Journal of Teacher Education, 22*, 133–140.

Habermas, J. (1979). *Communication and the evolution of society*. (Translated by T. McCarthy.) Boston: Beacon Press.

Hathaway, W. E. (1985). *Models of school-university collaboration: National and local perspectives on collaborations that work*. Paper presented at the Annual Conference of the American Educational Research Association, Chicago.

House, E. R. (1977). *The logic of evaluative argument*. Los Angeles: Center for the Study of Evaluation, University of California.

Karier, C. J. (1974). Ideology and evaluation: In quest of meritocracy. In M. W. Apple, M. J. Subkoviak, & H. S. Lufler (Eds.), *Educational evaluation: Analysis and responsibility*. Berkeley: McCutchan.

Krippendorff, K. (1980). *Content analysis: An introduction to its methodology*. Beverly Hills: Sage.

Lieberman, A. (1986). Collaborative work. *Educational Leadership, 43*, 4–8.

Little, J. W. (1984). Seductive images and organizational realities in professional development. *Teachers College Record, 86*, 84–102.

Lofland, J., & Lofland, L. H. (1984). *Analyzing social settings: A guide to qualitative observation and analysis*. Belmont, CA: Wadsworth.

MacDonald, B. (1976). Evaluation and the control of education. In D. Tawney (Ed.), *Curriculum Evaluation Today* (pp. 125–136). London: Macmillan Education.

March, J. G. (1972). Model bias in social action. *Review of Educational Research, 42*, 413–429.

March, J. G., & Olsen, J. P. (1976). *Ambiguity and choice in organizations*. Bergen, Norway: Universitetsforlaget.

Meyer, J. W., & Rowan, B. (1978). The structure of educational organizations. In M. W. Meyer (Ed.), *Environments and organizations*. San Francisco: Jossey-Bass.

Miles, M. B., & Huberman, A. M. (1984). *Qualitative data analysis: A sourcebook of new methods*. Beverly Hills: Sage.

Mischler, E. G. (1979). Meaning in context: Is there any other kind? *Harvard Educational Review, 49*, 1–19.

Oakes, J., Hare, S. E., & Sirotnik, K. A. (1986). Collaborative inquiry: A congenial paradigm in a cantankerous world. *Teachers College Record, 87*, 545–561.

Patton, M. Q. (1980). *Qualitative evaluation methods*. Beverly Hills: Sage.

Rossi, P. H., & Freeman, H. E. (1982). *Evaluation: A systematic approach*. Beverly Hills: Sage.

Sarason, S. B. (1971 and 1982). *The culture of the school and the problem of change*. Boston: Allyn and Bacon.

Schatzman, L., & Strauss, A. L. (1973). *Field research: Strategies for a natural sociology*. Englewood Cliffs, NJ: Prentice-Hall.

Scriven, M. (1967). The methodology of evaluation. In R. Tyler, R. Gagne, & M. Scriven (Eds.), *Perspectives of curriculum evaluation* (pp. 39–83). Chicago: Rand McNally.

Sirotnik, K. A. (1987). Evaluation in the ecology of schooling: The process of school renewal. In J. I. Goodlad (Ed.), *The ecology of school renewal*, 86th Yearbook of the National Society for the Study of Education, Part I. Chicago: University of Chicago Press.

Sirotnik, K. A., & Burstein, L. (1987). Making sense out of comprehensive school-based information systems: An exploratory study. In A. Bank, & R. C. Williams (Eds.), *Inventing the future: The development of educational information systems*. New York: Teachers College Press.

Sirotnik, K. A., & Oakes, J. (1986). Critical inquiry for school renewal: Liberating theory and practice. In K. A. Sirotnik & J. Oakes (Eds.), *Critical perspectives on the organization and improvement of schooling*. Boston: Kluwer-Nijhoff.

Stake, R. E. (1967). The countenance of educational evaluation. *Teachers College Record, 68*, 523–540.

Stake, R. E. (1978). The case study method in social inquiry. *Educational Researcher, 7*, 5–8.

Stufflebeam, D. L., Foley, W. J., Gephart, W. J., Guba, E. G., Hammond, R. I., Merriman, H. O., & Provus, M. M. (1971). *Educational evaluation and decision making*. Itasca, IL: F. E. Peacock.

Suchman, E. A. (1967). *Evaluative research: Principles and practices in public service and social action programs*. New York: Russell Sage Foundation.

Tikunoff, W. J., & Ward, B. A. (1983). Collaborative research on teaching. *The Elementary School Journal, 83*, 453–468.

Tufte, E. R. (1983). *The visual display of quantitative information*. Cheshire, CN: Graphics Press.

Weick, K. E. (1976). Educational organizations as loosely coupled systems. *Administrative Science Quarterly, 21*, 1–19.

Willis, G. (Ed.). (1978). *Qualitative evaluation*. Berkeley, CA: McCutchan.

# CHAPTER NINE

# Shared Problems and Shared Vision: Organic Collaboration

PHILLIP C. SCHLECHTY and BETTY LOU WHITFORD

As the preceding chapters demonstrate, collaborative arrangements between and among public schools and institutions of higher education have a long history and have taken a variety of forms. As these chapters also demonstrate, efforts to establish and maintain collaborative relationships are fraught with difficulties and frequently do not produce the intended effects. Yet, the idea persists that public schools and universities can and should collaborate. John Goodlad is clearly one of the most thoughtful and persistent advocates of collaboration. And, as this volume shows, there are many who share Goodlad's faith that if public schools and universities could somehow find more effective ways to work together, the quality of life in schools and universities would be enhanced, and the education received by children would be dramatically improved.

We count ourselves among the faithful. At the same time, our view of the problems and prospects of collaboration differ in degree, if not in kind, from the views set forth in most of the chapters in this volume. We agree that collaborative relationships can be formed on the basis of enlightened self-interest, and since this is the case, it is probably best to view these relationships as symbiotic. Our problem is that symbiotic relationships are inherently fragile, temporary, and even given to fickleness. Furthermore, symbiotic relationships call upon each party to spend considerable energy on attracting and holding an appropriate partner long enough to produce the desired effects. Pilot fish move from one shark to another, depending upon convenience, chance, and timing. The clown fish can choose any sea anemone that strikes its fancy. And, as the preceding chapters show, lack of permanence and stability is a continuing problem in educational symbiosis as well.

In our view, the cause of school reform would be much advanced if collaborative efforts moved from symbiotic relationships to organic relationships. In organic relationships, the parts fulfill unique functions, sometimes in a semi-autonomous fashion, but the purpose of these functions is to serve the body of the whole. Indeed, each part has a major investment in the survival of the whole because ill health of the body has potentially devastating effects on each of the separate parts. Thus, unlike symbiotic relationships, which emphasize mutual self-interest, organic relationships stress the common good above all else. Certainly, common interests are not entirely absent in symbiotic collaboration between public schools and universities; but they are either assumed or are so implicit that their identification and nurturance are left largely to chance or to the heroic actions of individuals. In organic relationships, on the other hand, explicit attention to the identification and development of common interests would receive the institutional support necessary to sustain the collaboration.

We now address these issues in more detail. Symbiosis can be characterized by a primary emphasis on mutual self-interest. As a result, each party agrees to address one or more particular problems that are "owned" primarily by one or another party. The situation approximates, "I'll help you with your concerns, and you'll help me with mine." In contrast, organic relationships focus on concerns or problems which are mutually owned; they are *our* problems. As long as the concerns or problems are defined in the context of any one collaborating organization, however, it is exceedingly difficult, if not impossible, for all partners to the collaboration to own them jointly. This logic suggests that the problems to which collaboration is addressed must be boundary-spanning. That is, they must be problems that no party to the collaboration can solve alone or over which no party has an exclusive monopoly.

### The Professionalization of Teaching: A Boundary-Spanning Issue

Institutional renewal and personal renewal are goals worthy of pursuit. To argue that these goals could well be achieved by public schools or universities operating in isolation from each other would be foolish and wrongheaded. At the same time, renewal of public schools is of more direct concern to those in the public schools than to those in universities and vice versa. Thus, other than with a strong sense of noblesse oblige or a more pragmatic quest for a quid pro quo, institutional renewal and personal renewal provide a fragile basis around which to organize collaborative efforts between universities and public schools.

What is needed is a problem area that lies "between" universities and public schools rather than one which resides within one institution that the other somehow comes to share. And further, the boundary-spanning issue must be articulated and embodied in the explicit goals of each collaborating party. Our candidate for mutual territory in the wide-ranging field of the education reform movement is the professionalization of the teaching occupation. At present, a critical problem with professionalizing teaching is that key components of teacher education *are divided* among different agencies with interests that sometimes force competition. The problem is *not* with *how* they are divided or how the separate functions could come to be shared.

For example, institutions of higher education are under considerable pressure to raise admission standards to teacher education, make the preparation of teachers more rigorous and perhaps require more time, and certainly demand that those who enter teaching commit more energy to professional development than is now typically the case. However, unless the structure of schools and the conditions of the teaching occupation are dramatically improved, the likely consequence of a university response to these pressures is that student enrollment in teacher education will decline. Moreover, unless invited to do so, universities have no legitimate right to intervene in the restructuring of schools, and public school personnel have no legitimate right to set university admission standards. In the long run, however, the conditions characterizing the structure of schools and the teaching occupation affect a university's ability to attract teacher education students, just as the quality of students the university makes available to the schools affects the schools' long-term capacity for self-renewal.

Put differently, in the areas of the recruitment, selection, preparation, and continuing development of public school personnel, universities and public schools are not independent agencies that could better achieve their tasks if they understood their mutual self-interests. They are interdependent agencies that could better serve the public if they concentrated on a common agenda. Serving the common good rather than self-interest should be the unifying theme around which collaborative efforts between universities and public schools are organized. At present, we believe that this common good is best served by concentrating on the renewal of the teaching occupation through the professionalization of teaching.

## On the Division of Responsibility and Authority

All occupations, especially those that aspire to professional status, must attend to several important social functions if they are to be successful in establishing and maintaining themselves. Among the more important of these are knowledge generation and codification, recruitment and selection, knowledge transmission, norm enforcement, and motivation. Generally speaking, in fully developed professions, these functions are unified and under the control of the occupational group (usually through professional organizations). This is not so in teaching. Rather, numerous agencies, groups, and organizations struggle to control each of these functions. For example, the American Association of Colleges for Teacher Education (AACTE) claims to speak for the unified interest of teacher education, while state agencies continue to control accreditation of teacher education programs; school boards and administrators control the conditions of work, and teachers' organizations exert pressure to gain more influence among all of these groups. The result is considerable confusion concerning the question, "Who is in charge of the maintenance of the teaching profession?" As Lanier (1984) puts the matter:

> The major problem that makes change and improvement exceedingly difficult in teacher education is the diffuse nature of program responsibility and accountability. Too many warring factions control various small pieces of the enterprise. Consequently, each of the participating parties is weak, and no single group is powerful enough to exercise responsible leadership that might significantly change the status quo. Coalitions rarely are possible, since the various actors share little mutual interest and trust. . . . The situation is analogous to the current scene in war-torn Lebanon, where numerous factions with multiple, contradictory, narrow, and self-interested concerns continue to fight and further a growing anarchy. The loser, of course, is the country as a whole. (p. 2)

Collaborative arrangements that are based on self-interest can lead to treaties among warring parties, and they may lead to some relatively permanent alliances. If, however, the goal is to promote the common good, it will be necessary to invent a boundary-spanning organization. This organization must have sufficient power and authority in its constitutional frame to compel actions and support from participating parties, even when it may not appear that it is in their short-term interest to do so. Symbiotic relationships can produce confederations, perhaps relatively strong ones, but perpetual unions will only develop when those who work to further the cause of collaboration articulate and pronounce the organic nature of the relationships necessary to renew and professionalize the teaching occupation.

## The Need for a Shared Vision

Dealing with present problems and concerns can produce cooperative effort among otherwise competing parties, but a shared view of a common future is necessary to develop and sustain a new organization or a new sovereign state. Management theorists refer to this shared view as corporate vision. Political scientists refer to a shared understanding of a common future as the general will.

Put differently, before separate and distinct political entities can constitute themselves for continuous, mutual action, there must be leaders within these entities who understand that the vision they have of the future can be realized only with perpetual cooperation and continuous interaction with those from other sovereign states. It is this recognition that generates the general will necessary for otherwise independent entities to bond themselves and willingly to forego short-term interest for long-term, common good. We believe it is time that leaders in universities, especially those concerned with the preparation of teachers and administrators, and leaders in the public schools, including school administrators and union leaders, work together to identify and articulate a vision of the future that will be sufficiently compelling to command the loyalty and support of all. And, as should by now be apparent, we also believe that such a common vision could be most effectively worked out if educational leaders collectively centered their attention on the problem of the professionalization of the teaching occupation.

Once educational leaders have committed themselves to the proposition that the future they envision cannot be fully realized until the conditions of the workplace are such that teachers and school leaders can operate as professionals, then the issue of institutional renewal takes on a different meaning. Once the professionalization of teaching is articulated as a common means to assuring that every child will be guaranteed educational excellence and equity in the context of a democratic order, then professionalization can take on a new meaning. Working out such a shared vision may not solve short-term problems. We are relatively confident, for example, that the thoughtful discussions necessary to produce such a shared vision would not improve test scores by 5% by next year. On the other hand, we are persuaded that without such a shared vision, collaborative efforts will not produce the results any of us hope for and anticipate, and the social experiment that is now going forward may well fail. The remainder of this chapter, therefore, examines some of the issues that must be jointly and thoughtfully discussed by university and public school educators as they develop a boundary-spanning vision which could serve to guide collaborative efforts.

## Good Practice: Who Decides?

Frequently in the preceding chapters, it has been observed that public schools and universities represent distinctive and not always mutually supportive cultures. The most important aspect of these cultures as they relate to school improvement as an institutional goal is the normative structure that contributes to the definition of what constitutes good practice. From the perspective of the university, the quest is for convincing generalizations that apply to the universal audience (House, 1977). From the perspective of public schools, the quest is for persuasive arguments that are relevant to a specific context. Thus, the university has a value preference for norms that are based in generalizations about schools and about teaching, whereas the preference of the practitioner is for norms that have specific application in the real world of a particular school.

One of the major difficulties in the preparation and continuing development of teachers and administrators is that there is not a clear image of who is, and who should be, norm senders. Officially, those who teach on college campuses are the norm senders. Yet, we all know that practitioners learn about teaching and schools from many sources other than the university. Thus, in the natural system of professional development, there are many norm senders other than those who are officially designated to play such roles.

The problems associated with the confusion regarding who is and who should be norm senders are compounded by three additional conditions. First, within schools of education where teacher educators are usually housed, it is not clear who is and who is not a teacher educator. Some education faculties seem to view all faculty members as teacher educators and even include liberal arts faculty in this reckoning. Other faculties clearly designate responsibility for teacher education to a more limited range of faculty members (e.g., departments of secondary education are responsible for the prospective secondary teachers, departments of elementary education for elementary teachers, and departments of administration for principals). Even when there is departmentalization, it is not uncommon to find some confusion. For example, is educational psychology part of teacher education, even when professors are housed in different organizational units? Or, is it the case that teacher education is best conceived as the exclusive purview of those who have responsibility for more clinically oriented subjects (e.g., methods, practicum, etc.)?

Partly as a result of internal confusion, a second problem emerges. This problem has to do with status. In fully developed professions, norm senders are usually viewed as high-status members of the occupation. Yet, it is not uncommon to find teacher education occupying one of the lowest status positions within a school of education, just as schools and departments of education often occupy low-status positions in the college or university generally. Indeed, in major research institutions, it is not uncommon to find some of the most potentially powerful socializing experiences (e.g., student teaching) relegated to the control of the lowest status persons in these systems, that is, to graduate students.

Within higher education, and especially in some highly prestigious universities, the prestige and status of a professor of education frequently seem to be inversely related to the degree to which he or she works directly with teachers and administrators in the schools. There is considerably more prestige and honor attached to conducting an on-campus graduate seminar for school administrators than is attached to supervising twenty student teachers or conducting a field program. Similarly, it is more prestigious to publish an article in the *American Educational Research Journal* than in *Instructor Magazine*.

A third problem is more subtle but equally important. Operationally, teacher and administrator education takes place in two distinct organizations, the university or college and the public school. Furthermore, the operational norm senders (campus-based educators and practitioners in schools) are accountable to different systems; they participate in different reward structures and generally in cultures that are distinctively different from each other and sometimes downright antagonistic toward each other. Thus, it should not be surprising that the norms and values campus-based educators attempt to transmit are sometimes spurned as "mere theory." Nor should it be surprising that campus-based educators jealously guard their right "to grade student teachers" and to certify administrators precisely because they have little confidence that practitioners would know good teaching or administrative practice if they saw it. (Educators do not write about this subject much, but anyone who has been around teacher educators or administrative departments on university campuses for a period of time certainly knows that at least some hold practitioners in low regard, especially when the practitioners of concern are principals or supervisors.)

The often-noted hiatus between educational theory and educational practice is at least in part due to the fact that theory tends to be generated in a culture where it does not apply (the university), and efforts to apply theory are undertaken in cultures where few theoreticians practice (the public schools). Indeed, efforts to apply theory often take place in environments where it is expected and required that one disavow allegiance to theory as a condition to full membership. One of the finest compliments practitioners can pay a campus-based teacher educator is that he or she is "down to earth and not too theoretical."

A second major difficulty revealed by a normative analysis of the current scene in education is that those who presently occupy positions that logically lead them to be norm senders (professors on university campuses, school administrators, and school-system staff developers) are frequently not in communication with each other. And even those who are part of the same system often have major disagreements about what constitutes good practice.

Sometimes this lack of agreement is accompanied by lack of knowledge. For example, some teacher educators probably fail to transmit research-based norms simply because they are unaware of the research. Sometimes, however, the disagreements are based on lack of moral commitment to the norms; that is, individual teacher educators know what others think the norms should be, but they personally disagree with these "others." For example, many teacher educators view the existing research on teaching to be too narrow and prescriptive to serve as an adequate basis for normative consensus in teacher education. Others, however, seem quite willing to embrace this emerging literature as an adequate legitimizing base for normative consensus.

We do not intend to disparage the organization of people around modes of thought; after all, such organization is at the heart of a coherent normative order. Furthermore, the emergence of a coherent normative structure does not preclude the continuation of diverse schools of thought and advocacy groups. For example, in medicine, cancer research and treatment continue to be typified by divergent schools, cliques, and advocacy groups as are other fields within medicine, law, theology, and architecture. The critical question is: are there agreed-upon norms (rules and procedures) for determining the ways in which normative consensus is to be sought? Indeed, is normative consensus viewed as an end worthy of pursuit? In the case of American medicine, the more deleterious effects of not attaining normative consensus were overcome when norm senders (those who taught in medical schools) and high-status practitioners (physicians who practiced medicine in urban hospitals rather than exclusively from their offices and the homes of patients) committed themselves to the normative proposition that practice should be research based and that disputes over preferred practice should be resolved by disciplined clinical trials. Such an agreement may have potential for the field of education as well.

## Professional Schools and Normative Consensus

The absence of normative consensus does not dismay all educators. Indeed some, especially those most committed to the culture of the liberal arts academy, make a convincing argument that such disagreements are what universities are about — the free play of ideas in a world of independent scholars.

However, there is a fundamental difference between the kind of normative order appropriate to disciplining ideas (the culture of the liberal arts institution) and the normative order appropriate to disciplining practice with ideas (the norms of professional schools). The search for "best practice" is central to the mission of the professional school, and rules for making short-term and long-term decisions regarding what constitutes best practice are at the heart of professional knowledge.

Given this view, campus-based educators must make a choice about which normative order to emphasize. Either they should acknowledge that their primary mission is studying schooling and teaching others how to study schooling, or they should commit themselves to the view that their primary obligation is to identify and transmit best practice to neophytes. If the latter choice is made, the norms of the professional school are most appropriate.

## The Dilemma for University-Based Professional Schools

Professional schools are organized to transmit to neophytes the norms of the occupation whose interest these schools are designed to serve. In addition, they are symbolic decision makers regarding what constitutes best practice and are the primary source of new knowledge upon which changes in practice are based. Indeed, professional schools are the basic institutional unit used to legitimize change in practice, first, by incorporating the change into the training programs for neophytes and, second, by updating established members regarding advances in the field.

In addition, professional schools are based on the assumption of relative consensus among norm senders regarding what constitutes good practice. Indeed, without this consensus, professional schools cannot fulfill their mission. Though total consensus is never fully present, it is widely perceived as a goal worthy of pursuit. Normative consensus is, in fact, so important that most professional schools (and most of the occupations served by professional schools) have elaborated rituals, procedures, programs, and protocols that must be followed when consensus has not been attained.

Professional schools are also an important part of the discipline and control structure established by the occupation to assure that best practice is upheld, not only by individual practitioners, but also by the organizations in which the practitioners operate. Because persons employed in professional schools are viewed as high-status members of the occupation, professional school faculty are frequently called on to serve on review boards and panels, to conduct or participate in malpractice procedures, and to establish and maintain standards for institutional accreditation.

The norms and values of the professional school are, therefore, idealized versions of the norms and values that are supposed to dominate the profession as a whole. It is expected that professional schools will uphold best practice, for professional schools are the arbitrators of what constitutes good practice. Most of all, it is assumed that the mission of the professional school is to discipline practice with an established and agreed-upon body of knowledge, lore, and tradition that has itself been disciplined according to some standards the members of the occupation find desirable (e.g., the clinical trial in medicine or the precedent-setting case in law).

The discipline and orthodoxy required by the normative order of a professional school is, in some ways, directly contrary to the norms and values that are implicit in the liberal arts establishment where the mission is to discipline ideas rather than to discipline practice with ideas. Professional schools may encourage the unorthodox or novel application of ideas to practice, but they do not encourage the application of unorthodox, marginally tested, or poorly established ideas themselves. The liberal arts tradition encourages one to pursue unorthodox and novel ideas and to submit these ideas to the discipline of the scholar.

Thus, there is an inherent clash between the values and norms of the professional school and the values and norms of the liberal arts academy. This clash in values is best summarized by the question, "Should practice be based on theory or should theory be based on practice?" The professional school answer to this question is the latter. Those who uphold the liberal arts orientation to teacher education are more likely to answer that practice should be based on theory. Willard Waller (1967), a master at taking established ideas and using them in novel ways to help to understand and discipline practice, put the matter this way:

Both the theory and practice of education have suffered in the past from an over-attention to what ought to be and its correlative tendency to disregard what is. When theory is not based upon existing practice, a great hiatus appears between theory and practice, and the consequence is that the progressiveness of theory does not affect the conservatism of practice. (p. 192)

Waller adds:

A central point of the teacher's training . . . should be the attempt to give him insight into the nature of the social reality which is the school. This is what teachers usually learn in the hard school of experience, and by those rules of thumb which experience gives, and this is another reason for the conservatism of educational practice. Prospective teachers learn all the new educational theories while they are in schools, but they must learn how to teach from horny-handed men who have been teaching a long time. But if theory is ever really to be translated into practice, theorists must learn to follow it through the social dynamics of the classroom. Only so can experience be fruitful in the understanding that will make possible a change of things that are. (p. 459)

It is more than coincidence that the effective teaching and effective schools research, which in some ways follows Waller's suggestion that "theory must be based on practice," has such currency among practitioners. Many practitioners find Madeline Hunter appealing because her primary claim is that what she provides is a framework for describing what good teachers have always known. The problem, of course, is that the teaching profession has yet to establish norms and procedures for testing the claims some would make for their particular "practice-based theory."

For example, now that we know something about what effective teachers do, how do we determine that if teachers do these things, they will be effective? Many states are developing evaluation systems and beginning teacher training programs based on the assumption that if teachers teach the way the "effective teaching research" suggests, teachers will be more effective. Is this so, how would we know, and who is empowered to say so? These questions, and questions like these, cannot be answered without increasing normative consensus among practitioners and norm senders.

Such normative consensus cannot develop outside of a professional school context, and therein lies the dilemma for campus-based educators. If a professional school context is to be established, the school must have sufficient autonomy to establish and maintain a normative structure that is in many ways different from the normative structure that typifies the liberal arts departments. Furthermore, the professional school and its faculty must be directly linked to the world of practice in fact as well as rhetoric. Status in the professional school should be associated, at least in part, with status in the teaching profession. The professional school should be at least as accountable to the schools served as to the university with which it is associated. Indeed, in professional schools, the norms and values of the occupation serve as the primary focus; the norms and values of the university are secondary.

To bring about the changes that are needed, one must face the political realities of power and cultural dominance. So long as campus-based schools of education are embedded in the liberal arts framework, as is now the case on most campuses, the values and norms of the liberal arts academy will prevail in those schools. Working in schools will continue to be devalued, especially at times when the rewards of promotion, tenure, and merit pay are distributed. Publications that are aimed at disciplining practice with ideas will be less valued than are publications aimed at disciplining ideas.

Proposals suggesting that schools of education should be organized as professional schools are not new. Such proposals have come from highly respected teacher educators and relatively powerful organizations such as the AACTE. Why then has little movement occurred? Perhaps the answer lies with the difficulty of determining whether the goal is to enhance the status, authority and performance of teachers and administrators or to enhance the status, authority and autonomy of campus-based educators. If the former is the goal, there is an excellent chance that campus-based educators can and will play a vital role in the professional preparation of teachers and administrators. If the latter is the goal, there is a very real prospect that campus-based teacher and administrator education will increasingly be viewed as irrelevant to the arguments about reform and revitalization of public schools.

## Implications for Collaboration

The most critical barrier to the effectiveness of the campus-based educator as a norm sender resides in the fact that few are located in positions where they can give believable demonstrations, engage in intense communication about what they are demonstrating, carefully monitor neophytes, and cause neophytes to review carefully what they have practiced. For example, many teacher educators, understanding this handicap, strive mightily to overcome it through videotapes and simulations and by "practicing what they preach" in their college classrooms.

The problem, of course, is that the situations described above are somewhat contrived and artificial. At best they are context oblivious. For example, such activities may demonstrate the importance of planning, but they are unlikely to demonstrate the limitations of planning. Even more important, demonstrations of isolated classes cannot take into account the history of the class as a sociological phenomenon. What is happening today cannot be properly analyzed without knowing what happened yesterday, and what one hopes will happen tomorrow. Understanding the anatomy of the classroom and of a particular class is as important for the teacher as understanding human anatomy is for the physician. One cannot understand the anatomy of a class by taking out a slice from its midsection. How the class as a social unit started is as important as understanding how today's lesson started.

Collaboration based on symbiotic assumptions will certainly address some of the issues we have raised here, especially when the focus is simultaneously on school improvement and the improvement of university training programs. If nothing else, such collaboration promises to develop a common language out of which a common culture might emerge. We are persuaded, however, that a common culture cannot be a by-product of collaboration; it should be its primary goal—in other words, the symbiotic must evolve into the organic. The systematic and continuous improvement of the quality of education cannot occur until education becomes a progressive profession rather than a traditional-based craft. And, education cannot become a progressive profession until those who prepare educators and those who practice in the field are bound by a common culture. The building of this common culture requires that those who now function on university campuses and those who practice in the schools join together in a common organization with sufficient autonomy from the organizations they now serve to work out their common destiny.

There is little doubt that campus-based educators know much that is of value to practitioners. There is also little doubt that campus-based educators are not now positioned to make what they know effectively available to practitioners. The question is: will campus-based educators be willing to participate in the creation of the new organization that would be necessary to increase their effectiveness? If they are not, it is highly likely that policymakers and progressive practitioners will simply abandon the university as a vital source of knowledge to guide practice. And some public schools will find it necessary to invent their independent responses to meet the needs that organic collaboration could easily fulfull.

## References

House, E. R. (1977). *The logic of evaluative argument.* Monograph #7, Los Angeles: Center for the Study of Education, University of California at Los Angeles.

Lanier, J. E. (1984). *The future of teacher education: Two papers* (Occasional Paper No. 79). East Lansing: Michigan State University, Institute for Research on Teaching.

Waller, W. (1967). *The sociology of teaching.* New York: Russell and Russell.

# CHAPTER TEN

# The Future of School-University Partnerships

JOHN I. GOODLAD and KENNETH A. SIROTNIK

Chapter 1 described the rationale for and the beginning of a large-scale social experiment: the deliberate joining of school districts and their schools with universities for the simultaneous improvement of schooling and the education of educators. Janus-like, the chapter looked backwards to earlier examples of relationships between higher and precollegiate education and forward to expectations for 14 school-university partnerships linked together in the National Network for Educational Renewal (NNER). In succeeding chapters, the history, problems, and possibilities of five selected partnerships (four of them members of the NNER) were reflected upon and recounted from the vantage point of people intimately associated with the efforts. This chapter, a cautiously optimistic review of the short history to date of the social experiment, benefits from these five case studies as well as from personal experiences with the other partnerships.

By the time this manuscript appears in print, all of these partnerships will have moved on to another phase in the change cycle. Consequently, it is important for this chapter to draw from experiences in them to date in such a way as to assist others seeking to draw schools and universities more closely together. The body of data available to the writers includes preceding chapters, visits to those partnerships constituting the NNER, individual and group meetings with executive directors, correspondence and telephone conversations with a variety of individuals involved with these partnerships, a miscellaneous array of reports and newsletters, and a round of correspondence with eight deans who responded to a series of questions raised with them regarding the school-university partnership to which each had made a commitment regarding his or her school or college of education.

There are, it appears, relatively common sets of issues and problems manifesting themselves in different ways. Some grow out of distrust between inhabitants of two different cultures — particularly distrust of the motives of university people on the part of school people. Some emerge out of the markedly different demands, expectations, and reward systems of the two types of institutions. Other problems and issues arise out of the larger cultural context in which schools and universities coexist—a context which separates university professors from public school teachers in a two-tier system of status and prestige, for example. The differences between schools and universities may be so great that establishing collaboration as a permanent way of life rather than as a series of projects may not be possible.

There are troublesome organizational and structural problems in school-university partnerships. These potential problems range from meshing regularities such as annual and daily work schedules to creating a governing and managing structure that represents the best interests of all participants. There are ticklish issues of authority and responsibility. Who is to determine whether a new program developed by a partnership is to be implemented? Do collaborative task forces just make recommendations to others who hold the power? If so, will not interest in collaborating soon disappear? Is there a point at which charismatic leadership becomes dysfunctional for the long-term interests of the partnership?

There are also both the classic problems of effecting change and the unique manifestations of these problems in the processes of schools and universities coming together in areas of mutual self-interest. High among these problems is getting beyond simply conducting old business better to conducting old business differently as well as better and at the same time redefining the basic educational functions of both sets of institutions. The gap between "unsatisfactory" and "excellent" in education is not necessarily closed simply by doing better. Some things must be done quite differently; others not at all.

The data already available on the early history of the partnerships noted above have produced evidence of all of these problem areas, issues, and more. Consequently, they can be addressed in rather concrete ways.

First, however, it is important to argue once again, from a somewhat different perspective, the case for the kind of collaboration proposed in Chapter 1. Even though what is transpiring in school-university partnerships can be thought of as social experiments and, therefore, in a way, the testing of a set of hypotheses, we argue now for the necessity of such collaboration *as a postulate*. In effect, we find ourselves closely aligned with Conant's (1964) explanantion as to why researchers are willing to spend lifetimes testing hypotheses: because they believe in them as principles.

After further discussion of the concept as a postulate, we turn to some of the issues and problems now causing or likely to cause difficulties for those embraced by symbiotic school-university partnerships. In concluding, we take the view that school-university partnerships may be an idea whose time is come — *if* the two cultures are able to go beyond cooperation to fusion.

## Merging the Two Cultures: A Productive Tension

Chapter 1 cites McNeill's contention that significant human progress can be traced again and again to the interpenetration of two cultures, one with the other. To the extent that one culture completely loses its identity, the productive tension between interacting cultures is lost. That chapter stresses the necessity of differences among institutions joining in a partnership and the necessity of retaining these differences. There is little to be gained if the characteristics of one accurately mirror those of all others. The differences must be appreciated by the partners even when they produce abrasions, as they undoubtedly will. As Schlechty and Whitford point out at the end of Chapter 9, public schools would find it necessary to invent what the university can provide if the latter were not part of an organic collaboration.

Educators in the schools are capable of coming up with increasingly better ideas about their work and workplace, particularly if they have opportunities to observe and converse with co-workers in their own and other settings — something the partnerships described are designed to promote. But the record of so doing and then implementing radically different ways of conducting business is not impressive. This limitation is noted in the discussion of the League of Cooperating Schools in Chapter 1. Blame this shortcoming on bureaucratic structure and rigidity, if you will, but there are few signs that such will go away. Bureaucracy is a condition to be worked with and around.

Getting beyond performing familiar tasks better is not easy. Wooden boat builders improve their craft by observing and interacting with one another. But they are (and were) unlikely to consider the possibilities inherent in fiberglass rather than wood. Indeed, many wooden boat companies saw fiberglass as a threat and went bankrupt fighting against its use. But the buying public on whom they depended was offered a choice.

If school personnel do not consider new ways seen by others to be better or worthy of attention and renew their institutions accordingly, either alternative ways will be thrust upon them or new institutions and educational delivery systems will emerge. Such already has occurred. Here is where the university is an obvious partner—an institution charged with the responsibility of being constructively critical of our civilization and, through inquiry, of providing authorized opinions as to how human affairs might be conducted differently and better. As Buch-mann (1987) proposes, the action-oriented culture of the school and the reflection-oriented culture of the university stand to benefit from inter-penetration.

The university has little to offer such a joining, however, if its faculty members create, in their ignorance of schools, some fictional characterizations of the precollegiate educational world. Schools of health must be linked with public health, schools of agriculture with agricultural productivity, schools of social welfare with social well-being, schools of theology with the role of religion in human experience, schools of education with the enculturation of our people and the culti-vation of the intellect in our educational institutions. But the implied connection between the scholarly endeavors of professors of education and the often-messy enterprise of educating all of the children of all the people appears not to mirror accurately the culture of all schools of education.

Near the beginning of this century, John Dewey urged our profes-sional forebears in the newly emerging schools and colleges of education to seek lessons from "the matured experience" of other professional callings (1904, p. 10). Law and medicine, for example, were well on their way to carving out their own niches, making certain not to be dominated solely or perhaps even primarily by the academic criteria of the arts and sciences departments. Dewey appeared to be suggesting a somewhat parallel role for schools and colleges of education.

Several decades later, however, Robert M. Hutchins (1936), while president of the University of Chicago, made it abundantly clear that communicating "the practices of the professions to the young" (p. 111)— whether of law, medicine, schoolteaching or administration—had no place in the university:

> The prospective lawyer would have exactly the same general education as the clergyman and the doctor. He would study metaphysics, because with-out it ethics, politics, and economics are meaningless. . . . He would also study the empirical and historical knowledge of society, the history of law and legal institutions, economics and economic history. . . . He would gain some knowledge of the physical world. . . . Anything further that he needed for the practice of his profession, such as familiarity with the roles of a particular jurisdiction, with methods of using digests and reports, with drafting legal documents, with writing briefs, or with the tricks of the

trade, he might acquire in a legal institute attached to the university. (p. 114)

Hutchins made it equally clear that those who staffed such an institute, whatever the profession, would have little or no voice in matters affecting the conduct of the university and the content of its work. It was characteristic of Hutchins to view compromise from a "plague-on-both-your-houses" perspective. He saw the university, as he conceived it, to be endangered by the intrusion of vocationalism. Simultaneously, he conceived such a university as inhospitable to the technical needs of professionals and, therefore, as not being fully capable of serving the professions. For him, then, a solution involving compromise was no solution at all.

But Hutchins' tidy view of the university was not to prevail. Three decades later, Clark Kerr (1963), in the Godkin lectures at Harvard, found it necessary to coin the term "multiversity" to connote the complex institution that the University of California, over which he presided, had become. And what both the Berkeley and Los Angeles campuses had become so also had all of the "flagship" public state universities and dozens of other institutions labeled "university." Today, a popular view is that the 10 to 15 professional schools on many campuses and the professionalization of the academic departments provide the direction and the driving force of the modern university.

Hutchins may well have been right. Both the university and the professions might have been better served by the former eschewing vocationalism and professionalism while hewing to a strictly liberal, general education, and the latter establishing institutions joined to but not of the university — as in a partnership. (Hutchins was vague on the organizational arrangements.) There would be today no need to create school-university partnerships; such would be redundant. An institute of pedagogy (or education) would be the bridge connecting the practice of teaching or administering with its conceptual and theoretical underpinnings. Dewey would have liked such an arrangement, we think. Yet Dewey probably was perceptive enough to note that the more mature professions were busily seeking to get the best of both worlds — to be part of the university and yet relatively independent of it. He wanted as much for a school or college devoted to preparing teachers for our children.

The relative success of schools such as medicine, law, and dentistry in achieving considerable autonomy within the university and the general failure of schools of education became particularly apparent to the first author while chairing a committee of the University of California

(University-wide Program Review Committee for Education, 1984). For the former schools, the committee found accommodations in the academic criteria for faculty advancement calling for recognition of clinical and professional demands. We found no such accommodations in the written criteria to be employed in evaluating education professors; indeed, the criteria were precisely those used in evaluating professors in the arts and sciences departments. In our discussion of this finding, a professor of political science on our committee posed a paradox: A graduate student or faculty member in architecture and urban planning is rewarded for designing a new school building; but a graduate student or faculty member in education would not be rewarded for designing the educational program to go into it!

Whether or not Hutchins was right, the multiversity prevails. The challenge to the unit charged with the study of education and the education of educators is to relate effectively to the practice of education in elementary and secondary schools, regardless of whatever other functions such a unit might serve. To do this effectively, there must be both accommodations within the university and permanent linkages with the schools.

We are proposing, then, not just a project in the reform of schooling or teacher education, but a way of life: a joining of schools and schools of education in a permanent partnership similar to those now imperfectly forged between most other professional schools and the settings where their graduates intern and practice. Like any marriage, the relationship will be marked by tensions, some of which will threaten to tear it apart. The more theory and practice fuse in both preparation programs and school settings, the more productive the tension and the more viable the educating in both schools and universities will be.

## Developing Trust and Ownership

The tensions that emerged early in the history of school-university partnerships, some described in preceding chapters, are more a question of developing trust than of solving tough problems of mutual interest. Lack of initial trust stems in part from the unfamiliar relationship between university-based and school-based people called for in the partnerships. This is exacerbated by the unknowns. What is to be gained? What is to be given up? What turf, if any, will be ours to control? Such questions do not always remain below the surface. And the way they sometimes manifest themselves does not immediately contribute to trust.

In the early beginnings of one partnership, several school administrators hotly resisted the idea of involving university professors in the affairs of their schools. "Professors either lecture to us or rework our problems so that they no longer are recognizable," said a school principal. Months later, when a professor was trying to back away from a full and equal partnership with schools, a superintendent spoke sharply, "You had better not; if there's word of a funeral for colleges of education or schools, rest assured that it won't be for the schools."

Inherent in the very nature of universities is a certain detachment, even mystique, that breeds some suspicion and distrust on the outside — the "town and gown" syndrome. Most teacher-preparing institutions recruit their students from nearby and place them as teachers in local communities. The student-professor relationship persists for years. Often, these same individuals come back to the university for graduate studies and once more are "students," sometimes of their former professors. And now, these professors are to treat them as equals in a school-university partnership? Come now!

This problem of institutions (and individuals) needing to be truly equal partners came sharply to the fore early in the Brigham Young University–Public School Partnership's task force on the principalship. (See Chapter 6.) Reflecting later on their early experiences, teachers and principals in this group were candid. Initially, they were reluctant to speak up in the company of professors. They were appalled at the time it took to get any agreements, especially among the professors. Minutes of meetings reveal the dominance of the latter. Thanks in large part to the patient, low-key leadership of the chair, the school-based members were drawn into the dialogue, agreements emerged, decisions were made. The plans that emerged and the new program for the preparation of school principals implemented during the 1986–1987 year were as much the work of teachers and principals as of professors.

A deep-seated concern, particularly of those in partnership schools working on committees and task forces, but also a view shared by some professors whether or not they are involved in collaborative activities, is that their hard work will end up in recommendations to others with veto power. A necessary condition pertaining to all partnership activities is not yet, we think, fully understood and respected: committees and task-force members are *not* making plans and recommendations for others who will then decide what to do with them; instead, they are making plans and recommendations for *themselves*. But it is not easy to think and act in this way. Making plans for others is indigenous to the education enterprise, just as it is in other areas of human affairs. It is all too easy to be unrealistic and irresponsible when someone else is to carry out the results of a committee's work. Conversely, it is all too easy to sidestep such results when the recommending body has no authority over those for whom the recommendations are intended and no responsibility for implementing them. Little is accomplished in either case. There is no point in perpetuating what is obviously futile.

Partnership working groups are not created to recommend to others. They are engaged in redesigning programs and practices, using their best judgment. This implies a great deal regarding both the membership and the authority of working parties involving school and university personnel. We are confident that the implications are not yet fully understood by those now involved. For example, we would wager that some professors of educational administration now joined with school personnel in rethinking preparation programs in this field are relaxed in the belief that they themselves will veto recommendations coming from the group when they are brought to the total faculty. The consequences would be devastating to a school-university partnership.

In the Brigham Young University–Public School Partnership, there is no doubt that trust on the part of school-based persons working on the principalship task force advanced markedly when the program they helped design became a reality. And, no doubt, a positive message was communicated rapidly to those involved in other working parties. The best guarantee of trust and willingness to participate is to see the results of one's efforts built into some part of the total enterprise. The uncertainties of investing time and energy are then changed into the satisfactions of ownership.

## The Change Cycle

Six years of experience with the League of Cooperating Schools (see Chapter 1; Bentzen, 1974; and Goodlad, 1975) impressed upon us the nature of a change process that differs markedly from the highly ordered, linear one often perceived as the one that works. The tidy model of change for research and development, particularly as it was employed to guide federally funded projects in the late 1960s, has been criticized by many (see, e.g., House, 1974).

We too observed a much less systematic approach on the part of persons in schools endeavoring to grapple with improvement. This somewhat erratic, stumbling course is not easily documented in the literature; but the complexity comes through in the five stages observed by Lieberman and Shiman (1973):

1. First, people talk about the possibility of bringing about some kind of change within the school. . . . The "tell us what to do" syndrome is rampant. . . . This stage is clearly Lewin's "unfreezing."
2. Activity ensues. . . . Usually a few people get excited about adopting a change, and with enough support they do it.
3. Out of such activity, teachers begin to ask questions. . . . "Is this better than what I did before?" Discomfort is great at this time.
4. The whole program begins to look shabby.
5. The large philosophical questions are asked. Teachers begin to deal with goals for the first time. (p. 52)

This last point is worth noting. Most reform models and efforts, including those criticized by House, *begin* with a statement of goals. Yet, as discussed in Chapter 8 and in the literature on organizations referenced therein, goals are more likely to emerge from human endeavor than to direct it.

To some extent, perhaps, the excessive setting of goals and refinement of those goals into precise objectives, so characteristic of the education enterprise in recent years, has caused educators to become weary, even skeptical of the process. In most of the partnerships, however, there has been considerable tension between the desire on the part of some participants to keep the dialogue open, thus delaying closure on a specific agenda, and the desire of others to get considerable closure on an agenda of relatively specific topics.

The latter occurred within the governing body of the Puget Sound Educational Consortium (PSEC) at one of its earliest meetings. At the suggestion of members of the group, there were individual conferences with each member of this body to assess areas of interest. Agreement on a list occurred at the first presentation of the summary that was prepared following these meetings. It is fair to say that there were no lengthy discussions of alternatives based on a careful analysis of national or local needs.

On the other hand, as Keating and Clark point out in Chapter 7, the formal creation of the PSEC was preceded by considerable discussion of critical issues by district and university personnel: The Educational Leadership Seminar, beginning in the summer of 1984, provided forums for reading and dialogue. Rarely, in our experience, have so many educators from so many districts and a university engaged so intensively in intellectual activity that was almost completely disengaged from goal-setting and academic credits. To a considerable degree, a norm of professional reading and dialogue within and across districts and across school-university lines had been in the making (and has continued). Presumably, the discussions regarding the agenda were influenced by what had transpired during the previous year.

But the urgency to get closure on an agenda is influenced significantly by other factors. First, superintendents perceive themselves not only to be in a decision-oriented role but also in a setting demanding a wide range of quick decisions. There is not time for much reflection—which is an argument for the role of university people in tempering these circumstances. Second, superintendents, on behalf of their districts, make a rather substantial financial commitment ($20,000 in the case of the PSEC) for an uncertain enterprise offering such intangibles as change, improvement, reform, and collaboration. Board members seem not to question the spending of much larger sums on such closely related matters as staff development, but these can be translated, usually, to fit norms and conventions. In a school-university partnership like the PSEC, a new venture not easily described or aligned with convention, there probably was some urgency on the part of the superintendents to identify the kinds of specific activities that could be readily subsumed under familiar rubrics. A task force on "excellence and equity," for example, may not denote specific activities, but at least the words are well worn and even high-sounding.

Herein lies a major problem in change processes. Because the very idea of change (and especially innovation) is threatening, particularly to persons who see themselves well served by the way things are, those involved often perceive a need to stay away from areas of controversy, at least initially. Sometimes, great care is taken to avoid language that too precisely defines the changes intended, especially if this language has been used before to describe initiatives seen as threatening or unproductive in some earlier era of reform. Yet, we know that using language that best fits both the circumstances to be changed and the changes to be effected tends to accelerate the process. Then, avoiding the controversial areas or coming at them very obliquely often means involving valuable human time and energy in matters that may not be worth the effort. Once thoughts of this kind intrude into the work setting, disillusionment and low morale quickly follow. Yet, to tackle head-on those long-standing, intransigent problems of institutionalized education may be to court disaster through the immediate arousal of all the many forces driven to resistance or outright opposition to anything likely to re-arrange or replace what now exists.

The mechanism of a school-university partnership may be uniquely suited to getting beyond this critical point of impasse and regression. For example, although the agenda initially agreed upon by the governing body of the PSEC did not appear to be, for the most part, very world-shaking, the working groups addressing the several topics have pushed far below the surface of each, revealing connections to issues of major importance. This may prove to be the rule rather than the exception when action-oriented and reflection-oriented individuals join in seeking to define and understand a problem. Whether this joining will then result in action involving a continuation of this inquiry remains to be seen.

This issue returns us once more to questions of involvement and ownership. We see in the description of the Southern California Partnership (Chapter 5) an effort—problematic, but not without successes—to extend involvement and ownership beyond the governing body and, indeed, expand the membership in this group to levels of responsibility in addition to top school and university administrators. The momentum of the group of school principals and second-level district administrators was sufficient to keep the partnership alive through the loss of its initial university partner and marriage with another. Extending involvement to teachers and faculty, in particular, is a virtually universal concern within all partnerships.

Perhaps it was Paul Heckman's experience with the problems of extending this involvement in the Southern California Partnership that led to a different approach in the genesis of the Southern Maine Partnership. In his role as executive director of the latter, he encouraged meetings that simultaneously involved superintendents, principals, and teachers. He was careful to avoid a pyramid-like structure, with a governing board of superintendents and the dean of the college of education directing all activity from the top. Instead, he sought activities that involved simultaneously the dean, teachers, professors, principals, and superintendents, pushing all the while for those most obviously responsible and best able to make decisions to have the authority to make them. Consequently, the several superintendents made decisions regarding paying the costs of activities that had been cooperatively agreed upon as desirable. Similarly, the necessity of freeing teachers from restraints limiting their teaching decisions was addressed not just by teachers or by administrators but by both groups simultaneously. Heckman modestly attributes some of the apparent success of this approach to the relatively small size of the partnership, but this way of proceeding appears to be applicable to even very large partnerships.

Yet it is also apparent that the approach to involvement of all levels of the schooling system did not assure participation by university personnel. The hope was that professors, instead of coming to the schools to make speeches or report on their research, would be drawn into ongoing work because their interests would be tapped and they would be viewed as having something to contribute. There is no evidence at this time, however, of professors in the University of Southern Maine being more involved than are professors in other university partnerships. Indeed, the dean sees greater involvement as a necessity and the lack of it as a serious problem.

Professors tend to be specialists, not generalists. One might expect them to be most comfortable in working on certain kinds of problems (teaching, administering, counseling, etc.) with certain educational professionals (teachers, administrators, counselors, etc.); they may less readily perceive how to become productively involved in more long-term, multilevel school improvement processes. Consequently, substantial participation by university faculty may be an eventuality to be anticipated once the agenda of educational improvement is reasonably well defined.

On the other hand, it has been our experience in at least several partnerships that three or four professors have been willing to participate initially in less well-structured inquiries that are likely to persist for some period of time. This reinforces the point emphasized by Lieberman (Chapter 3) and Heckman (Chapter 5) that coordinators need to assume a brokering function, capitalizing quickly on common interests as they emerge in the school-university collaboration.

The promising principle at work here is that all levels of a system, whether large or small, characterized by bureaucratic structure and behavior, function as in interacting ecology (Goodlad, 1987). In its ideal form, this ecological model would eliminate the need for one level to seek the "permission" of another after the necessary deliberations had taken place; all of those levels necessary for implementation would be party to the deliberations. Consequently, it becomes the responsibility of all involved to effect the implementation process, whatever its focus. But the problem of effectively including the university in the ecology still remains, as Schlechty and Whitford astutely point out in Chapter 9.

In most, perhaps all, of the school-university partnerships with which we are familiar, the potential of this multilevel approach rests with the committees, task forces, or working parties now functioning or being established. The obstacles are likely to be the chronic ones arising out of the need to hold on to power and to protect turf. Those involved must come to understand that power is not finite. Sharing it usually creates more to spread around. Crossing over turf boundaries requires belief in that third characteristic of a symbiotic partnership: satisfaction of the self-interests of other collaborators in a common agenda is essential to the satisfaction of one's own self-interests. Superintendents, for example, must come to see that a first-rate school system requires a very broad scope of curricular and instructional decision-making space for teachers. Professors of educational administration, to cite another group, must come to see that a first-rate preparation program for school principals requires close collaboration with people in the schools. Eventually, educators in schools and in universities, aside from their specific interests, must come to own the common agenda—the "organic relationship" proposed by Schlechty and Whitford. Such thinking is hardly revolutionary in character, but it has not been abundantly present in the educational enterprise.

## Developing a Common Agenda

An unsettling observation about schooling is that educators do not commonly engage one another in serious dialogue about their enterprise. Lortie (1975) has provided us with a sobering picture of the isolation of teachers from one another. But the problem extends far beyond teachers and, it appears, the isolating effects of physical space arrangements. In general, principals do not talk about their problems with other principals (Goodlad, 1975), and superintendents keep their professional thoughts, aspirations, and difficulties very much to themselves. No doubt, the pyramid-like structure of the system contributes to the isolation of those at the top, whether in a school or in a district. Moreover, those who have spent considerable time in universities—in colleges of education, for example—know only too well how the very same phenomena of isolation and closed communication are manifest in the same, if not a greater, degree.

One of the most important concomitants of a school-university partnership may be the stimulation of dialogue, not only between school and university personnel as intended, but among educators within these institutions who are not ordinarily accustomed to engagement beyond the niceties of formal communication. The possibilities for sharing knowledge and expertise clearly are envisioned by Sinclair and Harrison in the goals of the Massachusetts Coalition for School Improvement (Chapter 4). Indeed, the concept of using people inside the Coalition as resource persons in all partnership activities appears to be an operating principle. The school as the unit of change provides the setting where, potentially, the intellectual input of all actors is to be integrated into the decision-making process.

There is no doubt that the effort to join school districts and the two universities in both the Metropolitan School Study Council (Chapter 3) and the Southern California Partnership (Chapter 5) provided the superintendents with settings in which the discussion of significant educational trends, issues, and research findings relative to their work came to be expected and appreciated. As one superintendent in the latter expressed her satisfaction: "I would consider the partnership worthwhile if I received no further benefit than these stimulating sessions with my fellow superintendents." Similar views were expressed by secondary principals from a dozen districts in the Puget Sound Educational Consortium (Chapter 7), meeting monthly, as they had never met before, to address problems of mutual concern. Most of the executive directors of the school-university partnerships in the NNER have noted this kind of benefit relatively early in the history of the collaborative endeavor.

Schlechty and Whitford's critical appraisal of school-university collaboration (Chapter 9) suggests a necessary stage beyond the recognition in a symbiotic partnership that satisfaction of one's own self-interests requires the simultaneous satisfaction of the other partner's. Something resembling a new, organic, relationship combining features of the other organisms (institutions) must result from the collaboration. In effect, the culture of the school and the culture of the university go beyond interaction; they merge. Both are changed with the merger; both retain a large part of their independent identities; both share the creation of something new. But the nature of these synergistic processes and their outcomes is not at all clear. They constitute, of course, the major unknowns and challenges in the social experiment.

Chapter 1 advances the rather obvious proposition that the extension of the common school upward to include secondary education and outward to include large numbers of young people who lack support from other institutions, particularly from a fully intact family, has created chronic problems. Although, at the root, these problems remain essentially the same, their manifestations change over time. The necessary agenda of educational improvement requires that these manifestations are correctly diagnosed as leading to a deeper root and, therefore, are worth the commitment of human time and resources. A basic assumption of school-university partnerships is that representatives of the two cultures will engage in the inquiry essential to diagnosis and amelioration.

However, if the press to get early closure on any agenda is very strong — because, for example, a school board expects early results, perhaps in the form of higher achievement test scores — the necessary dialogue may be circumvented or aborted. In one instance, a district dropped from a partnership just as it was beginning, on the grounds that no "returns" were visible. In another instance, an agenda with accompanying task forces was put together in a matter of months and then summarily abandoned. In contrast to that experience, in another instance, a multilevel dialogue with some input from consultants was sustained for a year without formal agreement on any agenda. One partnership has been driven for several years by several large areas of common interest agreed to by its governing board during the first weeks of its existence. In almost every instance, there has been a search for an agenda specific enough to bind participants in a common enterprise but general enough to allow for individuality and creativity.

It is instructive to note that the 14 school-university partnerships constituting the NNER experienced a pressure beyond that of their own members: namely, the mission statement of the NNER. (See Chapters 1 and 8.) The problems of accommodating the interests of each partnership to the NNER agenda laid out in the mission statement in many ways paralleled those of determining a single partnership's agenda. The mission statement proved to be too general for some, too specific for others. Interestingly, extensive dialogue among the executive directors regarding the difficulties of effecting change, current activities within their partnerships, and anticipated areas of effort revealed extensive early overlap in the agenda of partnerships and the mission statement of the NNER. It is difficult — indeed, impossible — to determine how much this mission statement played the "alternative drummer" role in guiding the dialogue toward agreement on a dozen themes involving both process and substance. It is reasonable to suppose that the effort to assume considerable ownership of a common agenda was informed by both the purposes of the NNER and considerable sensitivity on the part of the executive directors and their partnerships to the critical educational problems of our time: the manifestations of deep, almost intractable, difficulties of educating all children, youth, and their teachers.

### Concluding Observations

It is too early in the social experiment to draw reasonably definitive conclusions about what is working and what is not working and, certainly, about the same effectiveness of school-university partnerships in addressing the tough issues motivating their creation. But it is possible and it may be useful to pass along to others some highly speculative observations on organizational structures, change processes, and the prospects for significant educational improvement.

*First, the role of executive director may prove to be crucial.* Clark (Chapter 2) borrows from Sarason, Carroll, Maton, Cohen, and Lorentz's (1977) description of Mrs. Dewar in reflecting on this leadership role. A primary theme in Lieberman's account of the history of the Metropolitan School Study Council bears directly on the issue of leadership and "idea championing." Interestingly, the several executive directors in the partnerships that constitute our experience base vary significantly in personality, background, status in their institutions, and so forth. There is no question that persistence, identified by Sarason as an important trait, is crucial. Beyond this, it appears that ability to relate in an open, honest way (to be "authentic," as the concept often is described) to a wide range of groups and individuals, *and to listen*, are important characteristics. One must be able to move readily back and forth between the culture of the school and the culture of the university, to have an understanding and an appreciation of the values of both, and to be perceived as contemptuous of neither. Increasingly, executive directors are learning the importance of being able "to walk both sides of the street."

Just how much the beginnings and development of a school-university partnership depend on the executive director as an "idea" person is not clear. Being deeply committed to a personal agenda for reform may be a liability. Perhaps more important than the promulgation of ideas may be the ability to draw ideas from others and move them into a common agenda and strategies for action. The ability to question and even challenge others without being threatening, to supply information and resources at critical junctures, and to foster the use of relevant data in all inquiry appears to be a productive, though perhaps rare, trait.

A personal need to stamp a partnership with one's own image appears at this stage to be dysfunctional. The executive director is caught between the need to be a leader, seen as competent and in charge, and simultaneously to be self-effacing, giving the credit to others. This may not be easy for professors in this role who have been highly entrepreneurial, independent, and competitive in academe. There are careers to be made and enjoyed in this new, hybrid position; but many who take it on, whatever their previous roles and successes, may find themselves to be square pegs in round holes.

*Second, whatever the governance structure initially established, it will create problems and probably will require later modification.* The bureaucratic structure of school districts and universities serves to invite bureaucratic solutions to educational problems even when bureaucracy is part of these problems. When one of the essential goals of improvement is the unshackling of the critical mass of human energy and talent at the base of the pyramid, there is an irony in governance being in the hands of superintendents and deans, as is generally the case in the partnerships. Yet, as discussed in Chapter 1, to sidestep those in these positions of authority is to court failure from the outset.

A conventional solution is to "represent" other groups such as principals and teachers on the governing board. But this is fraught with difficulties. Who picks them? Will they participate collaboratively, or will they try to lobby for the wishes of their respective organized groups?

Whatever the structure and membership of the governing body, there appear to be some minimum essentials for successful functioning. The board or council must be readily accessible to all groups involved. Consequently, the agenda must be open to all, and this is a condition that is significantly influenced by the executive director. Members of the governing board must be alert to the involvement of teachers, professors, and principals, as well as sensitive to board actions likely to discourage participation. The governing council of the Southern California Partnership came close to causing a serious rupture when it became overly zealous in criticizing the report of one of its own task forces. Subsequently, it opened up membership on this body to persons in addition to superintendents and the dean. In several partnerships, steering committees at levels below the governing body are serving to assure broader participation in leadership and the elimination of logjams in the governance agenda.

How best to govern and administer collaborations that are still in an amorphous, developing stage should continue to remain an open question. Superintendents and deans have many demands on their time; for some, partnership business is not yet central. Yet, for them to be on the sidelines and uninformed ultimately means trouble for the partnerships. Success requires their active interest and participation. But their role must be permissive and encouraging: stimulating grassroots involvement, securing the necessary resources, encouraging new ventures, and so forth. Ultimately, the governance structure must be broadly representative of those upon whom significant educational improvement depends.

*Third, the disparity between the rhetoric of expectations and the financial commitment of school-university partnerships raises interesting questions about the future.* Unfortunately, the variability among partnerships is not sufficient to provide insights into the effects of small and large budgets. Most budgets are small. A large, cash budget could heighten expectations for early closure on an agenda and quick returns. An imbalance in regard to source (e.g., most of the money from a university or from a grant) could distort both the agenda and the degree of commitment evidenced by some partners.

Clearly, if school-university partnerships are to fulfill the high expectations many of the partnerships hold for themselves, they must increasingly attract resources now committed elsewhere. This observation reinforces another: partnerships must address the central business of educating children, youth, and teachers. The agenda must not be "projects" around the edges. If new programs are undertaken, they must be seen as pilot efforts intended, once refined, to replace existing programs. The implication here is that the success of partnerships depends on the centrality of their agenda to areas of mutual self-interest and, therefore, their legitimate access to "regular" budgets. A major question at this stage is whether persons in strategic school district and university positions view their partnership in this way. If they do not, then the lofty expectations voiced by many will prove to be empty of significant results.

*Fourth, questions of involvement, participation, and representation must be resolved on shared turf: the individual school, on one hand, and the university's programs for preparing educators, on the other.* The concept of "representation" has been abused and misused in education. Although getting principals, teachers, and faculty, as well as deans and superintendents, on the governing board of a school-university partnership is desirable, such does not assure that those best able to make decisions and most likely to be held responsible for their consequences will be given the authority to make them. Merely representing all groups often accomplishes little more than compromise. Members of a governing group must move toward a process that best serves the total enterprise, not merely the special interests of various groups of actors.

This last statement means that there must be a coming together of all the actors on common ground. Children and youth are formally educated in school programs; teachers, specialists, and administrators are prepared in university programs. School-based and university-based individuals preparing educators have a stake in both. Renewing these programs is the work of those who teach in them. The rest of the educational system justifies itself to the degree that it provides support for this process of renewal, with each part contributing to the ecology of the whole (Frazier, 1987).

There is a sense among many of the actors that the success of school-university partnerships will be determined by the degree to which the implied centrality of focus occurs. Several of the deans have said that the danger lies in scurrying about to create "projects," instead of looking carefully for ways to get leverage on conventional ways of conducting schooling and preparing teachers. Some of the executive directors view collaboration between schools and universities as a way to get a different perspective on old problems. But they also view as formidable the difficulty of creating mechanisms through which individuals at all levels of the educational system will grasp the possibilities of getting beyond business-as-usual and will have the time, energy, and motivation required over the long haul.

*Fifth, for this time, energy, and motivation to be poured into creating parallel programs is to assure failure.* For a host of reasons, too many to examine here, postmortems on reform efforts repeatedly reveal that failure resulted from taking on double burdens — operating the old ship and trying to build a new one simultaneously — and then running out of energy. At one partnership conference, a university professor spoke in frustration of working for several months with teachers on a curriculum project, only to experience absenteeism from meetings and dying enthusiasm.

The teacher who does not wish to teach better and engage students in a richer curriculum is a rare person. But the interface between these worthy desires and reform initiatives almost always is a mismatch. Even at the site level, what principals see as needed usually is not what spurs teachers to accept willingly additional demands on their time. The successful strategy is one that converts pervasive dissatisfaction with existing programs into a belief that change not only is possible but also will produce greater job satisfaction. Once even a small group involved in the program comes to share this belief and experience some modest successes ("get some things on the scoreboard"), changes of a kind and magnitude not initially contemplated become part of the agenda.

*Sixth, if the necessary mechanisms are to be sensitively nurtured, the partnership must become self-conscious of the change process.* Understanding and promoting effective change has been identified as an area of common interest by the executive directors of all partnerships in the NNER. This is an encouraging sign. There is now no need to blunder along, assuming that since change is inevitable it needs no guidance. There is a substantial body of literature on change that reports both theory and research and the implications for practice. Since much of this is relatively recent, many who might assume coordinating roles may only be dimly aware of this work.

Some partnerships already have conducted conferences and seminars on the change process; others are contemplating them. Topics pertaining to understanding and effecting change are showing up in on-the-job training programs and institutes for principals. Increasingly, school-university partnerships must bring these kinds of activities to the attention of their members. This kind of encouragement, designed to make attention to change pervasive, is precisely what partnerships and networks should be best able to do.

*Seventh, the ultimate indicators of the success of a school-university partnership are not what gets marked up on the scoreboard, however important short-term accom-*

*plishments are as motivators. The nature and quality of institutional and individual renewal serve as the source for determining evaluative indicators* (see Chapter 8). If we have learned anything from the decade of educational reform following Sputnik, it is that the installation of innovations is, at best, a temporary, stop-and-go process that requires continuous fueling with promissory rhetoric, money, and fresh waves of proposals and reformers. This is not at all the same thing as renewal, as discussed in Chapter 1 and subsequently.

In brief, renewal is a process of readying the ship's crew for possibilities and emergencies, changing the compass in the light of new data on rocks and clear passages ahead, taking appropriate action as a way of bringing informed experience to bear in considering further possibilities. The analogy is far from perfect. But it illustrates, in a different context, the process of informed dialogue, decision-making, action, and evaluation to be developed in partnership institutions and joint programs.

The enemy of renewal is the quick-fix. The quick-fix syndrome surfaces early in almost all efforts to improve education. Perseveration with it and, more often than not, failure to get beyond it is the malaise to be reckoned with, whether in the reform of schools or of colleges of education. For the syndrome's appearance to emerge early in a school-university partnership should be taken as normal, not as cause for alarm.

What is gratifying to date in our experience with school-university partnerships is the widespread expression of the desire to go beyond. Indeed, some of those persons who have been serving in key roles view collaboration among cultures as *the* opportunity to effect the kinds of fundamental changes that so often elude us and that take us beyond practices seeming to become more rather than less entrenched as a result of hapless efforts in the past.

Getting beyond turf problems, calcified reward structures, trivial agenda, already-full schedules, and regularities designed to keep things the way they are will not be easy. But the general pressure in the surrounding society for doing much better has rarely been stronger. Unless educators take full advantage of the opportunities presented by our times, they will carry forward memories of what might have been. And those are the saddest memories of all. However, the opportunities for educational renewal are many. Among them, school-university partnerships may be an idea whose time is come.

## References

Bentzen, M. M. (1974). *Changing schools: The magic feather principle.* New York: McGraw-Hill.

Buchmann, M. (1987). Reporting and using educational research: Conviction or persuasion? In J. I. Goodlad (Ed.), *The ecology of school renewal*, 86th Yearbook of the National Society for the Study of Education, Part I, pp. 170–191. Chicago: University of Chicago Press.

Conant, J. B. (1964). *Two modes of thought*. New York: Trident Press.

Dewey, J. (1904). The relation of theory to practice in education. In C. A. McMurry (Ed.), *The relation of theory to practice in the education of teachers*, 3rd Yearbook, National Society for the Study of Education. Chicago: University of Chicago Press.

Frazier, C. M. (1987). The 1980s: States assume educational leadership. In J. I. Goodlad (Ed.), *The ecology of school renewal*, 86th Yearbook of the National Society for the Study of Education, Part I, pp. 99–117. Chicago: University of Chicago Press.

Goodlad, J. I. (1975). *The dynamics of educational change*. New York: McGraw-Hill.

Goodlad, J. I. (1987). Toward a healthy ecosystem. In J. I. Goodlad (Ed.), *The ecology of school renewal*, 86th Yearbook of the National Society for the Study of Education, Part I, pp. 210–221. Chicago: University of Chicago Press.

House, E. R. (1974). *The politics of educational innovation*. Berkeley, CA: McCutchan.

Hutchins, R. M. (1936). *The higher learning in America*. New Haven: Yale University Press.

Kerr, C. (1963). *The uses of the university*. Cambridge: Harvard University Press.

Lieberman, A. & Shiman, D. (1973). The stages of change in elementary school settings. In C. A. Culver and G. J. Hoban (Eds.), *The power to change*. New York: McGraw-Hill.

Lortie, D. C. (1975). *Schoolteacher: A sociological study*. Chicago: University of Chicago Press.

Sarason, S. B., Carroll, C., Maton, K., Cohen, S., and Lorentz, E. (1977). *Human services and resource networks*. San Francisco: Jossey-Bass.

University-wide Program Review Committee for Education. (1984). *The role of the University of California in precollegiate education*. Berkeley, CA: University of California.

# Index

227

# Contributors

*Richard W. Clark* is deputy superintendent of the Bellevue, Washington, Public Schools. Clark has taught graduate and undergraduate courses at three universities as well as high school and adult education courses in the public schools. He was a junior high assistant principal and a high school principal, and has held various central administrative positions. He is an author of four high school English and speech textbooks as well as a number of articles on curriculum and school administration issues. He has served as a consultant on teacher evaluation and school administration.

*John I. Goodlad's* current base for teaching and research is the University of Washington, as professor and director of the Center for Educational Renewal. Prior to this, for sixteen years, Dr. Goodlad was the dean of the Graduate School of Education at UCLA. Beginning his teaching in a one-room rural school, he has taught at all levels from kindergarten through advanced graduate studies. Goodlad's scholarly work has focused primarily on educational policy and practice and has resulted in more than 20 books, chapters in over 70 other books, and 200 or so articles in journals, magazines and encyclopedias. About half of his books have received awards, the most recent being the 1985 AERA Outstanding Book Award for *A Place Called School*.

*Anne Harrison* is an experienced elementary school teacher who served as a demonstration teacher in the laboratory school at Smith College. Ms. Harrison is at present associate director of the Coalition for School Improvement in the School of Education at the University of Massachusetts, Amherst. Her current research centers on determining the association between teachers' perceptions and their effectiveness in promoting educational renewal in schools and classrooms.

*Paul Heckman* is currently an assistant dean in the College of Education at the University of Arizona and the executive director of the Greater Tucson School-University Partnership. Previously, Dr. Heckman was an associate professor in the College of Education at the University of

233

Southern Maine, where he directed the Southern Maine Partnership. Prior to that he served as assistant director of the Laboratory in School and Community Education at UCLA, where he coordinated the Southern California Partnership. His primary interests and writings focus on the nature of curriculum and the process of school renewal and change.

*Pamela Keating* is the associate director of the Institute for the Study of Educational Policy, College of Education, University of Washington. She currently coordinates research initiatives and activities in early childhood education, educational leadership development, Pacific Rim Educational Systems, and policy studies. For the past four years she has also served as director of the Northwest Center for Research on Women, a collaboration between the U.W. College of Arts and Sciences and the Graduate School. There she directs a project integrating knowledge about racial minority women in undergraduate history and literature courses in colleges and universities in the region, and coordinates center inquiry in diverse areas.

*Ann Lieberman* is professor of education and the executive director of the Puget Sound Educational Consortium at the University of Washington. Dr. Lieberman was previously chair of the Department of Curriculum and Teaching and executive director of the Metropolitan School Study Council at Teachers College, Columbia University. Her work has been characterized by a unique blend of a sensitivity to the practical realities of school life and the ability to conceptualize fresh ways of restructuring and rethinking how to build a more professional culture in schools. Her written work exemplifies this blend, including *Teachers: Their World and Their Work, Rethinking School Improvement*, and, her most recent, *Building a Professional Culture in Schools* (in press).

*Phillip C. Schlechty* is the executive director of the Jefferson County (Kentucky) Public Schools/Gheens Professional Development Academy and professor of educational administration at the University of Louisville. Dr. Schlechty is a nationally recognized expert in the areas of recruitment and retention of teachers, career ladders, and the professional development of teachers. In April of 1985, he received the American Educational Research Association Award for relating research to practice. In July of 1985, he received the American Federation of Teachers Quest Citation for Outstanding Contributions to the Professionalization of Teaching. Dr. Schlechty has written more than 100 books, book chapters, monographs, and journal articles.

*Robert L. Sinclair* is an experienced elementary and secondary school teacher. He is presently professor and director of the Center for Curriculum Studies in the School of Education at the University of Massachusetts, Amherst. Dr. Sinclair is also director of the Coalition for School Improvement. His latest co-authored book, *Reaching Marginal Students: A Prime Priority for School Renewal*, expresses his long-term concern for helping public schools become responsive to children and youth who are not succeeding.

*Kenneth A. Sirotnik* is currently a research professor, College of Education, University of Washington. Previously, Dr. Sirotnik spent a number of years as a senior research associate in the Laboratory in School and Community Education and in the Center for the Study of Evaluation, Graduate School of Education, UCLA. He has participated as a senior member of many educational research teams, including the nationally recognized A Study of Schooling. His publications range widely over many topics including measurement, statistics, and evaluation, computer technology, and educational policy, change, and school improvement. His most recent, co-edited book, *Critical Perspectives on the Organization and Improvement of Schooling*, reflects a long-standing commitment to reconceptualizing and reconstructing inquiry and method in the context of educational practice.

*Betty Lou Whitford* is associate professor of secondary education in the School of Education at the University of Louisville and is currently assigned part-time to the Jefferson County (Kentucky) Public Schools/ Gheens Professional Development Academy. She works extensively with teachers and administrators on a variety of collaborative research and development projects related to teacher education, staff development, and school leadership. A specialist in qualitative field research, Dr. Whitford has published theoretical arguments and research about planned change, the professionalization of teaching, and the nature of public school–university collaboration.

*David D. Williams*, is an assistant professor of instructional science in the College of Education at Brigham Young University. Specializing in naturalistic inquiry and evaluation methodology, Dr. Williams is the editor of a New Directions in Program Evaluation Sourcebook entitled *Naturalistic Evaluation*. He is currently engaged in an extensive and detailed naturalistic study of the BYU–Public School Partnership.